RAISED
ON THE
'80s

30+ Unexpected Life Lessons
from the Movies and Music That Defined
Pop Culture's *Most Excellent* Decade

Praise for *Raised on the '80s*

"Never did I believe I'd learn my greatest life lessons through a man-child of the '80s, or by actually reading a real book with words. But here we are. Chris Clews's latest inspired work — *Raised on the '80s* — reminds us what a wonderful, totally awesome world we used to live in. This is a funny and unforgettable book."

Kevin Barnett
Hollywood Writer and Producer
The Heartbreak Kid, Hall Pass, The Do-Over, The Wrong Missy, The Righteous Gemstones ... and So Many Other Rotten Tomatoes-Producing Productions

"For many of us, coming of age in the '80s meant sneaking into R-rated movies, trying to find something interesting on one of only three broadcast television channels (although cable was quickly spreading across the US), attempting to record our favorite songs from the radio onto cassette tapes, and (gasp!) no internet. In this accessible and fun-to-read book, Chris Clews (O Captain! My Captain!) transports us back in time and provides insights, lessons, and fun facts that are both more useful than any of Coughlin's Laws and simultaneously applicable to the personal and professional lives of individuals from any generation."

Evan L. Kropp, PhD
Director, Online Graduate Programs
University of Florida, College of Journalism and Communications

"Chris Clews shows us — once again in his third book, *Raised on the '80s* — his firm but loving grip on the pulse of pop culture in our beloved decade: the '80s. The way in which he has found the life lessons in the movies we've adored for 40 years — and related them to his own stories of growing up in that magical era — is a priceless gift for all true nostalgia fans and those of us still hopelessly stuck in the'80s."

Steve Spears
Creator and Host
Stuck in the '80s Podcast

"Be prepared to be thrust into the depths of the most bodacious decade with the utmost of ease. Clews is a masterful tour guide on this nostalgic ride through '80s pop culture, all the while bringing meaning to the movies and music that may have once seemed purely entertaining. I'd get in line for this ride again and again."

Tamara Dever
Author of the *Ultimate Mix Tape* Series
TotallyCool80s.com

"We let Chris borrow our DeLorean last week and although he immediately vanished, this amazing book appeared. It's the perfect book for anyone who loves '80s pop culture like we do! And if you see Chris, please tell him we are stuck in 1985. Help ... maybe."

Zak and Dustin
Two Dollar Late Fee, the #1 '80s Movies Podcast

"Chris is the master at telling a story around '80s pop culture and making it fit life TODAY! This book is so much fun to read, especially the 'OMG' moments when like 'Wow, that's exactly how the hall-monitor kids acted, and how in the world did he spin that into an all-time one-hit-wonder Men Without Hats song?' Brilliant! This book is a must-read for all generations. It will have you researching, listening, and watching '80s TV, movies, and music with a whole new appreciation."

Robert "Bo" Brabo
Former Presidential Communications Officer for Presidents Bush & Obama, and Author of *From the Battlefield to the White House to the Boardroom: Leading Organizations to Values-Based Results*

"The way Chris uses movies from the '80s to teach us valuable life lessons is amazing! If our teachers would have used this in school, we all would have spent a lot less time in 'Saturday class' for whatever it was we did wrong."

Kyle, Jeff, and JD
Hosts of the *Back in Time* Podcast

"Chris Clews will reignite your appreciation for the '80s as he uncovers life lessons to learn from the pop culture we love. You'll see yourself in every memory he unlocks. This is the only book that inspires you to live a better future by flashing back to the past."

Brianne Fleming
University of Florida Instructor and *Making the Brand* Podcast Host

"Many of us have watched these '80s movies and can remember watching them for the first time on the big screen. This next generation may be discovering these films for the first time. Either way, Chris Clews does an amazing job of showing us lessons we can learn and apply to our everyday lives. We know these movies by heart but thanks to Chris, we're learning new lessons and enjoying these favorites all over again!"

Rob Faught
Host, *Living in the 80s* Podcast

"Chris Clews brings us invaluable golden nuggets of fun movie wisdom that we can use in our daily lives and proves that the '80s were — and always will be — totally awesome! This book is a must-read if you want to be clutch in life."

Patricia Stark
Author of *Calmfidence: How to Trust Yourself, Tame Your Inner Critic, and Shine in Any Spotlight*

RAISED
ON THE
'80s

30+ Unexpected Life Lessons
from the Movies and Music That Defined
Pop Culture's *Most Excellent* Decade

CHRIS CLEWS

SILVER TREE
PUBLISHING

Raised on the '80s: 30+ Unexpected Life Lessons from the Movies and Music That Defined Pop Culture's Most Excellent Decade

Book #3 in

The Ultimate Series on Essential Work & Life Lessons from '80s Pop Culture

Copyright 2022 by Chris Clews
All rights reserved.

Published by Silver Tree Publishing, a division of Silver Tree Communications, LLC (Kenosha, WI). www.SilverTreePublishing.com

Editing by:
Kate Colbert

Cover design and typesetting by:
George Stevens

First edition, September 2022

ISBN: 978-1-948238-41-0
Library of Congress Control Number: 2022914552

Created in the United States of America

Dedication

To my mom, Narda Anderson, who passed away from Alzheimer's on July 5, 2021. There is so much I could say about her. It would take pages to communicate what she meant to me and the degree to which the world lost a beautiful human being when she passed. She loved every animal — from the smallest ant to the biggest elephant and every one in between. She also loved Lady Gaga and *Cypress Hill* (yes, she really did) and could never understand the love my sister Ashleigh Clews and I had for Neil Diamond. She loved her work as a teacher and adored the kids she taught over the years. If you see a hummingbird today, that is her saying hello. She was the best. The poem by Robert Frost that is at the center of *The Outsiders* book and movie really says it all: Nothing gold can stay.

"I don't know where I'm going
but I sure know where I've been.
Hanging on the promises
in the songs of yesterday.
But I've made up my mind ...
I ain't wasting no more time.
Here I go again!"

– Whitesnake

Table of Contents

A Letter to My Reader

T hank you. It's totally awesome that you are reading this book right now, making an investment of your time in a guy who is likely an unknown author to you. Maybe someone recommended my books to you, or maybe you were once in an audience while I was on a stage. But maybe you're just taking a chance because you saw a book description and thought "This sounds interesting." Not everyone is willing to take the time to purchase and peruse a book by a substantially-less-than-famous author and speaker who happens to know a lot about a ton of *truly* famous people from the 1980s. I hope that by the end of this book, you will feel that I earned every penny of your investment in me and my content. I promise that I worked hard to make this a fun and meaningful book for you.

People often ask me: "Why the '80s?" The easy answer might be reminding those people that most people are nostalgic for their youth and that there were a lot of us who were "raised on the '80s." My formative years — from age 10 to 19 — were all in the '80s and I often say that everything I did for the first time in my life (good, bad, or indifferent) happened in the '80s, so it's a fun era for me to write about and reflect upon. All of this is true. But the truth of the matter is that, regardless of when I was born and what I experienced and witnessed firsthand, the '80s themselves are worthy of a book series. Millions of people agree — including you, apparently, which is totally awesome.

Movies, and Television, and Videos ... Oh, My!

The way I describe '80s pop culture is that it was like someone threw a glitter bomb against the wall and when it exploded, all these wonderfully bright and fantastic colors came spilling out all over the place. It was loud and colorful, bold, and unapologetic, and that glitter bomb left the world forever changed (as glitter — which is damn near impossible to clean up — is apt to do). Those glitter colors in this analogy represent the massive amount of variety, creativity, and innovation that is found in '80s pop culture. During the 1980s, genres of music like hip-hop, metal, and alternative were massively expanded upon with a multitude of entirely new splinter genres that helped to bring in audiences from all walks of life. The same is true for movie genres like rom-coms, slasher movies, big-budget action flicks, and high-school/coming-of-age films — all of which planted their flags squarely in the '80s.

Even in television, where things move a bit slower in terms of change, we saw the first new network launch since the early 1950s in attempt to challenge the big three. Fox Television launched in 1986 with most insiders in the media industry believing Fox would fail miserably. Fox proved the doubters wrong by producing shows with a bit more edge than the traditional networks, and endearing audiences to their content. The new network immediately made their impact felt across the entertainment industry with hits like *Married with Children*, *The Tracey Ullman Show*, *21 Jump Street*, *COPS*, *America's Most Wanted*, *In Living Color* (1990, but still one of this author's favorite shows), and *The Simpsons* (which is now the longest-running sitcom and animated series in history). *X-Files*; *Beverly Hills, 90210*; *Melrose Place*; and *24* would follow as well.[1]

As it turned out, traditional over-the-air networks were about to be challenged by cable stations, which would absolutely dominate by the end of the '80s. It's fair to say that cable television changed everything. Away went the "bunny ears" antennas on top of old televisions (which brought most of us just six networks) and suddenly we had almost 30 channels, including a 24-hour news station (CNN), 24-hour sports (ESPN), 24-hour music videos (MTV — which, thankfully, wasn't 24 hours of *Jersey Shore* and *Teen Mom* at the time), 24-hour movie channels (HBO, Showtime, Cinemax) and 24-hour, umm, "adult" channels that were covered with static and squiggly lines. Speaking of those "adult" channels, I have heard (wink wink) that with the right amount of tweaking on the cable box that "things" would become visible for a moment or two. Imagine that! Cable changed the television landscape forever and for us night owls, we no longer awoke on the couch in the middle of the night to the sounds of the national anthem and the American flag flying in the background signaling that programming was over for the day. Cable television never slept.

September 2019 -- Right after moderating an MTV VJ reunion panel with Mark Goodman, Alan Hunter, Nina Blackwood, and Jim (Poorman) Trenton, DJ/Creator and Host of Loveline on Los Angeles's KROQ-FM in the '80s.

---

1   https://www.britannica.com/topic/Fox-Broadcasting-Company

In the '80s, movies became our national pastime and I'm not just talking about HBO or trips to the movie theatre. In that fateful decade, we witnessed the rise of the local and national chain video stores where you could actually rent a movie (day or night), take it home to pop it into the VCR, and watch it as many times as you wanted. You just had to make sure to rewind it before you brought it back or you'd have to pay an extra buck. And don't even ask me what happened if you didn't return it at all. The horrors!

Oh, and arcades! So many quarters that were found between the couch cushions and in the clothes dryer were spent on games like Galaga and Dragon's Lair. The '80s also saw the cementing of video-game consoles as a standard appliance for every home when Nintendo, ColecoVision, Intellivision, and Atari were battling it out for home video-game supremacy. And let's not forget the rise of the personal computer in homes as well with names like VIC-20, TRS-80, and Commodore 64. That story is perfectly told by the phenomenal television series, *Halt and Catch Fire*. It's a must-watch for anyone who loves '80s pop culture. So is *The Americans*.

The 1980s was a decade of experimentation that led to a treasure trove of amazing pop culture. It was absolutely the last decade where pop culture wasn't manufactured. The creators created and just threw it out there. We told them what we liked, and they made more of it. Some things stuck and others simply didn't. What a spectacular time for the consumer of pop culture! It's one of the main reasons that we had so many totally awesome one-hit wonders in music.

The 1980s was a decade of experimentation that led to a treasure trove of amazing pop culture.

In this guy's humble opinion, the pop culture we've watched and participated in post-1980s has become more and more manufactured to the point where we are being *told* what we are going to like. You see, the conglomerates who create it need to make all that marketing money back and they need to do it quickly. And if advertisers are willing to pay for it, media outlets are going to keep making it. As Martin Scorsese said in a *New York Times* opinion piece and other publications:

> "That's the nature of modern film franchises: market-researched, audience-tested, vetted, modified, revetted and remodified until they're ready for consumption. Another way of putting it would be that they are everything that the films of Paul Thomas Anderson or Claire Denis or Spike Lee or Ari Aster or Kathryn Bigelow or Wes Anderson are not ..."[2]

Thankfully, I feel like the tide may be shifting here — now that it's the 2020s and we're more than 30 years past the close of the 1980s — and the power is going back to the independent creators and the consumers of pop culture. That's exactly where the control and influence should be.

'80s Pop Culture — Not Just for Gen Xers

"I love the '80s!" It's something I hear from readers and audiences all the time. I hear it from people who were alive in the '80s but were too young to remember it, and I hear it from Millennials and Gen Z and now from Generation Alpha (the generation whose oldest members are just 12 at the time of this book's release — those kids who invariably dressed up in neon crop tops, parachute pants, leggings, and fingerless gloves for '80s Day at their elementary and middle schools). Indeed, '80s pop culture

---

2   https://www.yahoo.com/entertainment\martin-scorsese-says-marvel-movies-have-no-mystery-and-no-risk-in-new-york-times-oped-essay-131919755.html

isn't just for Gen Xers. Not even close. Just look at the massive '80s pop culture renaissance we are having right now in 2022.

Nostalgia is supposed to come in 30-year cycles and only for a short time. For example, in the early '80s, we had a little 1950s resurgence that included pegged pants, slicked-back hair, movies set in the '50s — like *Diner* and *Back to the Future* — and music that was heavily influenced by the '50s sound from The Stray Cats and The Honeydrippers. There were additional nods to the '50s throughout the decade via movies such as *Stand By Me, La Bamba,* and *Dead Poets Society* but ultimately the influence was fairly limited.

Compare that with what we are seeing today. We are now 42 years removed from 1980 and 33 years from the last year of the decade (1989) and the influence of '80s pop culture is only getting stronger. *Stranger Things* (set in 1980s Indiana) and *Cobra Kai* (based on the 1984 movie, *Karate Kid*) are the most-watched shows on television; Kate Bush's 1985 song "Running Up That Hill" is #1 on iTunes while Metallica's 1986 masterpiece "Master of Puppets" sits at #5 on iTunes. Artists like The Weekend and Dua Lipa, amongst others, are embracing the '80s sound and becoming global megastars along the way. Movie sequels (not remakes — there is a huge difference) like *Coming to America 2, Indiana Jones 5, Beverly Hills Cop 4,* and *Gremlins: Secrets of the Mogwai* are using (or have used) the original main cast members, which was a lesson learned from *Cobra Kai.* Movies like *Deadpool, Guardians of the Galaxy,* and *Ready Player One* absolutely ooze '80s pop culture references and were massive box-office hits. Biopics on Madonna, Weird Al, and more are on the way. Remakes abound, unfortunately, both on television (*Magnum PI, MacGyver, Fraggle Rock, Dynasty*) and in movies like *Red Dawn, The Karate Kid, Footloose, Clash of the Titans, Poltergeist, Vacation,* and more. Unfortunately, there are way too many too list here so if you are curious about the ones remade and being remade there is a great list on IMDb. Remember that everything here in my overview of this '80s resurgence, minus the remakes, is really just covering the past six years (2016-2022) with most of the mentions post 2020. Yes, the '80s pop culture resurgence is just getting started. Buckle up.

And then there's the phenomenon of *Top Gun: Maverick.* As this book heads to press, *Top Gun: Maverick* has become Paramount's biggest domestic film in its 110-year history! It has earned $701 million in the US and a total of $1.4 billion world-wide as of Sept. 2022. Beyond the dollars that this '80s-inspired film has racked up, the buzz is a powerful reminder that the '80s are alive and well. I consistently hear from moviegoers that *Top Gun: Maverick* audiences stood up and clapped and cheered at the end. This happened when I went to see it as well. When was the last time that happened for you? A *Rocky* movie, perhaps? Standing ovations and audience participation in movie theatres happened a lot in the '80s. People would cheer or clap at the end of a great movie. *Top Gun: Maverick* has every other studio looking for their version of it — that lightning in a bottle. Unfortunately, this might mean more remakes, some of which are already in the works for classics like *Flashdance, WarGames, ScarFace, Weird Science, The Naked Gun, An American Werewolf in London,* and *Road House.*

Everybody Loves the '80s

To my surprise and delight (sort of), Gen Z is currently embracing some '80s fashion choices, including sequins, oversized blazers complete with shoulder pads, high-waisted and pale blue "mom" jeans (complete with front pleats), turtlenecks, bodysuits, and lots and lots of Magnum P.I. mustaches. Thankfully, the rumors of a comeback for parachute pants and Members Only jackets have been proven false. Please spare us (and your future self) by not embracing those '80s fashion faux pas.

And have we ever stopped talking about Jake Ryan? Nope. And we never will.

All of this is to say that the '80s pop culture resurgence is here to stay for the foreseeable future ... and I am here for it! Even the timeless and super-talented Cyndi Lauper is gracing us with her presence, both in person and song, in multiple television commercials. Speaking of commercials, our '80s Saturday mornings were full of cartoons and commercials, especially cereal commercials. General Mills just — in 2022 — announced that they are bringing back four classic '80s cereals — Franken Berry, Count Chocula, Boo-Berry, and Frute Brute Monster Cereals! Hopefully, the '80s cartoons are coming back with them.

When I speak at conferences, the two generations that are most interested in chatting after my keynotes are Gen Z and Gen X. Two generations divided by two to three decades, yet a love of '80s pop culture unites them. It's pretty remarkable, when you think about it. Kids born in the shadow of Y2K — which was the 119th time the world was apparently ending — finding common ground and shared "awesomeness" with people who at the exact same time Gen Z was being born were themselves anxiously waiting for their dial-up modem to connect so they could hop into an AOL chat room (or two or three). In households, communities, and workplaces, such connections between generations can be golden.

For me — and now for you — '80s pop culture can be as instructive and inspiring as it is entertaining and nostalgic. We can learn valuable life lessons from '80s pop culture, and I'm excited to share dozens of lessons that I think might make you go "Oh Yeah. Chick Chicka Chicka" in your best Yello — the band famous for the song made famous by Ferris Bueller – voice. I mean, that's why you're here, right? Together, we'll explore the iconic characters and plot twists and memorable dialogue from movies like *Road House, Can't Buy Me Love, Trading Places, The Breakfast Club,* and more. Oh, and we'll talk about a musician who loved the color purple. In the end, these movies and music that defined pop culture's most excellent decade can teach you how to live your absolute best life.

In the end, these movies and music that defined pop culture's most excellent decade can teach you how to live your absolute best life.

If you're not already an '80s pop culture fan, have no fear — '80s pop culture has something for everyone, regardless of your generation. In the words of Grace who was Principal Rooney's assistant in *Ferris Bueller's Day Off* (there's Ferris again) — when she was talking about everyone's love for Ferris the student: "The sportos, the motorheads, geeks, sluts, bloods, wastoids, dweebies, dickheads — they all adore him. They think he's a righteous dude." And they all adore '80s pop culture.

From *The Golden Girls* to *Fast Times at Ridgemont High* and everything in between, my favorite decade really did have something for everyone. That's what makes it so great. And this Gen X-er is so incredibly happy to share it with each of you. The pages that await you are going to be, in the 1988 lyrics of J.J. Fad, "Supersonic" — I promise!

At the Risk of Sounding Like a Rom-Com

Clearly, I love the '80s. The people, the stories, the fashion, the music, the films, the freedoms, the creativity, the innovation. It was a time like no other and its influence has shaped the man I have become. And because I'm *still* learning lessons from '80s pop culture, this era will continue to shape me forever. My love for the '80s, of course, is not blind; like every decade before it and every decade that will come after it, the '80s weren't perfect, by any stretch. But the pop culture absolutely *was* ... and that's why it isn't going anywhere.

I'm not going anywhere either. This is my 3rd book in *The Ultimate Series on Essential Work & Life Lessons from '80s Pop Culture* and, at the risk of getting all rom-com sappy, it really is a love letter to the '80s. I hope you enjoy reading it even half as much as I enjoyed writing it. And I hope you learn something really unexpected and powerful that you can apply to your life. You are most *certainly* going to learn a few unexpected things about *me*. Yikes. Here we go!

Enjoy the trip back to the '80s. As Doc Brown said, "Roads? Where we're going, we don't need roads." It's an honor to travel by your side.

Stay Rad!

CHAPTER 1

TRADING PLACES

"You know it occurs to me that the best way to hurt rich people is by turning them into poor people."

— BILLY RAY VALENTINE, *TRADING PLACES*

For several years, I worked in marketing roles within the financial services industry. It was fascinating — particularly for someone who sucks at math. I was surrounded by really smart people making lots of money without creating anything tangible. There was no product coming off an assembly line and nothing you could see, hear, smell, taste, or touch. Sometimes it all felt a little *Weird Science,* if you will — all these intangibles being analyzed and leveraged for the ultimate profit of our clients and ourselves. Where I worked, money made the world go 'round. No matter where *you* work or what you do,

I'm betting money plays a big part in your life too. Without it, fewer dreams come true. Fewer homes are purchased. Less stuff, more stress — unless, of course, you take the Jeff Spicoli approach to life and decide that "All you need are some tasty waves and a cool buzz and you're fine."

Good, bad, or indifferent, finances and the financial industry are integrated into our lives in critical ways. And with that in mind, let's talk about the '80s, shall we? Because the '80s had a lot to say about money — especially through iconic moments in pop culture. Let's be honest here — the three most popular subjects explored in music are love, sex, and money. Right? (Go ahead, think about any song you like. Does it touch on one of those themes?) In the '80s, musicians as diverse as Madonna, Dire Straits, Donna Summer, Pet Shop Boys, LoverBoy, Eric B. & Rakim, Cyndi Lauper, Boogie Down Productions, and Dolly Parton all had huge hits with their songs about ... you guessed it ... money. As it turned out, musicians weren't the only ones obsessing about the topic of money. The box office had its fair share of "money movies" in the '80s too. *Trading Places* was one of my favorite money/finance movies from the '80s and it was a star-studded affair with Eddie Murphy, Dan Akroyd, and Jamie Lee Curtis.

Trading Places was ahead of its time with its daring social commentary and useful life lessons, blended in artfully with the film's laugh-out-loud humor. There is a lot to unpack in this movie but, for our purposes, we're going to focus on the relationship between Billy Ray Valentine (played by Eddie Murphy) and the butler, Coleman (played by Denholm Elliott).

Let me ask you something: How many of you find yourselves a bit skeptical of the honesty and transparency of large institutions? Maybe it's just one specific institution and your skepticism is based on a negative personal experience that you endured, or maybe you were born skeptical about all big companies with big pocketbooks. My guess is that all of us — at one point or another — have had to navigate an impossibly complex and frustrating web of process and people to find an answer or get support for a problem caused by that same institution. I know I have. My teeth are grinding a bit just thinking about it. I swear a certain cable and internet provider is responsible for me having to wear a nightguard in my mouth when I sleep. But within those "evil" institutions are also people like you and me, who are just doing the job. Sometimes you find a person who is awesome, a kindred spirit of sorts, and you trust them to help you. It's in their approach and delivery. It's honest and genuine.

At one point in *Trading Places*, Coleman the butler — who has saved money for years likely afraid to invest it in the financial markets based on what he has seen from his bosses — trusts Billy Ray Valentine with those same life savings. Part of their conversation goes like this:

Coleman: "My life savings, sir. Try not to lose it."

Billy Ray Valentine: "Lose it? In a couple of hours, you are going to be the richest butler that ever lived, man."

In this moment, Coleman teaches us something profound:

Believing in the person over the institution provides the greatest return on your investment.

Ever heard the term "imposter syndrome?" I'm not sure it's something we said back in the '80s but it sure did take hold as a business buzzword in the 2020s. Imposter syndrome is the idea, developed in your own head, that you don't belong in the job or in the position that you are in — regardless of whether you have earned it and are smart and capable enough to do it well. It's that sense of faking it or not being "enough." We used to call this "being insecure."

Earlier in the movie, after Billy Ray Valentine is plucked off the street while doing his con man thing to do the job of a commodities broker (and after being trained very quickly by the firm), he is facing his first day on the job and is incredibly nervous. After all, he's never done this job before, and the reality of his inexperience is setting in. We have, however, already learned how incredibly intelligent he is from how quickly he picked up the commodities broker game, so from what we can see, his nervousness doesn't stem from inability or a lack of smarts. At this moment of unsteadiness, he has this exchange with Coleman:

> **Billy Ray:** "What if I can't do this job Coleman? What if I'm not what they expected?"
>
> **Coleman:** "Just be yourself, sir. They can't take that away from you."

If we just learned that being yourself is a key to happiness and success, we'd learn a lot from that exchange. But what we really learn in this moment is that:

 You can be good at what you do and still question yourself. Confident people question themselves. Arrogant people question others.

Now if you've read either of the previous two books in my series, then you also know that this is the time in each chapter where we jump in our time-traveling DeLorean and go back to the exact month the chapter's featured movie was released so we can see what else was happening in pop culture. Oh, and on more than one occasion, you'll get a little glimpse into why my dad had to say *"The village must have lost its idiot again"* multiple times during my formative years.

My Life in June 1983

I was 12 years old and just finishing 6th grade. If I recall correctly, we were going to be the last 6th grade class at the elementary school because the middle school was being reorganized to comprise 6th, 7th, and 8th grades. We most certainly dodged a bullying bullet there.

Graduating from elementary school was a big thing back in the day, especially if you avoided ever strapping on the bright yellow safety harness and sash. Oh, yeah — the iconic "hall monitor." In my school, the task of keeping order in the common areas of the school was basically relegated to kids who were selected to be "campus security." If you liked to tattletale on others, you were the perfect candidate. These pint-sized security wannabes put that harness across their chest that said "Safety" and suddenly they were all powerful and able to tell the other kids what to do, where to go, and how to dress. That last part is not true but given the opportunity, I bet they would have embraced and exercised that power. Did I mention that they all went on to become politicians? I'm sure you know the type. That being said, my bad memories of "safety kids" didn't ruin one of my all-time favorite one-hit wonders, 1982's smash hit "The Safety Dance" from *Men Without Hats*. Yes, you are singing it right now. "You can dance if you want to ..." (Go ahead. I won't watch.)

My fondest memory of elementary school was my phys-ed teacher, Duane Shaulis. (Do they even have Phys Ed anymore?) He was also the reason that I didn't want to graduate elementary school, because I knew that I would lose him as a teacher. Mr. Shaulis was one of a kind in so many ways. He was really the first adult I knew (besides my parents) who had a total passion and love for what he did for a living. Even as a kid, it was easy to see how much he truly loved teaching us. Now, as an adult, I appreciate what he did for us even more.

Headed off to school with a Star Wars shirt and what might be a Godzilla lunchbox.

The first time I met him was during my first week as first grader. He walked into the gymnasium and told us to have a seat on the floor. He was dressed in a way that we would soon learn was his "signature look." Black-rimmed glasses, slicked-back hair, tight athletic non-breathable shirt tucked into very short nylon polyester shorts, tube socks with colored rings at the top of the calf, and Converse tennis shoes. Oh, and he was never without his whistle around his neck. He also had two hearing aids, which was something that most of the kids, including me, had never experienced before. To us, he sounded a little different when he talked. This was great exposure at a young age for all of us to the wonderful variety of people who are the fabric of our communities and it taught us that it is our differences that make us stronger and what makes our planet totally awesome.

Throughout the course of our time at elementary school, we played a lot of really cool games and participated in some rad activities with Mr. Shaulis. Kickball, dodgeball, red rover, all types of tag, and — of course — parachute. If you're a Gen Xer, then you likely know this one. You walked into gym class and saw that huge colored parachute on the floor. Everyone would circle around it and you'd play games like Making Waves, All Change, Popcorn, Roller Ball, and Ball in the Bucket. (If you have no idea what I'm talking about, head over to YouTube to find a video. You need to know about parachute in gym class!) It was by far the best P.E. day. Mr. Shaulis also had climbing ropes of all lengths attached to the ceiling and other beams and he allowed anyone at any time to try and climb higher than they had before. Before we talked about "personal records" (as all our marathoning and weight-lifting friends do today), we were trying to break our own "PRs" on the ropes. Mr. Shaulis really challenged and encouraged all of us, but there were two things he did that made him unforgettable as a teacher and a human:

1. **He motivated us.** In the foyer of the school and right above the doors to the gymnasium were these wooden boards with school records for every event and sport you could imagine — long jump, high jump, fastest rope climb, shuttle run, 50-yard dash, 1-mile run, pushups, pull ups, sit ups, and so many more. Next to each record was the name of the student and the year that they set the record. They were also split by boys and girls as well as grade level. It made every one of us want to strive to see our name on the big wooden "records board." Some of the records had been there for 10 years or more.

   Apparently, Mr. Shaulis had these boards made to inspire us to set goals and strive to be the best we could be. The story goes that he personally paid for the production of the record boards. I never verified it but, based on who he was, it would not surprise me at all. Just the fact that he thought to have them built and displayed is really enough.

2. **He leveled the playing field and enabled our success.**
    I grew up just outside of the city of Baltimore. Our town
    did not have country clubs, golf courses, or high-end
    restaurants. We had public swimming pools, basket-
    ball courts, and McDonalds. We would have been
    more caddie than member at *CaddyShack's* infamous
    Bushwood Country Club and we liked it that way. But
    it also meant that some kids didn't have sneakers for
    phys-ed class. Mr. Shaulis knew this and believed so
    much in the importance of physical fitness — as well
    as the right of every child to have the basics — that he
    had a 10x10 room filled with every shape, size, and
    color of sneaker.

    I'll never forget the day he showed us the room and said
    that the sneakers were there for anyone who forgot to
    bring theirs on a phys-ed day. I mean sure there were
    days here and there where I'm sure students conve-
    niently forgot their sneakers, but that wasn't the real
    reason. He knew that we had a lot of students in need,
    and he didn't want them to feel singled out or embar-
    rassed. The ability for a child whose family can't afford
    sneakers that fit to say "I forgot my sneakers" was a true
    gift. That is just the highest-level humanity right there,
    and that was Mr. Shaulis.

He really truly cared about each one of us. I have no idea where
he is today but if anyone reading this knows him or his family,
please let him and them know what a positive influence he had
on me. I'll never forget him. He was a real-life *Uncle Buck* with
a dash of *Mr. Hand.* What more could you ask for in a teacher?

Pop Culture in 1983

Speaking of teachers, television was embracing educational
shows around 1983 ... sort of. *The Facts of Life* with one of my

teenage crushes Lisa Blair, *Head of the Class* with Howard Hesseman from the classic WKRP, and *Fame* (which is still influencing pop culture today) were all squarely in the top-15 most-viewed shows. And then there was the one-season wonder, *Square Pegs* starring Sarah Jessica Parker, which premiered in 1982 and ended in 1983 due to some supposed shenanigans behind the scenes that you can Google if you so desire.

In music, *Thomas Dolby* was bringing the classroom into the top five with "She Blinded Me With Science" while one of my favorite songs and videos from the '80s, "She's a Beauty" by *The Tubes,* was holding strong in the top 20. One of the really fun band names to say, *Kajagoogoo,* had their biggest hit with "Too Shy." They also had a cameo in *American Horror Story's* season titled "1984," which is a love letter to all things '80s campy horror. One of the most popular singles, "Come on Eileen" by one-hit wonder Dexys Midnight Runners, was ending its run while the staples like Michael Jackson, Prince, and Elton John all had taken up residency in the Top 40 as they often did.

At the box office, there were so many great movies all at once, as it seemed to be each and every week in the '80s. And unlike today, it wasn't all Marvel and DC Comic superhero movies. Yes, that is a dig at the lack of imagination today and the abundance of pre-packaged templated pop culture. I probably should have prefaced the last two lines with "Warning: Curmudgeon analysis incoming." So back to the box office in June of 1983. *Return of the Jedi* was at #1 while Roger Moore was reprising his James Bond role and premiering at #2 in *Octopussy*. Cheech and Chong were *Still Smokin* in real life and in popularity at the box office while *Valley Girl* was delivering on laughs and a great soundtrack. *Flashdance*, which I had to sneak into, and *WarGames,* which I didn't, were both attracting teenage boys to theatres for very different reasons. But it was the movie that premiered at #3 the week of June 10th that provides us with the lessons for this chapter.

Life Lessons from *Trading Places*

Trading Places — starring Eddie Murphy, Dan Akroyd, and Jamie Lee Curtis — told the story of Billy Ray Valentine (Murphy) and Louis Winthorpe, III (Akroyd), who are pawns in a bet by the Duke Brothers who own a commodities brokerage firm. Louis is one of their best traders and is also a snobby, privileged, and pompous human being. Billy Ray is a superb con man who is ultimately busted trying to pull one over on the Dukes and Winthorpe. The Dukes, being pompous and privileged themselves, come up with a bet — a $1 bet — that if they reversed the roles and fortunes of Louis and Billy Ray, that Louis might turn to a life of crime and Billy Ray might thrive in his newfound position in society. They promptly set up Louis with drugs and had him busted while they invited Billy Ray into the commodities brokerage and gave him Louis's job. While on the street, Louis meets a "lady of the night" named Ophelia (Curtis) who finds it in her heart to help Louis and keep him from getting himself killed while also working with him to find out exactly what happened. It's a very funny movie with generational acting talent, that was also way ahead of its time with a focus on some really important social issues.

■■■■■■■■■■■■■■■■■■■■■■■■■■■■■■■■

⚒ **FUN FACT:** The Duke Brothers have a small cameo in Coming to America as two homeless guys who Prince Akeem (played by Murphy) gives a pile of $100 bills. If you haven't seen Coming to America or if you just missed their cameo, it's good to see that karma put them exactly where they belonged.

■■■■■■■■■■■■■■■■■■■■■■■■■■■■■■■■

So what did a spoiled commodities broker, a con man, a butler, two pompous wealthy brothers, and a lady of the night teach us about life?

Believing in the person over the institution provides the greatest return on your investment.

Although there are several characters in the movie, I've chosen to make the interpersonal relationship between Billy Ray and Coleman the focal point of both lessons. The reason for this is that in a world of wealth, they've both been treated as if they don't really exist — that they really don't matter and are unimportant and just part of the unwashed masses simply because of their station in life. It's this commonality, which they also share with Ophelia, that really makes their interactions interesting and meaningful.

So, speaking of interpersonal interactions, who thinks one of the best things in life is when you must call customer service at a large organization? We all look forward to it, right? How about having to interact with a government agency? Been to a DMV lately? Okay, sorry for making everyone stress unnecessarily. If you read my 2nd book, then you can use one of the lessons that we learned from Mr. Miyagi to ease it a bit when he said, "Don't forget to breathe. Very important."

Ahhh.

Large institutions are part of our lives, like it or not. Big tech, big pharma, big government, and Wall Street are all around us all the time. Unless you go completely off the grid — which sounds intriguing and a bit romantic until you watch a show like *Alone, Naked and Afraid,* or anything set in Alaska — you really can't escape the influence they have on how you live. But this is not going to be a diatribe on all things "evil empire," nor will it be a state media piece on how they only bring positivity and happiness into our little common lives. I'll leave that conversation to the journalists, think tanks, and talking heads. Way too serious a topic for this "neo maxi zune dweebie," which was the label that Bender put on Brian in *The Breakfast Club* and which I gladly accept and embrace as my own.

On Malibu Beach in my *Risky Business* sunglasses after visiting *The Fall Guy* set, doing my best impersonation of Anthony Michael Hall as Brian in *The Breakfast Club*.

Towards the climax of *Trading Places* — not to be mistaken with *Klymaxx*, the all-female R&B group from the '80s that brought us the awesome ballad and couples-skate favorite, "I Miss You" — Billy Ray and Louis have joined forces to bring down the Duke Brothers. To put their plan into action, they need Coleman the butler and Ophelia to put their trust in them ... and give them their life savings, which prompts this exchange:

> **Coleman:** "My life savings sir. Try not to lose it."

> **Billy Ray:** "Lose it? In a couple of hours, you are going to be the richest butler that ever lived, man."

> **Ophelia:** "I worked real hard for this, Louie. I hope you know what you're doing."

Louie: "Thank you, Ophelia."

As I've alluded, the complexities of the commodities market are a little too much for a Simple Mind (now you're humming "Don't You Forget About Me") like mine to understand or explain to anyone else. Same goes for Coleman and Ophelia, but what they did know — with great confidence — was the character of these men, Billy Ray and Louis. And that's what they were really investing in. Not the financial markets or institution and certainly not the commodities market. They invested in the human beings who worked within the institution. They trusted *them* with their life savings. Their cold, hard cash. Their money. But let's think about investing in a different, broader way.

Let's go back to the customer-service question I brought up at the beginning. Very few of us have the connections to go right to the top when we're seeking to close a transaction to our satisfaction or when we have an issue with an institution like a consumer services company (cell phone provider, the electric company, etc.), a big retailer (like Amazon or Target or WalMart), or even a big non-profit (like a university or a hospital). Most of us don't have pull or contacts even at small or mid-sized companies, let alone the giants. Large institutions have multiple layers and you are a "liar, liar pants on fire" if you say that you've never yelled "customer service" or "representative" multiple times into the phone at the automated choose-your-own-adventure extension tree.

■■■■■■■■■■■■■■■■■■■■■■■■■■■■■■■■

🕹 **FUN FACT:** Choose Your Own Adventure books were written in 2nd person and allowed the reader to take on the role of the protagonist. Every few pages, you were given several choices to solve a problem or challenge and then told to turn to the corresponding page where you would learn the impact of your decision. Would your story continue,

or would you perish and have to start over? Most
were in the fantasy genre and their popularity
soared in the '80s. Over 250 million copies have
been sold[3] and there are very real rumors about a
"Choose Your Adventure" show being greenlit at
a large studio!

■■■■■■■■■■■■■■■■■■■■■■■■■■■■■■■■■■

Now let's expand this example beyond customer service and
broaden our focus to the people with whom we interact in general
at these large institutions. Many of us — including me — enter into
these interactions with a bit of a negative attitude. Our experience
has shown us that whatever we need to get out of said institution
is going to be a challenge (at best) and a near impossibility (at
worst). In the case of the large institutions that require a monetary
investment from us or other tangible resources, they've absolutely
earned a healthy suspicion and skepticism from even the most
patient and trusting among us. We're not apt to believe in the
institution, but can we overcome our reticence to believe, instead,
in a person or a group of people? Remember our lesson:

**Believing in the person over the institution provides the
greatest return on your investment.**

What I hope you have noticed so far in this lesson is that I've
focused on the institution and not the people — except to
mention that we have interactions with them. Coleman and
Ophelia made their monetary decision based on the *people*
with whom they interacted and not the institution itself. But as
I mentioned before, not every investment we make with large
institutions or organizations is monetary. Sometimes we invest
time and energy — sometimes a lot *more* of our free time than we
signed up for when we chose to interact with a large entity on the
promise that they would provide their service or product to our

---

3   https://www.smithsonianmag.com/arts-culture/choose-your-own-adventure-
    40-years-old-180973084/

expectations (and the expectations they instilled in us through their marketing/advertising).

Over the 2021 holiday season, my sister gave me a totally awesome gift that I desperately needed. I live in South Florida but travel often to cold weather environments for speaking gigs and I don't have, as the British would say, "a proper" jacket. So my sister went to one of the most well-known outdoor outfitters on the planet and got me a fantastic one. This is a company that prides itself on making a rugged, high-quality product that is designed to hold up and thrive in the very worst of elements. From the outside, the company's reputation is stellar and I've always held them in very high regard, so I was surprised when the zipper on the jacket broke after it had been worn just four times. I mean, come on folks, it wasn't like I was climbing Kilimanjaro as it rose "like Olympus above the Serengeti" (as Toto sang in their 1982 hit, "Africa," which — if re-released today — would probably go to #1 on the charts once again). I just wore it on two flights — one to Chicago and the other to Lexington, Kentucky — and thankfully we didn't experience any of the external elements inside the plane at 35,000 feet. The jacket was clearly just a faulty product that should be pretty simple to address and resolve with this global outdoor company. I was about to find out that the process for exchanging or having a faulty item fixed could have been what Ozzy was singing about in his 1980 metal classic, "Crazy Train." Here's how it went:

1. Search heaven and earth Belinda Carlisle style for a contact number.

2. Call, wait patiently through multiple choose-your-own-adventure phone trees and then sit on hold for an *hour*.

3. Share my story with the representative, who then tells me that I will need to pay for shipping to send the jacket

for their review. Read that again — I have to pay for the shipping for their faulty item.

4. The review process will take 6 to 8 weeks from the time that they receive the jacket. Meanwhile, no replacement jacket to keep me warm while I wait.

5. There will be no communication between the company and me throughout the process.

6. They will either fix the jacket or send it back unrepaired if they determine the broken zipper is not their responsibility.

What?! Needless to say, I was not part of the "Shiny Happy People" who R.E.M. sang about when I was informed of the process. Knowing that it was the institution/organization and not the person, I pushed back politely and respectfully and ultimately got them to agree to pay for the shipping — which they really should have done all along. I explained to the representative that I did not blame her one bit and that her company had put her in a really tough position. It was pretty clear that upper management did not consider or care for the people on the front lines or, as it seemed to me in that moment, their customers.

Fast forward eight weeks and I received my jacket back. Yay! I opened the package with the same zeal that Ralphie opened his Red Rider BB Gun in the 1983 now cult classic, *A Christmas Story*. But unlike Ralphie, I didn't get what I wanted. Inside the package was my jacket ... still with a broken zipper and a letter that said they could not process my request because the case number was not included inside the package with the jacket. A case number that was in multiple emails, along with my name and contact info, which was also on the *outside* of the package. A case number that was in their system associated with all my information. But apparently you also must include it on a piece of paper inside in the package that you send. Of course, no one told me this. Worse yet, this company thought the best course of action was just to hold the jacket for almost two months and then return it to me still broken. No one bothered to even try to match my contact info with the claim number. Needless to say, I was dumbfounded and after reading the letter I was dropping "F" bombs like Neal Page at the rental car counter in *Planes, Trains and Automobiles.*

But here is where we get to the lesson that we learned from our characters in *Trading Places.* After "F" bombing around my house, I collected myself and called the company to explain my situation. The person I got on the phone was amazing from the first moment she picked up and immediately set me at ease. I trusted her right away and knew that she was going to resolve this situation to my benefit. After educating herself on my case (including that ever-loving case *number*!) and a bit of back and forth with her manager, she said she was going to see this all the way through for me. She walked me through a very thorough process and told me to put her name on the outside of the package as well as on the inside on a piece of paper with my case number. She said that she would personally handle my item and would make sure that the jacket was fixed and sent back to me in an expedited fashion. She apologized for my inconvenience at least five times throughout our call. She took full responsibility for a situation that she did not cause and that was in no way her fault — which is a lesson in and of itself for all our dear "leaders" today. In a manner of minutes, my confidence was restored because of a single person inside a large, impersonable retail company. I trusted Samantha even when I trusted no one else in her company.

You should know that I did receive my jacket back in half the time that I did the first go-round and it was fixed. No more broken zipper! There was also a note inside from Samantha, apologizing again for something that was not her fault as well as saying that she hoped my friends, family, and I would continue to support the company that she worked for. I will do that. I will buy from them, and I will encourage my friends and family to do the same.

You're probably wondering why on earth I would patronize this company again. It's simple, actually. It's because of Samantha. I'm investing in her, not the organization. She is a human being doing a tough job at a company that clearly doesn't value her and her teammates like they should. But currently her income and livelihood is predicated on this company generating revenue to support positions like hers. Oftentimes, punishing the institution or organization has less of a negative impact on the leadership and decision makers within the institution or organization overall and more on the people who are just trying to do a sometimes difficult or impossible job (thanks to arbitrary or inane rules set by those who don't have to deal with the consequences that their rules or policies create).

Having said that, I did let her know that if she ever leaves the company that she should feel free to email me and let me know because at that point, I will not buy from them any longer and I will not recommend them to anyone I know. The human I invested in and the one who invested in me would have moved on and I would have no reason at all to invest in the organization at that point. I have no idea if she will actually do that, but if she does, I will gladly be true to my word. At the very least, telling her how I felt about the situation conveyed how much her efforts on my behalf really meant to me. I appreciated her, and she deserved that appreciation.

There's a great Depeche Mode song — well, a lot of great Depeche Mode songs — and the lyrics go like this:

> *"People are people*
> *so why should it be,*
> *you and I should*
> *get along so awfully?"*

I don't think they were talking about the humans you interact with inside of large institutions or organizations, but it's good to remember those words when you do. Actually, we'd be much better off if we just made that a core life principle. That's for another day or lesson, I suppose.

Okay, on to our next *Trading Places* lesson!

 You can be good at what you do and still question yourself. Confident people question themselves. Arrogant people question others.

If you read my first book, then you know that I am not a fan of buzzwords. Every company and every group of friends unfortunately has a guy or gal we will call Buzzword Bob or Buzzword Betty. You know the person in a meeting who says, "Let's *table that* while we *drill down* into these *bowling pins* and see if we can *move the needle* with *limited bandwidth*. But, for now, let's *take it offline*, because I need a *bio break*, so make sure to *put a pin in it* and *ping me later*." Ugh.

There is one recent catchphrase that I think represents something real and tangible — *imposter syndrome,* a concept we introduced at the beginning of this chapter and which I'd like to explore more deeply now. If you are unfamiliar with "imposter syndrome," it's basically the feeling that you don't deserve the success or opportunity that you have been given and earned. Maybe you feel like an imposter after earning and receiving a promotion, being offered a new job at a higher level than you've had before, being asked to be interviewed as a subject-matter expert by a media outlet, or — in my case — being paid to be a keynote speaker and author. People who experience imposter syndrome struggle with the idea that they have been chosen to do something over others no matter how much more qualified they are through their own hard work, experience, and effort. You'd be surprised how many people actually feel this way. Maybe you've felt it or are feeling it now. That's a good thing, actually.

At one point in the movie *Trading Places*, Billy Ray and Coleman are having a conversation about — you guessed it — imposter syndrome. It was the night before Billy Ray started the new job as a commodities broker. Now prior to this conversation we've seen how intelligent, resourceful, and capable he is and how quickly he picked up the inner workings of the commodities market. Nonetheless, he has this vulnerable exchange with Coleman:

> **Billy Ray:** "What if I can't do this job, Coleman? What if I'm not what they expected?"

> **Coleman:** "Just be yourself, sir. They can't take that away from you."

Now if our lesson just ended with "always just be yourself," that would be pretty good advice to take with you on your life journey. But we are going to go deeper than that. Deep like a lyric-writing class taught by Chuck D or Morrissey. (Bet you never thought you'd see those two referenced together. Different backgrounds. Different genres. Same musical and lyrical genius.)

Like most of us, Billy Ray was nervous the night before starting something new and that is totally understandable. Regardless of how prepared you are, there are a lot of unknowns when you step into a new role — particularly when it is in an entirely new area of your career or life. Now this may sound a little counter-intuitive, but the more you question yourself, the more prepared you are for the new opportunity that is presenting itself to you. It's also a pretty good indicator that you are — or are going to be — a very good leader. I can see some of you tilting your head to the side like a dog does when they are trying really hard to understand what you are saying. Am I confusing you like geometry confused me?

The more you question yourself, the more prepared you are for the new opportunity that is presenting itself to you.

Let me explain. There aren't many concrete truths in this world, but you can be certain that you absolutely cannot get better at something without questioning yourself. After all, the only other options are never questioning yourself (because you are, of course, perfect in every way to which Enid Strict, aka The Church Lady, would tell you "Well, isn't that special!") or constantly questioning others (which is what arrogant people tend to do). So, if you aren't perfect and you're not arrogant, then at some point you will have imposter syndrome through the very simple and humble act of questioning yourself, just like Billy Ray.

Now for us to get everything out of this lesson, it's going to require sharing the ending of the movie with you. This is your spoiler alert but let's be honest here — '80s movies typically had a happy ending (no, not *that* happy ending, you "sinners" .... in my best Chris Farley voice). We were all hoping for "happily ever after" in every '80s movie, so it should come as no surprise that Billy Ray, Louis, Ophelia, and Coleman all win in the end. This wasn't the '90s, where we find out at the end of *The Usual Suspects* that the violent mastermind criminal Keyser Soze is actually Verbal Kint, who is portrayed as the weakest and most feeble of the characters. Neither is it the 2000s with movies like *Gone Girl*, where the little girl isn't dead or missing but "adopted/kidnapped" by the police chief to replace his child who passed away. For those who haven't seen either of those movies, I'd imagine your spoiler hate for me is pure at this point. Are you picturing me as the most hated of characters in '80s movies — Todd/Tad, who was always the bully with perfect hair and a neatly tied sweater around his neck. You know the guy ... he dated the girl who the introverted, awkward, geeky, and super sweet main character had a crush on. I never understood how bully behavior, perfect hair, and a sweater tied around your neck went together. If you really want to see a realistic bully in the '80s, take the time to watch the very underrated *Three O'Clock High,* where Richard Tyson plays Buddy Revell — who, for my money, is the best bully of all time.

Okay, back to the spoiler for *Trading Places.* Thanks to how quickly Billy Ray was able to learn and excel at commodities trading, he and Louis partner to own the commodities market and drive the Duke brothers out of business and into bankruptcy. There's a great article on NPR that explains in real terms exactly how Billy Ray was able to pull it off.[4]

Billy Ray wins the day by replacing a crop report on oranges (that the Duke Brothers had bribed someone to obtain before the market opened) with a fake one that tells them to do the exact opposite of what they should. This created an environment where everything the Duke Brothers did made things worse for them and their clients. Like the upside-down world in *Stranger Things,* Billy Ray had to drive up the price, sell to the less-capable brokers on the floor, then wait for the real report to hit the market, thus driving the price down. Billy Ray and Louis essentially bought low, got rich, and bankrupted their enemies. The money that they used to invest from Ophelia and Coleman make them both millionaires multiple times over and Billy Ray and Louis go on to start their own firm while the Duke Brothers go bankrupt.

---

4   https://www.npr.org/sections/money/2013/07/19/201430727/what-actually-happens-at-the-end-of-trading-places

Ultimately, *Trading Places* tells us the story of an intelligent and underrated guy who just needed an opportunity to showcase his abilities —a guy who thought he wasn't good enough to do the job. A guy who questioned himself rather than others. A guy with imposter syndrome.

■■■■■■■■■■■■■■■■■■■■■■■■■■■■■■■■

🕹 **FUN FACT:** Trading commodities on inside **information obtained from the government wasn't actually illegal when the movie came out, but it's illegal now. It was banned in the 2010 finance-overhaul law, under a special provision often referred to as the Eddie Murphy Rule.**[5]

■■■■■■■■■■■■■■■■■■■■■■■■■■■■■■■■

As we get closer to finishing up this lesson, you may have noticed that I haven't spent any time talking about the arrogant people who question others. There are several reasons for that:

1. **Arrogant people don't read books.** They know everything already. This lesson and this book is for you, the person who questions themselves rather than others.

2. **Arrogance and arrogant people can only survive and thrive when talked about.** A big part of arrogance is talking about yourself, whether alone or around others.

3. **Arrogance and arrogant people promote negativity and negative energy.** Confidence and confident people promote positivity and positive energy. I'd rather focus on the latter. That's my tribe. Those are the people I dig.

4. **We all know arrogant people.** They suck. I didn't think it would do any of us any good to spend time and energy on describing why they suck. My goal with this lesson

---

5   https://www.npr.org/sections/money/2013/07/19/201430727/what-actually-happens-at-the-end-of-trading-places

was to let you know that questioning yourself isn't a lack of confidence. On the contrary, it's that very confidence that allows you to question yourself and that makes you totally awesome and not at all sucky like those arrogant sweater-around-the-neck dudes and dudettes.

In his 1982 hit song "Change," which was also on the soundtrack for Chapter 2's movie *Vision Quest*, John Waite sang:

> *"Do you remember*
> *When you got your lucky break?*
> *You're looking back now*
> *And it seems like a mistake ..."*

Your break — whether it has already happened or is in the making — is not entirely lucky or a mistake. You earned it. You made it happen. But it's always a good thing to keep a little head-space reserved for questioning yourself. That's how you'll keep from sitting back on your laurels and how you'll continue to get better at what you do. And when you ultimately make it to the top, that questioning headspace will also keep you humble. A bit of imposter syndrome is a good thing. The unfortunate truth is that the rarest talent in the most talented of humans is the ability is to show humility. When the time comes, be rare.

**Your break — whether it has already
happened or is in the making — is
not entirely lucky or a mistake. You
earned it. You made it happen.**

CHAPTER 2

VISION QUEST

"It ain't the six minutes ... it's what happens in that six minutes."

— ELMO, *VISION QUEST*

L ife is full of moments. Take, for example, the moment you sit down and begin typing the first words for your first book. The initial moments of becoming an author can be surreal. You are beginning a journey that has a lot of unknowns and your initial plan will most certainly change. (And not just once. Multiple times.) And you'll find that what you *thought* made sense at the beginning really doesn't once you get to the middle. And the *ending*? Well, that will likely change as well. You may keep the conclusion but the lead-up to it could look very different. The path is uncharted. Every single time.

So why am I telling you this? Is it to help you understand the trials and tribulations of a writer or the complexities of the book-writing process (because that's admittedly front of mind for me)? Nope. This is about you ... not me. Writing a book is just an example of a goal-driven journey that requires our open-mindedness and our willingness to do things differently, sometimes midstream. As it turns out, writing a book is no more difficult than anything else you may want to accomplish (and it's no more special than many of the things *you* have already achieved). I discovered that, when writing a book, it starts and ends with me and the choices that I make with my time, for better or for worse. Make the time to write and then voila! Sooner than I thought it possible, I became a published author. It's as easy today as it has ever been. Self-publishing tools, author coaches, and collaborative publishing models are right at our fingertips and they're designed to make the process as seamless and simple as possible. The world of publishing is not nearly as scary or as mysterious as it once was (thank goodness!). And the old way of doing things is not always the best or most accessible way anymore. The great news is that you don't need the big traditional publishers to publish your book today. Options like indie publishing (i.e., self-publishing) and hybrid/collaborative publishers, of which there are many, are the great equalizer. And the coolest thing in this scenario is that you really get to keep your voice and your identity. Surely, the folks at Random House — had I approached them instead of my current publisher — would have been like, "This dude is obsessed with the '80s. He was wearing checkerboard Vans at his first meeting with the editorial team! Are we sure about this? Can we get him to wear penny loafers instead?"

My reason for sharing the broad basics of the writing journey is to provide a practical example of the different ways in which we can spend our time — our proverbial 15 minutes of fame or our powerful opportunities at work and in life. *Are we making the most of those minutes?* As I sat down to write this 3rd book in my series, the COVID-19 pandemic had essentially shut down the global economy and, in the short term, had changed the way we lived — even with things as simple as a trip to the grocery store. Before everything went a bit haywire, I took off with a friend on a cross-country trip from my home in South Florida to hers in Pagosa Springs, Colorado. We essentially went from population 4.5 million to population 2,000 and I have to say that it was delightful (but my thoughts on big city vs. rural living or beach vs. mountains is for another time). You see, as we drove across the big, beautiful United States — with all its magnificent splendor and diverse landscapes and populations — we passed many a small town.

March 2020, on a road trip from Florida to Colorado with a stop on the famous Route 66.

This network of small towns is often referred to as the fabric of America and as we drove through and by, we noticed a distinct small-town trend. Most of the towns had a welcome sign — usually on a water tower but sometimes on a little green sign — that included a nod to the local high school sports heroes. They said something like "Home of Central High School State Football Champions: 1968, 1993, and 2016" or "Home of the High School State Champion Monarchs Girls Volleyball Team: 2000, 2015, and 2018." Some of the welcome signs focused on individuals who grew up in the town and went on to play professional sports — recognizable names like Mickey Mantle and Jerry Rice. And yet other towns touted athletes who may not be recognizable to outsiders but who will forever have their place in home-town history for centuries to come — names like Timmy Gast, Jane Wright, and Louden Swain. Did you catch that last one, '80s fans? I sure hope so.

Now we didn't *really* see a welcome sign with a "Home of Louden Swain, State Wrestling Champion 1985," but I can assure you that if we had, that sign would now be hanging in my house, laws about stealing roadside signage be damned. I would have gladly paid the fine and spent the weekend in a county lockup — institutionalized — for that prized possession.

■ ■

🕹 **FUN FACT:** Suicidal Tendencies sang "They stuck me in an institution / Said it was the only solution" in their timeless 1983 punk rock classic "Institutionalized." Hmmm ... and to think all he wanted was a Pepsi.

■ ■

On that note, let's talk about Louden Swain and one of the all-time greatest sports movies, *Vision Quest*. The night that Louden is going to wrestle his nemesis, Shute, for the state championship, he visits Elmo (the short-order cook at the hotel restaurant where Louden has a part-time job) at Elmo's small apartment. Elmo is taking the night off to watch Louden compete and when Louden says he is nervous and not sure if can go through with the match, Elmo gives one of the most impassioned, inspiring, and under-rated monologues in movie history. Within the monologue he says, "It ain't the six minutes ... it's what happens in those six minutes." Now he was talking about a wrestling match, but the concept applies to our whole lives. Some of us only get one minute while others get the full six minutes (or 15!). Ultimately though, it comes down to how we use the time we're allotted.

 It's not the minutes we are given; it's what we are willing to give to those minutes.

When we think about 18-year-old high-school wrestlers, we don't typically presume they might provide us with philosophies on life. But Louden Swain, like many unlikely heroes from iconic '80s movies, teaches us quite a bit through his grit, determination, and his never-quit attitude in the face of incredible adversity. At the beginning of the movie, he says, "My name's Louden, Louden Swain. Last week I turned 18. I wasn't ready for it. I haven't done anything yet. So I made this deal with myself. This is the year that I make my mark." Through his words and his actions, he teaches us a lesson that I'd like to impart here to you:

 There are really two ways to live your life: You can mark the time or make your mark.

Imparting wisdom. Look at me. All grown up.

So, before we dive deeper into musings on the value of life and time, and the lessons we can learn from high-school wrestlers, lets hit 88 mph in the Delorean and travel back in time!

It was February 1985 and I was in the second half of my freshman year in high school. Over the previous summer, I had a bit (insert sarcasm here) of a growth spurt. In a few months' time, I went from 5'5" and 130 pounds soaking wet to 5'10" and 170 pounds. The additional height was incredibly welcome, considering I was already wearing size-12 shoes (British Knights and Vans, if you are curious) — which, at my previous height, created a bit of a waddling gait, hence the nickname "Duck, Duck, Clews." Yeah, I know ... as aggravating as that nickname was, I do have to admit it was pretty good.

> *Reminiscing on my British Knights has brought up our first Digression Alert. For those who are picking up one of my books for the first time, welcome to my tendency to digress from time to time. Kind of like the whole "dog sees squirrel" thing. I promise to call out the Digression Alerts like the one below, to both make you, the reader, aware that we were going off track for just a bit and give me the opportunity to chase the proverbial squirrel up a tree before resuming our morning walk around the neighborhood.*

DIGRESSION ALERT

Many of you know the brand name Vans — at least I hope so. I mean they are really one of the only pieces of fashion that remain from the '80s, for very good reason. But you may not know the shoe brand British Knights, which hit the streets in 1983. Their tagline was "The shoe ain't nothin' without the BK button" and they were one of the first brands to use hip-hop artists as endorsers when they signed Kool Moe Dee (famous for "How Ya

Like Me Now") to introduce the brand on television.[6]
I did love my BKs, especially my black-and-white
faux-snakeskin shoes.

■■■■■■■■■■■■■■■■■■■■■■■■■■■■■■■■■■

So back to "Duck, Duck, Clews" and the second half of my
freshman year of high school. One thing I was thankful for was
that my voice had finally begun to change, and I was no longer
singing alto soprano solos of "Tomorrow" from *Annie* or "Send in
the Clowns" by Judy Collins in the school choir. I'm surprised that
I made it out of that era relatively unscathed. I still can't believe
I wore a mock turtleneck and sang The 5th Dimension's semi-hit
"Aquarius/Let the Sunshine In" while dancing and clapping in
front of the entire school. Good lord.

Luckily for me, there was a cavalcade of pop culture to distract
my high-school peers from my changing voice and ridiculous
feet. The Top 40 was as eclectic as ever, showing once again the
awesome diversity in genres and sounds that made the '80s music
landscape a true product that might be called "of, by, and for the
people." It was the '80s, so — of course — Prince and Madonna
had entries on the charts but, after that, the variety was awesome.
New Edition was "dialing their baby's number and getting a click
every time" with "Mr. Telephone Man." Glam metal band and
one-hit wonder, Giuffria, was on the charts with their ballad "Call
to the Heart." John Fogerty was building on his success from
Creedence Clearwater Revival in the late '60s and early '70s with
his folk-style hit "The Old Man Down the Road." Frankie Goes to
Hollywood was creating what would be a club song for decades to
come and telling us all "don't do it" with their hit single "Relax."
The HoneyDrippers (led by Robert Plant) were bringing '50s
rock back with "Rockin' at Midnight." Morris Day and The Time
said they needed to show us their "Jungle Love" — "oh we oh
we oh." And, last but not least, Journey's hit "Only the Young,"

---

6   https://en.wikipedia.org/wiki/British_Knights

from this chapter's movie, *Vision Quest*, was in its fourth week on the charts.

In television, MTV was getting some competition with the launch of VH1 in the United States; we all had a stool next to Norm in *Cheers;* Tubbs and Crockett were making really bad fashion fashionable in *Miami Vice;* two American families, the Huxtables (*The Cosby Show*) and the Keatons (*Family Ties*), were responsible for the two most popular shows of the year; and Betty White was just being her totally rad and awesome self in *The Golden Girls.*

At the box office, Eddie Murphy was once again #1 and making it rain $2.00 movie tickets. This time around, he was putting bananas in tailpipes as Axel Foley in *Beverly Hills Cop.* A brain, an athlete, a basket case, a princess, and a criminal were putting a spotlight on teen angst and were well on their way to becoming the poster children for Generation X in *The Breakfast Club.* A lot of people were actually paying good money for a history lesson with *Amadeus.* And Kelly Preston was dazzling us in yet another '80s coming-of-age movie, *Mischief.*

But our life and work lessons in this chapter come from a sports movie about wrestling — a sport that made headlines more for its scripted matches and colorful characters like Andre the Giant, Hulk Hogan, and Randy "Macho Man" Savage than for the athletes who grinded it out *for real* (not just for entertainment) in the squared circle in competitions throughout the world for thousands of years. On February 15, 1985, *Vision Quest* premiered in theatres across the country with very little fanfare. Directed by Harold Becker and starring Matthew Modine, Linda Fiorentino, and Michael Schoeffling (Jake Ryan from *Sixteen Candles*), the movie tells the story of a high-school senior and wrestler named Louden Swain (played by Modine) who doesn't feel like he has accomplished anything in his life. He sets out to do something that no one thinks is possible — drop several weight classes to wrestle and beat the undefeated Brian Shute, who was the best high-school wrestler in the state of Washington. Louden faces a variety of challenges along the way, but has his best friend Kuch (played by Schoeffling) supporting and encouraging him throughout. Besides Kuch, Louden also has two additional people in his corner who believe in him. The first is an older co-worker named Elmo (played by J.C. Quinn) and the second is Carla (played by Fiorentino), who is a mysterious drifter renting a room from Louden's father.

■■■■■■■■■■■■■■■■■■■■■■■■■■■■■■■

⌨ FUN FACT: Here's one for those of you who aren't old enough to have experienced the '80s in real time but who still love '80s pop culture. **Matthew Modine, who plays Louden Swain in *Vision Quest*, is also Dr. Brenner in the Netflix mega-hit, *Stranger Things*.**

■■■■■■■■■■■■■■■■■■■■■■■■■■■■■■■

Vision Quest is an inspirational movie and has elements of multiple genres including coming-of-age, romantic comedy (romcom), and drama. It is, without a doubt, one of the most underrated movies of the 1980s and boasts a top-five movie soundtrack that includes Journey, John Waite, Sammy Hagar, Ronnie James Dio, Foreigner, Don Henley, Style Council, Red Rider, and Madonna, who makes a cameo in the film as a singer in a bar performing her hit "Crazy for You."

So, what can an 18-year-old wrestler and his team of outcast supporters teach us about life?

It's not the minutes we are given; it's what we are willing to give to those minutes.

The night of his match with Shute, Louden is nervous and decides to visit his friend, Elmo — the short-order cook from the hotel restaurant — at his apartment. Elmo is decades older than Louden and it's also clear that Elmo does not have a lot of money. Throughout the movie, he is a bit of a father figure to Louden, whose actual father isn't overly supportive and doesn't seem to have a lot of time for him.

When Louden gets to Elmo's apartment, Louden sees that Elmo is getting dressed up and tells him that when he went by the hotel, they mentioned that Elmo was taking the night off. Elmo says to Louden, "Of course I'm taking the night off, dummy. Isn't this the night that you wrestle Shute?" Louden looks a little shocked and, knowing that Elmo will get docked his pay for the evening, he says, "You took the night off for that?" Elmo replies, "Money ain't everything, kid." Now if this section were to end right here, we could walk away with a very valuable life lesson. From the outside, people might think that Elmo choosing to forego some wages when he can least afford it is simply crazy. Why make that sacrifice? Why face those consequences? Elmo's support for his friend didn't come with conditions, parameters, or what-ifs — and that's exactly how it should be.

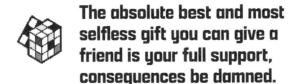

The absolute best and most selfless gift you can give a friend is your full support, consequences be damned.

That is friendship, at its purest, and that is likely your first lesson ever from a movie about wrestling.

But this is not where our discussion of *Vision Quest* ends and, thankfully for all of us, this was not where the scene ended either

— as this scene ultimately delivers one of the most underrated monologues in cinematic history.

Louden continues to look perplexed as to why Elmo would be willing to make this sacrifice for him and this classic exchange takes place:

> **Louden:** "It's not that big a deal, Elmo. I mean, it's six lousy minutes on the mat, if that."
>
> **Elmo:** "You ever hear of Pelé?"
>
> **Louden:** "Yeah, he's a soccer player."
>
> **Elmo:** "A very famous soccer player ... I was in the room here one day ... watchin' the Mexican channel on TV. I don't know nothin' about Pelé. I'm watchin' what this guy can do with a ball and his feet. Next thing I know, he jumps in the air and flips into a somersault and kicks the ball in — upside down and backwards ... the goddamn goalie never knew what the fuck hit him. Pelé gets excited and he rips off his jersey and starts running around the stadium, waving it around his head. Everybody's screaming in Spanish. I'm here, sitting alone in my room, and I start crying. That's right, I start crying. Because another human being — a species that I happen to belong to — could kick a ball, and lift himself, and the rest of us sad-assed human beings, up to a better place to be, if only for a minute. Let me tell ya, kid — it was pretty goddamned glorious. It ain't the six minutes ... it's what *happens* in that six minutes."

Six minutes.

As of today's writing, I am 51 years old — which looks much older on paper than I actually feel or act. That's now over half a century that I've been on this big, beautiful planet of ours. That's also a lot of six-minute segments. In fact, my handy-dandy calculator tells me that it is 4,467,600 six-minute segments. I've always liked the word proverbial, so I am going to use it here. Those six minutes encompass the totality of a wrestling match. Those *proverbial* "six minutes" really represent the time you have in life to give something a shot. To go out on the limb or the cliff's edge or any other cliché of your liking that represents the Rocky "go for it" mentality that was his answer to Drago in *Rocky IV* when Drago said, "I must break you."

■■■■■■■■■■■■■■■■■■■■■■■■■■■■■■■■■■

🔨 **FUN FACT:** Dolph Lundgren, who plays Ivan Drago in Rocky IV, has a master's degree in chemical engineering and attended MIT on a Fulbright Scholarship. I've heard it said he has an IQ of 160. The lesson here is "don't judge a book by its cover," kiddos.

■■■■■■■■■■■■■■■■■■■■■■■■■■■■■■■■■■

Now, unfortunately, not everyone gets the full "six minutes" of life — those epic make-it-or-break-it moments — and some who do get the full six minutes don't really and truly experience it to its fullest. What do I mean by that? Although I didn't wrestle growing up — beyond trying out one year and quickly being dismantled and twisted up through a move called the grapevine (pretty painful move, actually) by Chris Boyle who was a contender for the state championship at the time — I can certainly see the parallels between life's big opportunities and a wrestling match. We start in the neutral position with our life in front of us; we feel out our opponent or, in this analogy, our life; some of us carefully and gradually work our way across the mat while others race in, grab hold, and attempt to lock horns; we then find ourselves managing what life throws at us in the form of takedowns, escapes, reversals, penalties, and even illegal holds (which can lead to a disqualification for ourselves or another); we score points and we have points taken away; in some situations, we start on top while others find us starting from the bottom;

we sometimes find ourselves pinned on our backs, hearing the slap of the mat signifying a loss on our part while other times we find a way to break free before the match is called and reverse the momentum into our favor; and, if we are lucky enough to go the full six minutes, we will ultimately find ourselves feeling exhausted and drained but experienced and accomplished. To use the words of the hip-hop prophets Rob Base and DJ E-Z Rock all the way back in 1987, we will definitely experience "joy and pain." That's life and it is wonderful in all its messiness. What are you willing to give to your six minutes?

Mark the Time or Make Your Mark

Now let's go back to the 4,467,600 six-minute segments I mentioned a few pages ago. Each of those moments has been an opportunity for me to work toward achieving something, attaining a goal, or doing something to better myself. Although I have been very goal-oriented throughout my life, it wasn't until about the 3,700,000th six-minute segment that it really and truly clicked for me. As we find out at the beginning of the movie, Louden Swain figured it out much sooner than that. When we first meet him, he says:

> "My name's Louden, Louden Swain. Last week I turned 18. I wasn't ready for it. I haven't done anything yet. So, I made this deal with myself. This is the year that I make my mark."

The first week of my 18th year on this planet also happened to be my first week at college and I almost burned down our dormitory — Talking Heads-style "burning down" — during a pretty intense fireworks battle (which I promise to tell you more about in Chapter 5, when we get nostalgic about the Tom Cruise classic, *Cocktail)*. Contrast that with Louden Swain's first week of his 18th year, when he was already disappointed in his lack of life accomplishments and contemplating how to make his mark. We all mature at different speeds, I suppose.

Louden planned to make his mark by dropping down a weight class to 168 pounds to wrestle a guy named Shute who was a three-time state champion and remained unbeaten. Louden took the "what — are you crazy?" approach, which is exactly what is needed to make your mark. Now when we meet Shute, he is walking up the bleachers at his high school's stadium with what looks like a telephone pole resting across his shoulders. His physique resembles a smaller Dwayne "The Rock" Johnson and he looks all of 200 pounds while Louden's physique is more of the beanpole variety. Louden and his best friend, Kuch, are standing in the bleachers, watching with concern and admiration as Shute goes through his telephone-pole workout regimen. Louden decides this is the time to let Shute know that it is "on like Donkey Kong," as we used to say in a nod to the classic arcade game. He is Louden's goal and Shute needs to know it.

> **Louden:** "Hey Shute!"
>
> **Shute:** "Yeah. Do I know you?"
>
> **Louden:** "Louden Swain. Thompson High."
>
> **Shute:** "Think you'll make the weight?"
>
> **Louden:** "I don't know. I hope so."
>
> **Shute:** "I hope so too."

If Louden was looking to gain some sort of edge or outright intimidate Shute with his cutting words, he quickly realized that wasn't going to happen. The conversation between the two wrestlers couldn't have been more blasé even if they'd commented on the mild weather. But if we look and think deeper, we realize that intimidation isn't why Louden showed up at Shute's high school.

He showed up because he wanted to validate his goal by making it tangible and visible — the challenge he had in his mind needed to be moved from the category of "what could easily just become another fanciful wish or pipe dream" to something real and achievable. Once he interacted with Shute and made him real in the physical sense, there was no turning back.

How many times in our lives have we all set a goal or positioned ourselves for a challenge — talking a big game and dreaming a big dream — but never followed through? The initial excitement and enthusiasm shoots through our bodies and minds like the opening of Motley Crue's 1987 heavy-metal hit, "Wild Side." We run out to our local grocery store and buy a case of the original energy drink, Jolt Cola. "This is it," we think to ourselves. "This is where I am going to make my mark."

And then, just as quickly as we imagined ourselves the heroes of our own stories, questions begin to fill our head:

- ➤ Can I really do this?

- ➤ Will people think I'm crazy?

- ➤ Will it work?

- ➤ What if it doesn't work?

- ➤ What do I do then?

- ➤ What if I fail and everyone sees it?

Unless we're truly courageous and determined, we often find ourselves ultimately submitting to the uncertainty that surrounds our crazy goal, quickly moving from the lightning and rocket fuel of Motley Crue back to the comfort and safety of a Kenny G song from his 1986 debut, *DuoTones*.

■■■■■■■■■■■■■■■■■■■■■■■■■■■■■■■■

🕹 **FUN FACT:** Jolt Cola hit the market in 1985 and
billed itself as the soft drink with "All the sugar,
and twice the caffeine." It survived through several
dramatic business challenges until it officially
ceased production in 2019. Anecdotally, I can tell
you that there was a Jolt Cola can on every desk in
every dorm room during my college years in the late
'80s and early '90s.

■■■■■■■■■■■■■■■■■■■■■■■■■■■■■■■■

Such is the reality of modern living — just as we are determined
to "make our mark," we acquiesce. We conform, we comply,
we avoid making waves. We eliminate the risk by eliminating
the possible glory. We go back to marking our time (instead of
making our mark) and back to "the mass of men [people] who
lead lives of quiet desperation," as Henry David Thoreau so
eloquently stated. We've all done it. We're human. And there are
a million reasons why we sometimes can't or won't put our necks
out there. But what if we approached our craziest ideas and most
ambitious goals in a direct and unflinching way by channeling
our inner Louden Swain? Instead of just making more space in
our head so we can move our goal from one side of our brain to
the other with no real intention of chasing it, what if we made
it *real* and achievable through meaningful action? I know that
sounds obvious and you are probably thinking "Well duh, Chris.
I mean, of course we need to take action to accomplish a goal or
face down a challenge." And I agree. Honestly though, it's easier
said than done. The gap between said and done — the difference
between *thinking* about doing something and actually *doing* it —
is akin to the difference between Magnum P.I.'s cherry-red Ferrari
and the cherry-red Fiero that occupied at least one driveway in
every '80s suburb. Yes, that gap is rather large.

What if we approached our craziest ideas and most ambitious goals in a direct and unflinching way by channeling our inner Louden Swain?

And I should know. You are currently reading the words in my 3rd book, but it likely could have been my 10th if I would have taken Louden's approach and wasted no time in making that dream a reality. But you know what? It's okay. In fact, it's better than okay. It doesn't matter when you do it, it just matters that you do. I learned a lot while I was "marking my time" in a career as a corporate marketer. I wasn't ready 20 years ago or even 10 years ago to become an entrepreneur, to build a speaking business, and to write and publish books that required Jolt-Cola-level energy and never-quit tenacity. I didn't have the drive to do something on my own and on a personal level, I was really enjoying my 20s and 30s but I was most certainly in that "quiet desperation" mode. I just didn't know it.

As Loverboy stated in their 1981 hit, I was definitely "working for the weekend." Honestly, if I would have tried to force it — if I had tried to start a business when I didn't have the experience or maturity to make it work — I may have ultimately been so disappointed and frustrated that my ability to chase this dream later in life might have been permanently quashed. My brain may have been wired to "make my mark" but, at that point in life, I just preferred to "mark my time." My epiphany, at 46 years young, only happened because I opened my mind to it. It also helped that I was in a job that I hated, so I wasn't blinded by a sense of security or comfort. My eyes were open, and I was looking to the future — for something better and something utterly and unapologetically me. In the past, I've said I was in a job that "just wasn't working out," but the reality is that I truly hated it. And I needed that to shake me out of my complacency. Of course, it most certainly helped that the day I decided I'd had enough of everything, *The Breakfast Club* was on TV and Bender said those 12 words that would change the trajectory of my career (and, more importantly, my life): "Screws fall out all the time. The world's an imperfect place." And, yes, there will be more about that later in the book, in Chapter 10, entitled, you guessed it, "The Breakfast Club."

In the end, we all have but one journey on this big, beautiful planet of ours. Even if you believe that we are actually here multiple times with different lives (which feels more likely to me each passing day), it's equally likely that you won't remember any of the previous ones, so we are back to your one shot as Eminem so eloquently riffed in "Lose Yourself." I know, I know. Not '80s, but still a brilliant song.

I'll leave you with this from REO Speedwagon, but first a little lead-up. *Vision Quest* has an amazing soundtrack, as many '80s movies did — because musicians wanted to get the exposure and it was cool to have a song(s) attached to a movie. Madonna, John Waite, Journey, and REO Speedwagon were just a few of the iconic musicians represented on the soundtrack. REO's song was "Time for Me to Fly," which is about leaving an unhealthy personal relationship and to this day, a lot of people talk about the inspiration or push they needed to make a big leap, like finalizing a divorce or initiating a break-up. (And it's not just personal. We often need a push to break up with a career or job.) For those who are ready for the next phase in their life — personal, career, or both — this song is an anthem:

> *"Time for me to fly,*
> *Oh, I've got to set myself free.*
> *Time for me to fly,*
> *And that's just how it's got to be ..."*

Where and how do *you* want to fly? In what way are you "marking your time" instead of "making your mark?" And is now your time? Spoiler alert! Yes, it *is* your time. "Right here. Right now," as Jesus Jones sang in 1991 (so close to the '80s).

And here's another spoiler alert! Or is it? I mean, it was the '80s after all and the vast majority of movies ended exactly the way that the audience hoped they would. So yeah, Louden made his mark. He beat Shute — actually pinned him — to win the state championship and send Shute to his first defeat of his high-school career. Everyone in the Thompson High crowd goes crazy and Louden's hand is raised as the winner while Journey's "Only the Young" plays in the background. With a still-bloody nose from the match, he screams "Yeah! Yeah!" while his teammates pick him up and hold him above their heads as he pumps his fist into the air where the movie freeze-frames on Louden and we hear this narration from him:

> "I think a lot about those six minutes with Shute and the time that I spent with Carla that season. Kuch had it right. It was a Vision Quest but all I ever settled for is that we're born to live and then to die and we gotta do it alone. Each in his own way. I guess that's why we gotta love those people who deserve it like there's no tomorrow. Because when you get right down to it, there isn't."

Man, '80s movie endings were just chock full of awesomeness. The protagonist wins, a hit song plays in the background as he is being lifted in the air, and we get an inspirational narrative before they roll the credits.

Make your mark and go create you. If an 18-year-old high-school wrestler can do it, so can you. Let everyone else mark the time.

CHAPTER 3

CAN'T BUY ME LOVE

"I mean he went from totally
geek to totally chic."

— PATTY, *CAN'T BUY ME LOVE*

'm going to start this chapter off with another confession.
Just like I've never seen *Dirty Dancing* [insert audible gasps
and raised voices with shaking fists], I've also never seen an
episode of the wildly popular television show *Grey's Anatomy*.
I don't know if that quite rises to the level of betrayal that is felt
when I mention a lack of interest in seeing Johnny and Baby dance
together, but I do feel like there might still be some disappointment upon learning that I've shunned yet another pop-culture
Americana classic — this time one from the incomparable Shonda

Rhimes and a show that has been running for 19 seasons as of the publication of this book. As it turns out, I don't have to be a *Grey's Anatomy* fan to know the iconic name "Dr. McDreamy." But what does Dr. McDreamy have to do with this chapter on the 1987 romantic comedy, *Can't Buy Me Love*? Geek to chic.

The main character in *Can't Buy Me Love* is Ronald Miller, and he is what most would refer to as a geek, a nerd, or as John Bender so eloquently put it, a neo maxi zoon dweebie. We will get into how much of a geek, nerd, or neo maxi zoon dweebie he truly is at a later point in the chapter, but suffice to say he would have fit in very nicely as an additional cast member on *The Big Bang Theory*. He also happens to be played by Patrick Dempsey who also played — yes, you guessed it — Dr. Derek "McDreamy" Shepherd in *Grey's Anatomy*. From a geek who girls have nightmares about to a neurosurgeon they have dreams about — all in the span of 20 years. So there, my friends, is your first lesson: anything is possible.

Now something that I consistently mention about the '80s is that it gave rise to new genres in all areas of pop culture or took an existing genre to a completely new level. The romantic comedy (or rom-com as it is called today) had seen some success on the silver screen throughout the decades, due (in large part) to Marilyn Monroe and her movies in the 1950s — including *Some Like It Hot, The Seven Year Itch,* and *How to Marry a Millionaire*, which also starred Betty Grable and Lauren Bacall. If you only know Marilyn Monroe through what you've read, posters you've seen, or from short clips of her media interviews, I encourage you to watch her movies. She was a supremely talented comedic actress with great timing, and, in my humble opinion, I think we've done her a great disservice by not talking more about her comedic talent. Comedy is the most difficult of all the acting genres and she did it very well. The 1960s had movies like *Where the Boys Are* and *The Courtship of Eddie's Father,* which became a television show in the 1970s. The '70s also brought us rom-coms like *10* and *Annie Hall*.

But it was the 1980s when the romantic comedy genre really become an integral part of the pop culture and movie landscape for generations to come. Movies like *The Princess Bride, Say Anything, Sixteen Candles, When Harry Met Sally, Mystic Pizza, Bull Durham, Big, Romancing the Stone, She's Gotta Have It, Tootsie, One Crazy Summer, The Sure Thing, Roxanne, Mr. Mom, Skin Deep* (a favorite underrated one of mine starring one of my favorite actors, John Ritter), *Blame It on Rio, Splash, Coming to America, Overboard, Pretty in Pink, Valley Girl,* and — of course — *Can't Buy Me Love.* And there are so many more.

'80s rom-coms have had such a long-term impact that in the 2010 movie *Easy A,* the main character, Olive Penderghast, says:

"Whatever happened to chivalry? Does it only exist in '80s movies? I want John Cusack holding a boombox outside my window. I wanna ride off on a lawnmower with Patrick Dempsey. I want Jake from *Sixteen Candles* waiting outside the church for me. I want Judd Nelson thrusting his fist into the air because he knows he got me. Just once, I want my life to be like an '80s movie, preferably one with a really awesome musical number for no apparent reason. But no, no, John Hughes did not direct my life."

For the next 30-60 minutes of your life, it's the "ride off on a lawnmower with Patrick Dempsey" idea that we are going to focus on.

Getting a Little Creative with the Truth

Have you ever wanted something so much that you were willing to embellish a bit? Maybe tell a little white lie to enhance your position? Most of us have. Think about the first job that you applied for at the start of your career. Not your first summer job — mine was washing dishes in a restaurant — but the first position you applied for to start a career. Remember how so many of the job descriptions would say something like "Entry-level position; some experience necessary." So essentially, they were looking for someone looking for their *first* job who already had *experience* in said job. Huh???? Or as Arnold Drummond used to say, "Whatcha' talkin' 'bout, Willis?" Quite the "chicken or egg" dilemma. So, like me, you probably embellished a little in the hopes that you would get the position and could then figure it out later. You pretended you know a little something about restaurants (because you'd eaten in them before) or that you had bookstore experience (because you'd been to a library, and how much different could it be?). You faked it just a little bit and that's perfectly fine. The "just a little bit" is what's important here.

When it comes to Ronald in *Can't Buy Me Love*, faking it puts his entire life on a new trajectory — for worse and eventually for better. Ronald, as you may know, is decidedly outside of the "popular kids" bubble and he desperately wants in. But he has no shot of ever being accepted of his own accord, so he "pays" the most popular girl in school, Cindy Mancini, $1,000 dollars to be his girlfriend for a month. The ruse works (until it doesn't) which leads us to this lesson:

✦ **Don't fake it to make it. The fall can be fast and unforgiving.**

In the '80s, $1,000 was a *lot* of money. (Hell, in 2022, it's a lot of money!). To earn that kind of coin, Ronald mows lawns and does general landscaping. He's saving up for a telescope that he has wanted for years. Remember doing that at some point in your life? Maybe you did tons of babysitting so you could buy a Benetton sweater or did chores around the house to earn enough for a Cabbage Patch Kid or a new skateboard. I did it with a dishwashing job at 13 years old so I could purchase a boombox complete with a dual-cassette deck. That summer holds many fond memories for me, even though I didn't have a "band that tried real hard" until "Jimmy quit and Jody got married" like Bryan Adams did during his "Summer of '69," which, if you do the math on his age, you quickly realize that he is not talking about the summer of 1969. Adams has admitted as much.[7]

In *Can't Buy Me Love*, we consistently see Ronald on his riding mower, and we also see the pride he takes in the job that he's been doing for a year and a half, specifically when one of the popular girls, Patty, says to him: "Didn't you like, used to mow our lawn?" Ronald responds: "Yes, and you have the nicest pair of rhododendrons in town!"

Double entendre like "Summer of '69?" Maybe. But based on Ronald's personality and character, it's more likely that he was legitimately complimenting her parents' landscaping. (The movie's writers, on the other hand, knew exactly what they were doing.)

When we see Ronald at breakfast with his family, he proudly tells them that he has actually saved $1,500 (needing just $1,000 for the telescope) and plans to put the additional $500 in a money market. Ultimately, a challenge presents itself to Ronald when it comes time to purchase the telescope, which we'll get into later, but *within* Ronald's challenge, we learn that:

🎲 ***Doing* the thing is greater than *buying* the thing.**

At this point in this book, you hopefully know the drill. It's time to travel back in time via a mode of your choice and, for some of us, to a summer job during August of 1987.

Now, one thing that you should know about me is that although I *did* have a job putting skateboards together during my youth, I am not what you would call the handy type. I have been known

---

7   Henry Yates, "Bryan Adams: The Surprisingly Sexual Story of Summer of '69," *Louder*, Future Publishing Limited, July 1, 2020, https://www.loudersound. com/features/bryan-adams-the-surprisingly-sexual-story-of-summer-of-69.

to DIY my own home-theatre system, but my toolbox and the
tools within it have been used about as much as Milli Vanilli used
their real voices ... which is to say *never*.

Circa 1985, wearing my Chucks while on one of my Powell Peralta skateboards.

So that summer, I took a job doing what any non-handy person
would do — painting the exterior of houses using 25-foot ladders
and dangling from very suspect cables to reach the furthest
corners of old colonial homes. I worked for a company that
hired high school and college students to do the work (which,
in retrospect, was pretty brilliant from a profit-margin perspective). But based on the friends who I worked with, the painting
company's vetting process for summer employees left a bit to
be desired. I have no idea how my two knucklehead friends and
I pulled it off, but we did manage to paint six houses that summer
and, if I recall correctly, we only had complaints logged on two
of them. (Okay, maybe complaints on a third of our work is not
so great!) One of those complaints was from a lady who kept
yelling at us every day about the perceived lack of detail that we
were putting into the work. My buddy who was our supervisor —
that's laughable — would have to listen to her each day and do his
best to calm her down and reassure her. He'd then come to us and
tell us that we would have to redo a portion of the house that she

felt wasn't up to her "standards" — which, of course, were set at level Michelangelo.

At one point, I was in a sort of safety harness, dangling precariously about 20 feet above the ground and doing my best to paint the soffit, which extended about three feet from the main portion of the house. I'll be honest, I was terrified. I am not afraid of heights but, as you might recall, I struggle to use a hammer and nail properly and the harness I was dangling from was fastened by me using whatever mediocre ropes we had available, along with some metal carabiners to keep said ropes from slipping. I just wanted to get through this portion of the project as quickly as possible and, of course, without the demon-seed owner yelling at me for some "lunatic fringe" reason (as Red Rider sang in their 1981 hit by the same name, which also happened to be a main track on the *Vision Quest* soundtrack — look at me getting all nostalgic about Chapter 2 when we're only in Chapter 3!).

Everything was going surprisingly well, and I was about halfway through my portion of the overhang when, out of the corner of my eye, I saw a flash of movement. It was slight but enough to give me pause for a second or two and then it was gone. Maybe a fly or another summer bug with wings, of which there are many. Back to work I went and there it was again. This time, my instinct was to swat it away, which caused my makeshift harness to sway considerably more than I would have liked. And again, it disappeared. But, of course, now I started to see and feel it all around me. I jumped several times at absolutely nothing, cursed at myself and at the now-imaginary bug.

And then it happened. There's a classic line in *Raiders of the Lost Ark* when Indy and Sallah are looking down into an underground tomb and Indy drops a torch into the darkness that lights up the floor of the tomb, revealing a lot of snakes. Hundreds of them. And Indy says this:

"Snakes. Why did it have to be snakes?"

Indy hates snakes. He's terrified of them and wants to be as far away as possible from anything that resembles them. Now, if I was cast as Indiana Jones, which would have been totally awesome by the way, and they wanted to get my real fear on camera, they just would have had to replace snakes with spiders. How terrified am I of spiders? Well, let's just say that if someone wanted to rob me, their best shot would be not at gunpoint but at what I call "spiderpoint." Tell me to give you my wallet while putting a tarantula in my face and you'll be able to take anything you want, because I will be passed out on the concrete from sheer fright. Like 1985 vampire movie *Fright Night* fright. Imagine the kind of fright typically reserved for the moment when a character realizes that Jason, Michael, or Freddy is about to send a slight bit of pain and agony in their direction. For those in the back, "I hate spiders."

Tell me to give you my wallet while putting a tarantula in my face and you'll be able to take anything you want, because I will be passed out on the concrete from sheer fright.

So, of course, as I dangled in my makeshift harness, I realized to my horror that what was now crawling on my shoulder toward my neck at a rapid pace wasn't a winged summer bug or the traditional and annoying fly. No, what was making a beeline for my jugular was a hairy, eight-legged soulless nightmare of a creature that those without a case of arachnophobia would simply call a spider. I began to flail about, taking swipes at the creature as it moved ever-closer to the base of my neck. I screamed and

screamed again while my harness and I began swinging danger-
ously from side to side and while the creaking from the roof
overhang became louder like the sound of the heart under the
floorboards in Edgar Allan Poe's famous short story, *The Tell-Tale
Heart*. My friends heard my screams and ran to my side of the
house, likely expecting to see lots of blood or at least a broken
bone or two. Then suddenly and without warning, the hairy
and soulless creature leapt onto my face as if to claim me as its
property. I let out one last scream and then I passed out, my life-
less body hanging within my makeshift harness almost 20 feet
above the ground.

After what I imagine was at least a minute or so of chuckling
by my friends on the ground, they convinced the demon-seed
of a woman to allow them into her house, where they opened
a window and pulled me in. Once inside and acclimated to my
surroundings, I quickly realized that I would forever be branded
with this debacle. I was and, of course, it was well-deserved.

Now that I keep feeling something crawling on me, I need
a distraction. So let's talk about the music that flowed from
Walkman devices and boomboxes in August of 1987. LL Cool
J (Ladies Love Cool James — bet you didn't know that) was
moving up the charts with "I Need Love," which definitely has
a place in the Mixtape Hall of Fame, while "Touch of Grey" by
The Grateful Dead was cementing its place in the Hacky Sack
Hall of Fame. Gloria Estefan and The Miami Sound Machine
were warning us that the "Rhythm Is Gonna Get Ya" while
Debbie Gibson was singing the anthem of my Heather Thomas
posters that adorned my walls with "Only in My Dreams." The
immortal George Michael had the #1 video on MTV and the
#3 song overall with "I Want Your Sex" and this little band
from Ireland named U2 continued their billboard dominance
with the #1 song for that week in "I Still Haven't Found What
I'm Looking For."

In television, the summer was typically a very quiet time. Lots of re-runs as the networks geared up for new seasons and new shows in the fall. And, of course, we were several decades from streaming content so we actually had to go play outside and use those totally awesome imaginations of ours. But there *was* television, and sitcoms were all the rage. In fact, eight of the top 10 shows were sitcoms, including *Cheers, Golden Girls, The Cosby Show, Night Court, A Different World, ALF, Growing Pains,* and *Who's the Boss. Murder She Wrote* and *60 Minutes* were the only two non-sitcoms within the top 10. There were some absolute classics that rested just outside of the top 10, including *Magnum P.I.* (my favorite and in its second-to-last season), *Moonlighting* (Cybill Shepard and Bruce Willis with a bit of hair left) and *21 Jump Street* (with a young Johnny Depp who was also a multiple *Tiger Beat* cover alumni).

And at the box office the week of August 14, 1987, was a mix of cult classics and traditional classics. '80s kids were in movie heaven with *The Monster Squad* and *Masters of the Universe* while The Fat Boys were proving that musicians could still make the leap to the big screen with *Disorderlies*. Several underrated '80s comedies were bringing the laughs at the box office with *Stakeout* at #1 and *Summer School* just outside of the top five. One of my favorites and, in my humble opinion, the greatest vampire movie of all time, *The Lost Boys* (Chapter 4 in my 2nd book — shameless plug) was continuing to highlight the box office power of the two Coreys (Haim and Feldman) while a cinematic classic, *Full Metal Jacket*, was showing us the somber, human, and very dark side of war.

But it was a geeky kid on a riding lawnmower who stole our hearts and pushed the romantic comedy *Can't Buy Me Love* to the #2 spot in its debut week. Starring Patrick Dempsey as Ronald Miller and Amanda Peterson as Cindy Mancini, the movie tells the story of your typical nerdy kid and his undying crush on the most popular girl in school. Ronald makes his money mowing lawns and doing landscaping for neighbors, including Cindy's family. He's saving money to buy a telescope that costs $1,000 dollars and when he's at the mall getting ready to purchase it, he sees Cindy in a clothing store with a look of desperation on her face. In the previous scene, we saw Cindy at a party wearing her mom's new white suede dress — ah, '80s fashion — and lo and behold, red wine is spilled all over it. I mean, I remember Bartles & Jaymes, pony kegs, $5.00-a-case beer, a bit of grain alcohol, and maybe some NightTrain or MadDog 20/20 at high-school parties, but I don't recall big, bold Cabernets or palate-pleasing Pinot Noirs making the rounds. Hey, I may love the '80s, but I can still call out a suspect plot line.

It was geeky kid on a riding lawnmower who stole our hearts and pushed the romantic comedy *Can't Buy Me Love* to the #2 spot in its debut week.

Annnywaayyy ... Ronald goes over to the store where Cindy is having a bit of a breakdown and ultimately finds out that the dress cannot be returned and a new one will cost, you guessed it, $1,000 dollars — which Ronald just happens to have. Just as Cindy seems to have given up and has come to realization that she is going to have to tell her mom that she has ruined her new dress, Ronald steps in and this little conversation unfolds:

Ronald: "I want to rent you."

Cindy: "You want to rent me?"

Ronald: "Yeah. You pretend you like me, and we go out for a few weeks ... and that will make me popular."

Cindy: "Just going out with me is not gonna make you popular."

Ronald: "Well, I have a thousand dollars that says it will."

Cindy: "I think you've mowed one too many lawns!"

After being declined a few times, Ronald begins to walk out of the store when Cindy decides to take him up on his offer. Their negotiations begin and they settle on one month of "dating" (those are air quotes, if you were wondering), no hand-holding, no kissing, and some lunches together at school as well as a few Saturday nights thrown in. So, Ronald got what he wanted (or so he thinks) and the shenanigans begin in earnest. Ultimately, Ronald finds out that you can't buy popularity and you can't buy love.

■■■■■■■■■■■■■■■■■■■■■■■■■■■■■■■■

FUN FACT: One thing that I always enjoy when I'm doing my research, which is primarily just watching '80s movies (yes, you are jealous — I know you are, and it's okay), is looking up the cast to see if there were any future stars in small roles or someone unexpected in a larger one. *Can't Buy Me Love* has both. Seth Green plays Ronald's little brother, Chuckie, and Gerardo Meija plays Ricky, one of the star football players. Yes, that Gerardo. The one who rapped his way up the charts in 1990 with the hit song "Rico Suave." Oh, and because you will see this weird *Children of the Corn* connection running through this book, Courtney Gains (who plays Ronald's best friend Kenneth in *Can't Buy Me Love*) also played Malachai who was one of the demon-seed children in *Children of the Corn*. No relation to the evil woman whose house I nearly hanged myself from during Spidergate.

■■■■■■■■■■■■■■■■■■■■■■■■■■■■■■■■

So, what did a nerdy kid on a riding mower who tried to buy his way to popularity teach us about work and life?

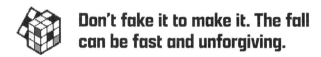

Don't fake it to make it. The fall can be fast and unforgiving.

Most of us have heard some version of "fake it 'til you make it" and we've likely heard examples of how someone rose to success by saying they could do something they couldn't — to get a job or contract — and then figured out how to do it *after* the fact. It's certainly true that businesses and people have been built by saying "yes we/I can do that" when they had little or no experience in what was being asked of them. It's also likely true that, in each of those stories you've heard, the person or business was expanding their skill set into an area that was just outside of their scope or a "quick learn" that didn't require a wholesale change to themselves or the business. It's also likely true that whatever they were doing at that time, even if they did it well, wasn't initially built on a wholesale lie with absolutely no experience or fact behind it.

I've said it before, and I'll say it again: most of us are guilty of embellishing things from time to time. I mean, who hasn't expanded the truth a little bit during a job interview when you are asked some of those tired and nonsensical questions like, "What do you consider your biggest career achievement?" or "Where do you see yourself in 10 years?" I always liked that second one. Ten years? You probably said something like, "Well, I hope to be here at Company Stupid Questions in a leadership position just like you." Ugh. Hey, I'm sure I said it at some point. It's what we figured they wanted to hear and even if it is a little fake, it's not a wholesale lie. Maybe you will be. Maybe not. But no one is worse off, including you, because you faked your answer a bit. It's not as if you fenagled your way onto a team of aerospace engineers only to find yourself the only one available when a few astronauts were stuck on the International Space Station with a hole in it that needed to be repaired. That would be unfortunate.

The arrangement between Ronald and Cindy is all about faking it. She's going to replace her mom's dress with a second, identical dress to fake her way through her big mistake with the red wine. And Ronald is going to fake his way into popularity with a fake relationship. When Ronald offers Cindy the $1,000 to purchase the new dress so her mom doesn't find out what she has done to ruin it — in exchange for fake dating him for one month so he can be popular — he sets into motion a disaster that will not just engulf him, but also his friends and Cindy as well.

As they initially discuss their dating arrangement and agree to terms, they have this little exchange:

> **Cindy:** "Whatever happens to your popularity, stay yourself. Don't change to please others."
>
> **Ronald:** "Me, change? Never!"

At first, Ronald is as nervous, unsure, and devoid of confidence as he was before, but it doesn't take long for him to begin relishing in his new-found popularity and it only takes one day hanging out with Cindy for the popular kids to quickly change their minds about him. He's no longer the geek and because of this, he quickly begins to shun his lifelong friends for the popular kids who had — just days before — ignored him and, on occasion, physically bullied him. He stops showing up for his weekend card games with his friends, ignores them in the hallway (yes, he "walks on by" as Simple Minds so famously sang in "Don't You Forget About Me"), stops sitting with them at lunch because they sit at the loser table, and laughs at the jokes and pranks that the popular kids play on them. None of these things mattered to Ronald in the moment. He was popular and it was all he had ever wanted. Suddenly, he's going to the best parties, girls are flocking to him, and he's a trendsetter with his fashion and with his dance moves at a school dance. (Dance moves, by the way, that he learned in a panic by watching a television show that he thought was a dance show in the same vein as the groundbreaking *Soul Train* or *Solid Gold* but was actually a PBS show on the Ancient Anteater Mating Ritual.) He was so popular in this moment that, even though it was an incredibly bizarre dance, everyone at the school dance thought it was cool and mimicked his moves.

At the same time, we still see the real Ronald and the real Cindy when they are alone and away from the popular crowd. We realize that Cindy, like Ronald, is putting on a show and is very different from the group she hangs out with at school. She's actually more like Ronald and is doing her own "fake it to make it" as all she's ever known is being popular. Now we know that Ronald had fallen for Cindy well before their little scheme, but we now see that she is also falling for him, and they are *both* forgetting that it isn't supposed to be real.

Oh, How the Mighty Fall

Things do become very real for Ronald when he is invited — along with a few of the football players — on their annual Mischief Night prank, which involves attacking the same house with eggs, rotten tomatoes, miscellaneous spoiled food items, and what they call a "shit bomb" (which is basically dog shit in a paper bag that explodes when it is thrown at the front door). The family that they target has been putting up with it for years and has finally decided to set up traps in the hopes that they can catch one of the culprits.

As they drive toward the address in what looks like an A-Team van, Ronald asks about the address and is horrified when he realizes that it's his best friend Kenneth's house. He tries and fails to convince them to try another house. Because he is the newb (gamer slang for the new guy/gal), they task him with throwing the shit bomb at the front door. He does without any hesitation — which is surprising and disappointing, considering it is his best friend's house. As Ronald is running away, Kenneth pulls one of the traps and captures Ronald in a net as he screams, "I got one! I got one!" Kenneth runs up to the net and as he pulls it aside, he falls back in shock when he sees that it is Ronald — who then takes advantage of the opportunity to escape.

The following day, Ronald sees Kenneth in the arcade playing Pole Position, which was one of the first great arcade racing games until it was bested by Outrun. Ronald tries to apologize several times, which Kenneth ignores until his anger comes through and he jacks Ronald up against one of the games and says: "You shit on my house! You shit on my house!"

And with that, he walks out, and Ronald has lost his best friend in his quest to be the popular kid. Of course, it gets worse from there. The day has come for Ronald and Cindy's official break-up and while Cindy wants to do it subtly, Ronald wants to make a scene (thus prolonging his popularity by being the guy who broke up with Cindy Mancini in public). Ronald insists and instigates a dramatic break-up in front of everyone.

A few nights later at a house party, Cindy rips Ronald in front of everyone and lets all of them in on their little secret with this little monologue:

> "You! Even Bobby thinks we went out. Great, huh? Ha! All of you thought we were a couple. What a joke! Ronald Miller paid me a thousand bucks to pretend I like him. What a deal, huh? $1,000 to go out with him for a month. This guy. Oh, God. He bought me. And he bought all of *you*. He was sick and tired of a being a nobody. Yeah, and he said that all of you guys would worship him if we went out. And I didn't believe that. I was, like, 'No way!' And he was right! No, leave me alone. He was right. Our little plan worked, didn't it, Ronald? The dance. That stupid dance! What a bunch of followers you guys are. I mean, at least I got *paid*!"

That moment is a painful turning point. All the popular kids turn their backs on Ronald, and he is *persona non-grata* faster than a 1980s one-hit wonder musical group. His younger brother, Chuckie, sums it up perfectly when he sees Cindy at the mall and says: "You took him from geek status to king status to no status." Indeed.

■■■■■■■■■■■■■■■■■■■■■■■■■■■■■■■■

FUN FACT: The '80s were known as the decade of one-hit musical wonders. In fact, when *Rolling Stone* held a reader poll in 2011 for the Top Ten One-Hit Wonders of all time, five of the 10 were from the '80s with A-Ha's "Take On Me" claiming the #1 overall spot. The other four from the '80s were The Vapors with "Turning Japanese", Soft Cell with "Tainted Love," Big Country with "In a Big Country," and Dexy's Midnight Runners with "Come On Eileen," which took the #2 overall spot.[8]

■■■■■■■■■■■■■■■■■■■■■■■■■■■■■■■■

"No status" really translated to no friends. Ultimately, Ronald found himself losing every new relationship he'd built through his fake popularity and every real relationship he had prior to giving Cindy the $1,000. But the '80s being the '80s, Ronald recovers at the end with a passionate speech in the lunchroom directed at one of the football players who had quickly befriended him when he was fake popular and dropped him even more quickly when he was found out. In front of the entire school, Ronald says:

"Nerds, jocks. My side, your side. It's all bullshit. It's hard enough just trying to be yourself."

---

8   Andy Greene, "*Rolling Stone* Readers Pick the Top 10 One-Hit Wonders of All Time," *Rolling Stone*, May 4, 2011, https://www.rollingstone.com/music/music-lists/rolling-stone-readers-pick-the-top-10-one-hit-wonders-of-all-time-14391/.

■■■■■■■■■■■■■■■■■■■■■■■■■■■■■■■

🕹 **FUN FACT:** An astonishing 183 high-school movies in the '80s had an ending where the high school ultimately rallies around the sympathetic character who just wants to fit in. Okay, I'm embellishing a bit ("faking it to make it!") with the overall number, but it *was* a recurring theme in '80s movies. A few examples are *Lucas, Just One of the Guys, Three O' Clock High,* and *Teen Wolf.*

■■■■■■■■■■■■■■■■■■■■■■■■■■■■■■■

In the end, Ronald unites the entire high school, rekindles his friendship with Kenneth, and rides off into the sunset on his lawn tractor with Cindy, tying up this true '80s rom-com complete with a Hollywood happy ending. Most real-life "fake it to make it" stories, unfortunately, end with the fast and unforgiving fall from grace without a riding mower to cushion the collapse. We've had some pretty public examples.

I mentioned Milli Vanilli in the opening. I still like their music. Don't tell me that you haven't found yourself singing "Blame It on the Rain" or "Girl You Know It's True" while doing that little shuffle dance of theirs. You know you have ... and I'll bet you're even humming one of them right now. But again, my handyman tools and their real voices have that never-been-used thing in common. Give me a hammer and a nail and I'll show you four different ways to ruin a nail.

The duo of Rob Pilatus and Fab Morvan (i.e., Milli Vanilli) *did* record an album with their voices after they were exposed and lost their Grammy for "Best New Artist." The album was called *Rob & Fab* and sold just 2,000 copies in the USA.[9] Looking back, it's interesting that they lost everything for lip syncing — for agreeing to perform on stage and in studio with the voices of three other uncredited "ghost-singing" vocalists — and we see

---

9   https://en.wikipedia.org/wiki/Milli_Vanilli

so much of that in today's music. Today, we just call them entertainers and one thing you can't take away from Rob and Fab is that they were most certainly excellent entertainers. But Rob and Fab were just the face for this "fake it to make it" scheme. The producer of Milli Vanilli's music, Frank Farian, most certainly knew the intricacies of the ruse, and you would suspect that most people working around them knew as well, but Rob and Fab — who likely were talked into the scheme — took the hardest fall. Their fame came fast but the fall was faster and, almost literally overnight, they found themselves stripped of their Grammy and suddenly becoming the butt of jokes in shows ranging from *The Late Show with David Letterman* to *In Living Color*. The musical duo tried several comebacks but were never taken seriously again. Rob passed in 1998 from a suspected overdose and Fab hasn't really been heard from in terms of music for decades. It's really tragic to think of it. I mean, if what is suspected is true, then their manager/producer was really the conductor of the Milli Vanilli "fake it to make it" train. I mean who's to say that any one of us wouldn't have taken the bait like Rob and Fab did for a chance to be worldwide megastars? You're lying to yourself if you wouldn't at least contemplate it.

"Faking it" happens in every industry. There are even Fortune 500 executives whose careers were built on a combination of hard work, talent, and a bit of "fake" on their resume (which eventually caught up to them). Former Yahoo CEO, Scott Thompson, was busted for saying he had both a computer science and accounting degree when he actually just had the accounting degree. When found out, he resigned after just roughly five months at the helm. Marilee Jones, who was the dean of admissions for 10 years at MIT claimed that she had three degrees and faked it for almost three decades until she was busted and forced to resign. And David Edmondson, who did not have a college degree, falsely claimed to have two degrees and was appointed CEO of RadioShack in 2005. He resigned in 2006 after his "fake it to make it" behaviors came to light.[10] Of course, we can have a debate over whether these transgressions involving some embellishment of their college degrees earned should really be offenses that result in termination. Some might say, "You have to be able to trust your leaders and if they misrepresent something that is so obvious, what else might they be misrepresenting?" Others will say, "Hey, they could clearly do the job better than most, regardless of this degree or that credential, which is why they held the esteemed positions that they did."

No one denies that everyone mentioned above had earned their way to the top and, in the case of Marilee Jones, she must have been very good at what she did considering how long she held the post. But even the biggest of us — after years of hard work and results — can be brought down overnight by the desire to "fake it to make it." One small or medium-sized fake when we are young and dumb can result in a lifetime of scandal and consequences.

But just like Ronald, who eventually got a second chance with Cindy and his best friend Kenneth, there are also people in the real world whose mistakes don't haunt them forever. Second chances happen for people like George O'Leary, who was a successful head football coach at Georgia Tech University. He won the Bobby Dodd National Coach of the Year in 2000 and was offered the head coaching job at the University of Notre Dame in 2001, which is one of the most prestigious jobs in all of sports — both professional and collegiate. Five days after accepting the job, he resigned when it came to light that he had indulged in resume padding in the late 1960s. He explained the transgression by saying: "In seeking employment, I prepared a resume that contained inaccuracies regarding my completion of course work for a master's degree and also my level of participation in football at my alma mater. These misstatements were never stricken from

---

10 Priya Anand, "5 Big-shots Who Lied on Their Resumes," *MarketWatch*, September 20, 2014, https://www.marketwatch.com/story/5-big-shots-who-lied-on-their-resumes-2014-09-18.

my resume or biographical sketch in later years." O'Leary did get a second chance and landed at University of Central Florida in 2004, where he was the head coach until 2015 when he resigned after a slow start to the season.[11]

When the "Fake It to Make It" Fall Hurts Them All

In the instances I mentioned previously, the impact was mainly contained to the individual. Sure, some people or administrations had egg on their faces, but the organizations were large enough to move past it without much of an economic or reputational impact. That's not always the case for smaller businesses and the "fake it to make it" scenarios that don't make the news.

When I was a kid, my dad had a small but successful production company that focused on corporate video and some television commercials. Actors and others in the entertainment business are notorious for "embellishing" on their resumes — even adding skills to match a part that is being cast. "Juggling and circus skills needed?" Sure! "Seeking an actor with voice-over experience." Well, kind of! The idea is, of course, that if you check the box or add a mistruth to your resume that you will figure out how to do said skill if you end up getting the part. You just want to be given a chance, right? This works for things like a bartender role mixing drinks but doesn't work for a skill like horseback riding and, well, that was the dilemma that my dad found himself in. He had just hired an actor who was perfect for the role in all aspects — including his experience on horseback (or so he said). Now maybe today, with all the video we have access to and with a company that has larger budgets for pre-production, you could verify whether someone had experience with horses or have them show you themselves on an actual horse. But this was 1982 and

---

11 "George O'Leary," *Wikipedia*, Last Edited December 19, 2021, https://en.wikipedia.org/wiki/George_O%27Leary.

they didn't have a big budget, so they trusted the actors, and took their assertions at face value.

Circa 1981, my dad explaining to me that I had to go back home to school in Baltimore after doing some acting and spending time with him on a Coca-Cola shoot in Atlanta.

The first day of the shoot required the main character to be on a horse — and not just sitting on but actually *riding* the horse. It was clear from the onset that the actor had never been on a horse before and didn't even know how to mount into the saddle. Equestrian skills aren't something you can teach in an afternoon and the production didn't have time or money to recast because the cash register was already ringing for the cast, crew, location, etc. Instead, they had to rewrite multiple shots on the fly to avoid showing the actor on the horse, which was a huge challenge because more than half the shots involved dialogue while on horseback. Additionally, the three big "hero shots" (those would be shots without dialogue that make a scene memorable like the ending in *The Breakfast Club* when Bender walks across the football field and pumps his fist) were all on a horse — trotting, riding, or sitting with the actor facing the camera.

The "fake it to make it" attitude of the actor caused a lot of stress for all involved, disrupted the shoot on multiple occasions, created issues with the client, impacted the final product visually, and put the production over budget. And that's the difference between an embellishment and full-on "faking it." Beyond yourself, the full-on fake tends to impact others in a negative and sometimes irreversible way and that is exactly the impact that *Can't Buy Me Love*'s Ronald Miller had on everyone around him.

■■■■■■■■■■■■■■■■■■■■■■■■■■■■■■■■

FUN MAYBE FACT: So, I'm not sure if this is completely accurate, but back in 1982 when MTV was exploding across the world, a band reached out to my dad, requesting that he shoot their new music video. Rather than fake it 'til he made it, he politely declined as he said it wasn't a strength of his company. As the story is told, the band was *Duran Duran* and the video was for their smash hit "Rio." I'll never really know if that was the band that actually had the request of my dad and his company, but it's cool to think about regardless.

■■■■■■■■■■■■■■■■■■■■■■■■■■■■■■■■

What many of these "fake it to make it" stories have in common is that the fakers had been using the inaccuracies for such a long time that the dishonesties had become real for them. Decades of the same embellishment or lie became their "real" life story and, at a certain point, there was really no turning back. With Ronald in *Can't Buy Me Love*, he so desperately wanted to be popular that he began believing that his fake persona was his real self and that, regardless of what happened, he would never be a geek again. What he didn't realize was the very people who he wanted to like him were as fake as his popularity.

And, of course, '80s pop culture can be quite prophetic and almost always has an answer for everything and every situation.

In wrapping up this lesson, we turn to the King of Pop himself, Michael Jackson, who was most certainly waxing philosophic in his 1983 smash hit, "Billie Jean," when he said:

"Be careful of what you do because the lie becomes the truth."

Listen to Michael. He knew.

 ## *Doing* the thing is greater than *buying* the thing.

Before we dive into this lesson, let's take a "New York Minute" (as Don Henley sang in 1989) and think back to the first thing you wanted as a kid that you eventually earned through hard work. What was that thing for you? Mine, as you might remember, was a dual-cassette boombox that I earned through washing dishes for $2.30 an hour in a restaurant kitchen when I was 13. The minimum wage was $3.35 so yeah, I should have some backpay coming my way in 3 ... 2 ... 1 ... Nope.

■■■■■■■■■■■■■■■■■■■■■■■■■■■■■■■■

FUN FACT: *3-2-1 Contact* was an educational science show for kids on PBS, which premiered in 1980 and ran for seven seasons. It was one of my favorite shows in the early '80s but lost its luster for me in 1983/84 when I replaced the posters of planets and rocket ships on my wall with those of Heather Thomas, Heather Locklear, and Phoebe Cates. (Check out a photo of me getting ready for prom in front of those posters at the end of the chapter!)

■■■■■■■■■■■■■■■■■■■■■■■■■■■■■■■■

Whether you are a kid with a summer job or an adult entrepreneur hustling to build something remarkable, it is an equally cool feeling when your hard work earns you something that you really want or desire. There's a reason that restaurants and a lot of small businesses frame their first dollar and proudly display it prominently on their wall. That first dollar represents all the proverbial (or literal!) blood, sweat, and tears that it took to get to the first customer purchase. The initial return on investment (ROI) or in marketing terms, the cost per acquisition (CPA) will not look good on paper. Getting started is hard. Tens or even hundreds of thousands of dollars invested along with sleepless nights and 20-hour days all for that one initial dollar. I hope it goes without saying that the short- and long-term goal is more customers and more revenue but ask a restauranteur or any small business owner which earned dollar they remember most and it's not the 1,000th or the millionth — if they should be so lucky — and it's not anywhere in between. It's that first dollar. We all remember our first customer or client — the first product or service we sold, and under what circumstances. Go ahead and ask a business founder and you'll see their eyes light up like a kid in a candy store. You can almost see the journey they took flashing through their pupils, and you won't even have to ask how that dollar came to be. They will tell you without even missing a beat.

■■■■■■■■■■■■■■■■■■■■■■■■■■■■■■■

FUN FACT: There is actually a band from the '80s named Dollar and I just found this out. They were a pop new-wave duo from the UK who saw incredibly limited success in the US but fared much better in Ireland and the UK. My advice to you is to YouTube the band Dollar right now. Their music videos are the essence of the early '80s and it looks like they may have shown the glam band Poison how to properly or improperly use Aqua Net.

■■■■■■■■■■■■■■■■■■■■■■■■■■■■■■■

Can't Buy Me Love is a movie that's all about the difference between *doing* a thing (i.e., *earning* a thing) and *buying* a thing. When we first meet Ronald, he is in his happy place on his riding mower and, if we didn't know he was a high schooler working a summer job, we'd think that this was his life's work and his mission. He's happy, smiling, and carefree as he meticulously maneuvers around a perfectly landscaped yard that, as a homeowner myself, I envied. Then he sees Cindy and his demeanor shifts quickly from carefree to "Caught Up in You" (*.38 Special* style circa 1982). He's completely enamored but feels as though being the caretaker for her family's yard is as close as he will ever get to her. When he snaps back to reality, he starts his mower, and the bag of grass blows right into his face as the mower backfires. To make things worse, this happens in front of Cindy and her friends — which just adds to his "loser" status in their eyes. But we've spent most of this chapter outlining Ronald's struggles to be cool, so let's put our big-kid pants on and focus a bit on what *does* make him very cool from the beginning of the movie.

Fitting In and Standing Out

From a high schooler's perspective, Ronald was all the things that represented uncool. He was super smart, and his fashion sense was lacking considerably. He was unathletic and he talked about astronomy with the same passion that the other kids were talking about the upcoming house party. He worked as a landscaper instead of at a trendy store at the local mall. He was saving money for a telescope with the rest going into a money market for college. And, to make matters even dorkier, he even sits on the visitors' side during football games, as if he knows and accepts that he's an outsider.

> **Ronald:** "I just think it would be more fun to party with those guys our senior year ... go to the games."
>
> **Kenneth:** "We go to all the games."

Ronald: "We sit in the visiting section, Kenneth ... at our own school."

So yeah, maybe Ronald was uncool from the perspective of a teenager. But from the perspective of an adult, Ronald had a lot of the qualities that you'd hope for in a child: smart, kind, hard-working, and financially responsible. Ronald valued a hard day's work and appreciated the journey as much as the end result. He was a teenager who appreciated the power of now but also planned for the future. He was mature and thoughtful before he was old enough to have peers who realized that maturity was cool.

Now, as we learned before, the way Ronald spent his earnings — his "end result" for all his hard work — was a little different than he had anticipated. He went from planning a telescope purchase to using those earnings to save Cindy from a very awkward and likely expensive conversation with her mother about the suede dress she had ruined. I mean a $1,000 suede dress in today's money is likely close to $5k or $6k and that is no cheap "raspberry beret that you'll find in a second-hand store," as Prince sang back in 1985.

And in that moment of offering his earnings to someone else in exchange for a "boyfriend experience," he learned a lesson that it takes many of us decades to figure out. He learned the difference between *buying* the thing and *doing* the thing. He discovered the difference between the value of a new possession vs. the value in a new experience — creating memories vs. collecting stuff. Now that's not to say that it isn't admirable to set a goal to earn a thing that will just make you generally happy because you want that item. We've all done that and will continue to do so throughout our lives. In the case of Ronald, the telescope he was working toward earning would have made him happy and could have propelled him forward into an astrophysicist career and I think we can all agree that it would have been worth it.

But stargazing might have just been one of the *many* paths of interest that a teenager has available to them. And even if it did lead to a career or just a passionate hobby, the telescope would have eventually been discarded or set aside for a more advanced model. But the experience that Ronald created from taking the $1,000 and helping Cindy, albeit with a bit of an ulterior motive, could never be traded in or traded up.

Let's do a quick exercise. Go back to when you were 17 years old. I want you to think about two things and the memory that each has created for you:

1. Something cool you purchased.

2. Something positive or fun you experienced.

Now think about two more things related to each:

1. Which of the two triggered more of your senses?

2. How many times have you told the story of each to others in your life?

I'm no Tangina Barrons, the medium/mind reader in the 1982 horror classic *Poltergeist*, but I'm going to venture a guess that the experience you thought of triggered more senses and is likely a story you've told countless times. I know it does for me.

When I was 17, back in 1987, I bought my first mountain bike, which I used to move myself here and there around Ocean City, Maryland, that epic summer. The bike got me from point A to point B in a cool fashion and was one of the biggest investments that I had ever made. But fast-forward to 2022 and I honestly couldn't tell you what color it was, its size, model, or any interesting stories that my bike and I shared during that summer. Now that same summer, I lived on my own for the first time with six other guys in a two-bedroom apartment right off the beach on 10th Street in Ocean City, MD, and just typing those words brings a wave of emotions flooding all my senses:

1. **Sight** — I can see the apartment in all its glorious splendor. Well, not glorious at all, actually. It was on the first floor of two with a putrid green exterior and wooden steps that were beginning to rot away. It had plain white walls with a tiled floor that didn't get cleaned all summer. Our two bedrooms each had three twin beds and we used bed sheets as curtains. I can still see the three ratty couches with dust bunnies underneath and upholstery holes from anything you can imagine. I remember the kitchen with appliances from a 1930 Maytag catalog, complete with a refrigerator whose contents shall remain top secret. When I close my eyes, even now, I can see the magnificent sunrises and sunsets while sitting on the beach and I'll never forget the visual of the ceiling fan that fell twice during the summer (once during a larger-than-expected house party).

2. **Sound** — We lived in the middle of one big party across multiple blocks — a party that raged on pretty much every night. It's horrifying to think about it now as a 52-year-old but it was a Jeff Spicoli "totally awesome" way to live at 17. I can hear Def Leppard blasting from one apartment while The Cure and Yaz blasted from another. I remember the clinking of bottles and the bounce of a ping pong ball during games of Beer Pong (of course I was 17, so I stayed away from those shenanigans). In the background, I hear Chris Berman and the late great John Saunders anchoring ESPN Sportscenter, which was on in our house at all hours — day and night. On the odd quiet night, the crashing of the waves on the beach just 100 yards away filled our ears. And on even odder early mornings (what teen boy gets up early?), the house was consumed by the sound of the seagulls as they hunted sand crabs. I remember the variety of electronic sounds coming from the boardwalk arcades mixed in with the swoosh of a skeeball and the clinking of an

air-hockey table. And, of course, there were all the sounds
– that will also remain top secret — that emanate from an
apartment with seven guys all under the age of 21.

3. **Smell** — I'm going to skip right over the smells from
    inside the apartment that, just like the house that
    Talking Heads sang about in 1983, are currently
    "burning down my nostrils" as I recall that summer.
    Externally, the smells were pure happiness and
    freedom. I remember the ocean salt water, which is
    such a calming smell; the smell of the salt and vinegar
    from the world-famous *Thrasher's® Fries* on the board-
    walk; the multitude of *Fisher's* popcorn flavors as they
    popped in the steaming hot storefront where one of my
    roommates worked; the rubbery smell of t-shirt decals
    of all kinds — from ones that said OC, MD (Ocean
    City, Maryland) to bands like Van Halen to some very
    naughty ones — being pressed in t-shirt shops on the
    boardwalk by the hundreds; the smell of beer from
    Miller Lite to Budweiser to Pabst Blue Ribbon because
    that is all the beer there was back then; the smell caused
    by a pressure drop as a storm rolls in off of the ocean;
    and, of course, the intoxicating aroma of Old Bay spices
    sprinkled on Maryland steamed crabs. Ahhh ...

4. **Touch** — I can feel the sand between my toes every
    single day. In my hands, the buttons and joysticks on
    arcade games like Galaga, Dragon's Lair, and Time
    Pilot. The sticky floors and countertops of our very
    unclean apartment. The smooth, cool metal of the
    scoopers that we used to measure candy at Candy
    Kitchen where I worked. A cold Pabst Blue Ribbon in
    my hand that I pretended to drink to be "cool." The
    steering wheel of my friend's Mustang almost too hot
    to touch from the August sun. The silky-smooth fur of
    our neighbor's Golden Retriever. The summer heat of

an over-crowded apartment with no air conditioning. And the 2nd-degree burn I received on my hand from a juvenile trick gone wrong.

Circa 1983, hanging out with a friend at the local arcade in front of my favorite game, Galaga, complete with a sweet winged and feathered haircut.

5. **Taste** — So many of my favorite tastes were also my favorite smells. The delicious vinegar and salt of Thrasher's Fries; the caramel of Fisher's Popcorn; the interesting texture of Gummy Rats (so much more daring than a simple gummy *worm*); the melting hot cheese on a double-cheese pizza from The Dough Roller; the one-of-a-kind seasoning flavor from putting Old Bay on everything including potato chips; the spaghetti the girls that lived above us made for me one night (which was my only home-cooked meal all summer); the cheeseburger subs at 2:00 a.m. from Mitchell's Market; and the raw eggs that I cooked in a frying pan, which hadn't been washed in a week after being used as a raw meat container, unbeknownst to me

until it was way too late. Yeah, think the pie-eating scene in *Stand by Me* and you'll get the picture.

Wow, I am feeling super nostalgic now and for some reason Warrant's 1989 hit "Heaven" is front of mind. The opening lyrics are eerie but something everyone will feel at some point when they break through the 40-year barrier:

> *"Got a picture of your house*
> *You're standing by the door.*
> *It's black and white and faded*
> *And it's looking pretty worn ...*
> *The memories are gray but man they're*
> *really coming back ..."*

It's a great song and you should look up the music video on YouTube, which has been viewed almost 50 million times!

So, I hope you did the sensory exercise as well and I hope that it is bringing back some really great memories for you. It's a pretty simple way to see the difference between *buying* the thing and *doing* the thing. Life really comes down to our experiences, not our possessions.

Okay, back to our protagonist Ronald Miller and his doing of the thing. Although Ronald experienced an embarrassing verbal undressing in front of a large group of his classmates and he found himself on the cusp of losing his best friend, he also gave an impassioned speech that ultimately united all the cliques in the high school when he said:

> *"Nerds. Jocks. My side. Your side. It's all bullshit. It's hard*
> *enough just trying to be yourself."*

You can bet that the adult version of Ronald never regretted trading in the potential purchase of a telescope to date the most popular girl in school. The experience changed him. I mean, he does ultimately get the girl in the end (and she gets her guy). It was an '80s movie, so of course it had a happy ending. But the lessons are powerful even if the happily-ever-after is predictable. And it was the journey and the experience that couldn't be replaced or upgraded — which would have likely been the case in a few years with his telescope. The telescope would have helped him see the stars; the experience of becoming momentarily popular helped him see himself — and all the people around him.

Now I do recognize, to a certain extent, that this lesson has a bit of a complex crossover with the first one, as it was that very "faking it to make it" that also allowed Ronald to learn that "doing the thing is greater than buying the thing." I also recognize that technically he had to "buy the thing" in order to *do* the thing when he purchased the dress for Cindy to replace the one she ruined that was really her mom's. Okay wait … digression alert.

■■■■■■■■■■■■■■■■■■■■■■■■■■■■■■■■■■■■

DIGRESSION ALERT

My god, the "whole doing the thing, buying the thing" thing is really starting to sound like Lloyd Dobler's answer to the question of "What do you plan to do with your life?" — which was posed to him by Diane Court's father in the 1989 classic, *Say Anything*. Lloyd responded with:

> "I don't want to sell anything, buy anything, or process anything as a career. I don't want to sell anything bought or processed, or buy anything sold or processed, or process anything sold, bought, or processed, or repair anything sold, bought, or processed. You know, as a career, I don't want to do that."

■■■■■■■■■■■■■■■■■■■■■■■■■■■■■■■■■■■■

In Ronald's quest to be cool in *Can't Buy Me Love*, he stepped into an experience that would no doubt awaken his five senses every time he thought about it for the rest of his life. There would be plenty of time to buy telescopes but very little time to find love and true friendship, to find himself, and to make it into the high-school history books, which is exactly what he did.

There's a great Expedia commercial that launched during the NFL's 2022 Big Game (you know the one, but I can't say it because the NFL will hit me with a lawsuit harder than a Lawrence Taylor sack) that stars the magnificent Ewan McGregor and featuring a final line that really sums up the idea that doing the thing is greater than buying the thing. He's walking through a sound stage, talking about the "stuff" we buy and upgrade as we go through life. He then says, "Do you think any of us will look back on our lives and regret the things we didn't buy?" He pauses as he walks towards a stage door that he opens, revealing a beautiful beach scene with what looks like the rock from *The Goonies* in the background. He walks onto the beach, turns back to us, and says, "or the places we didn't *go*?" Stuff vs. experiences.

Just do the thing.

Oh, and now I remember. My mountain bike was white. Does it really matter, though?

One final lesson from *Can't Buy Me Love*'s leading man himself. As I mentioned at the beginning of the chapter, Patrick Dempsey went from a geek mowing lawns (and a nerdy pizza delivery boy in the 1989 comedy, *Loverboy*) to the studly Dr. Derek McDreamy Shepherd in *Grey's Anatomy* and one of *People Magazine's* most beautiful people in 2007, so I guess anything is possible. The sky is the limit, my friends! Onward and upward!

My posters, in all their glory. (You didn't think I forgot, did you?) And just to be clear, they are no longer on my walls ... and haven't been since 1988!

CHAPTER 4

PRINCE AND SUZANNE VEGA

"Dearest Suzanne ..."

— PRINCE

n life and in business, there are times where you will need to change up your formula a little bit. It may be because things are a bit stagnant or maybe you just need the spark that comes from trying something new. Sometimes it might just be that something better has come along and that's exactly the place where I found myself when I first heard this magnificent story about the greatest musician the world has ever known — Prince.

So how did I change my formula? Well, if you've read either of my first two books, please accept this huge thank you from the bottom of my heart. And if you haven't read one or both of those books, it's my job to entertain you enough with this 3rd offering that you'll consider adding one or both of the previous books to your collection. Once you've read all three books, you'll note that I changed my formula a bit as the book series has continued to evolve and attract readers, fans, and keynote-speaking audiences. I've started giving more homage to '80s *music*, which I love as much as I love the movies. Up until this very chapter here in what is my 3rd book, all the lessons have come from '80s movies and the characters and scenes that defined them. But '80s pop culture encompasses more than just movies. It's music and television and Music Television (MTV) and literature and fashion, which was really bad (except for Vans, of course). This is the first chapter where I explore lessons that are derived from outside of '80s movies. This represents a change in my formula, and what better way to institute change than using an example from the pop culture icon who so loved and adored the color purple? I've always felt a great tribute would be if Crayola would name one of the crayons in their 64-color or 128-color sets "Princely Purple." That would be "cooler than cool," as Elvis (played by Val Kilmer) said in the 1993 film, *True Romance*. Not an '80s movie, but a near-perfect movie, nonetheless.

■■■■■■■■■■■■■■■■■■■■■■■■■■■■■■■■■

FUN FACT: The color purple and crayons have a long history in literature. Believe it or not, Prince was not the first pop-culture icon with one name to embrace the color purple. In 1955, Crocket Johnson released a children's book called *Harold and The Purple Crayon* about a boy and his purple crayon, which he used to draw his own adventures. It's one of my favorites from my childhood and a movie with the same name is in production and scheduled for a release in January of 2023!

■■■■■■■■■■■■■■■■■■■■■■■■■■■■■■■■■

Okay, back to our musical icon with one name who loved the color purple. In 1987, Prince was the king of music and pop culture. We call Michael Jackson the king of pop and he can have that moniker. Prince was the king of music. He was on the biggest stage in the world and entertaining us with his singing, writing, composing, acting, directing, and talents for expertly playing enough instruments to legitimately be a one-man symphony orchestra. At the same time, there was an alternative rock singer named Suzanne Vega who was not known by one name and was moderately known at that time and generally in circles of people who listened to college radio or dissected the soundtracks of John Hughes films. That was me, of course, and I have always admired Suzanne Vega's talent from her voice to her songwriting to the magic she creates with her guitar. My first recollection of hearing her music was the song "Tom's Diner," which was released in the early '80s. The song centers around the NYC restaurant, Tom's Restaurant, whose exterior was eventually used as the exterior for Monk's Café in the classic television show, *Seinfeld*.[12] Her song, *Left of Center,* was on the soundtrack for the 1986 movie *Pretty in Pink* and then in 1987, she released the song "My Name Is Luka" — a song about child abuse — that became an international hit.

When Prince heard the song, he was so moved by it that he penned a handwritten note to Vega that is the basis for this chapter. And with this noble and simple gesture, he taught us two lessons for life and the workplace:

   1. **Leaders share the stage of success.**

   2. **Encouragement doesn't cost a thing.**

All I will tell you for now is that if you liked Prince before you hear the entire story, you are going to *love* him now. And I mean the

---

12 "Tom's Diner," Wikipedia, Last Updated August 20, 2022, https://en.wikipedia. org/wiki/Tom%27s_Diner.

kind of love that you would create a mix tape for, complete with Air Supply, REO Speedwagon, and Sade. Yes, that kind of love.

My Life in 1987

Now before we dive into the totally awesome details of this hand-written note, let's get to the clock tower before the lightning strike and go back to 1987. Typically, we would go back to a specific date that coincided with the release of the movie for that chapter, but the exact date in 1987 of Prince's handwritten note is unknown, so let's just go back to that year in general.

1987 was an interesting year for me. It encompassed the 2nd part of my junior year in high school and the 1st part of my senior year. I had finally gotten my driver's license, which meant two things when it came to my social life:

1. I no longer needed to sneak out of my bedroom window, jump onto the small roof below, and then jump off the roof, grabbing the rim of my basketball hoop on the way down to break my fall enough so I didn't break another bone or end up in the ER with more stitches. Yes, I actually did that multiple times. I also snuck onto the roof (I know there's a lot of roofs in this story) of our middle school — Franklin Middle — in the middle of the night to drink a Bartles & Jaymes "Thank you for your support" wine cooler and retrieve all the kickballs that resided there.

2. My mom would never again need to drive me to and from a date. Such an incredibly horrifying time in my life, those adolescent moments pre-driver's license. Even at 52, it still embarrasses me.

My attire during this epic period ranged from the fresh combination of Georgetown Hoya sweats and an Adidas Sport Lore sweatshirt (complete with a gold stitched logo) to a pair of pegged Z Cavaricci jeans and a "who farted" t-shirt that actually did get me kicked out of Spanish class and suspended for a day. And regardless of my attire, I was slathered in Drakkar Noir cologne, especially for those slammin' Saturday nights at Sportsman's, our local roller-skating rink. Unfortunately for me, I had to wear those putrid beige rental skates with the orange stopper, but at least I smelled good (or so I thought). The lack of a partner during couples' skate should have been the signal that maybe the half bottle of hair gel that made my spiked hair as sharp as icicles — combined with showering in Drakkar — was a recipe for a solo backwards skate or a night standing in front of the Galaga arcade game with no girls in sight.

■■■■■■■■■■■■■■■■■■■■■■■■■■■■■■■■

FUN FACT: Roller skating was invented in 1735 by a Belgian named John Joseph Merlin. Roller skating became so popular in the 1980s that in 1983, then President Ronald Reagan declared October to be National Roller Skating Month.[13] I can also tell you that in 1983, my invitation to join me for a couples' skate was turned down a record 10 times in one night at Sportsman's Hall and Skating Rink in Reisterstown, MD. If you are looking for a great comedy routine on roller skating in the 1980s, go Google comedian Bret Ernst's "roller skating bit." Bret also stars in the *Cobra Kai* series, so there's a lot of '80s happening with him.

■■■■■■■■■■■■■■■■■■■■■■■■■■■■■■■■

Pop Culture in 1987

If we take away my proclivity for bad fashion, worse hairstyles, and a severe misunderstanding of proper cologne usage, 1987 was a very good year for pop culture. Wrestling fans were treated

---

13 "Roller Skating," *Wikipedia*, Last Edited September 20, 2022, https://www.en.wikipedia.org/wiki/Roller_skating

to the largest wrestling event in history (at the time) when more than 80,000 fans packed into the Pontiac Silverdome to watch what some were calling "Hulkamania Running Wild" as Hulk Hogan retained his WWF title by defeating Andre the Giant at *Wrestlemania 3*. Beyond the physical ring, sports were also the rage in video gaming as Nintendo released a boxing video game called *"PunchOut"* with characters like Glass Joe, Don Flamenco, King Hippo, Bald Bull, and some other guy named Mike Tyson. The goal of the game was to get your guy — Little Mac — through all the contenders so you could fight Tyson for the championship belt. Why anyone would want to fight Mike Tyson — real or imagined — is the question to be asked here.

If we take away my proclivity for bad fashion, worse hairstyles, and a severe misunderstanding of proper cologne usage, 1987 was a very good year for pop culture.

On television, *The Simpsons* made their debut as a series of short, animated segments on *The Tracey Ullman Show* while Frank Sinatra made his last credited screen performance as a guest on *Magnum P.I.,* which was my favorite '80s show. Man, did I want to be just like Thomas Magnum. Never actually happened. Damn. The groundbreaking *Hill Street Blues* and the incredibly entertaining and underrated *Gimme a Break* ended their very successful runs, but perhaps the most impactful TV event of 1987 was on October 15, when Bob Barker stopped dying his hair brown and made his first appearance on *The Price Is Right* with white hair. Okay, it wasn't as impactful as someone being less than $100 from the price of their showcase in the Showcase Showdown, thus winning *both* showcases, but the audience did give him a one-minute standing ovation for his foxy white hair, so there's that.[14]

In a word, 1987 for movies was *spectacular*. From the dark and disturbing grittiness of *Less Than Zero* (with a cast that boasted James Spader, Robert Downey, Jr., and Jami Gertz) to the heartfelt and hilarious combination of Steve Martin and John Candy in *Planes, Trains and Automobiles*, 1987 was awash with modern classics. *The Princess Bride* (which has a chapter in my 2nd book — shameless plug), *Wall Street, Full Metal Jacket, Predator, Hellraiser, Lethal Weapon, The Lost Boys* (another chapter in my 2nd book and another shameless plug), *Three Men and a Baby, La Bamba,* and so many more. It also gave us a few of the most underrated films from the '80s in the form of *The Gate, Hollywood Shuffle, Three O'Clock High,* and *Can't Buy Me Love,* the last one of which you've already seen in this book and which I hope provided you with some totally awesome life and work lessons. *Three O' Clock High* also gave us one of the best bullies the big screen has ever seen in the form of Buddy Revell. Alas, 1987 also gave us one of the biggest box-office bombs in history with the star-studded comedy *Ishtar,* which cost $55 million to produce and brought in just $14 million at the box office. Ouch.

For those who know and "like" your 1987 movies in the same way that Mikey "liked" his Life Cereal, then you may be wondering why one very prominent movie from 1987 wasn't included in my modern classics list above. It pains me to even type the name of it, but here we go — *Dirty Dancing*. Now for those of you who have read my previous books, you know how much I love Patrick Swayze. I love him so much that my rescue pit mix is named Bodhi after his character in *Point Break* (which is not an '80s movie but is awesome nonetheless). So, you know those dirty little secrets that everyone has? Yes you. You know you have them. Well, besides singing Kelly Clarkson's song "Since You've Been Gone" at the top of my lungs in my house, shower and car, I have

---

14 https://en.wikipedia.org/wiki/1987_in_American_television

another dirty little secret around *Dirty Dancing* in that I've never seen it. That's right. Me, an '80s pop culture freak. A guy who makes his living from '80s movies has never seen *Dirty Dancing*. I'm proud to admit that I actually *did* "put Baby in the corner" and I left her there. Oh man, I can see the pitchforks in hand, ready to march on my home and demand that I watch the director's cut on VHS or Betamax so I can truly appreciate its greatness. But before you take my '80s card from me, please see below for a little fun fact about me and *Dirty Dancing*. I hope it helps. Please let it help.

■■■■■■■■■■■■■■■■■■■■■■■■■■■■■■■■■■

FUN FACT: I graduated high school in 1988. The theme for our Senior Prom was "I've Had the Time of My Life" from ... you guessed it ... *Dirty Dancing*. I wanted "Home Sweet Home" from *Motley Crue* as our theme but, alas, I did not get the votes necessary. Our ultimate "time of my life" theme was on all the party favors — glasses, coasters, pins, etc. — and we were tortured with that song at least 150 times that night and that is not an exaggeration.

1988: Trying to look suave in front of our prom limo
with my date, Melanie, getting ready to listen to
"I've Had the Time of My Life" a million times.

It is seared into my brain and not in a good way.
To this day, I still have night terrors and wake up
sweating profusely as I hear Bill Medley and Jennifer
Warnes singing, "Now I've ... had the time of my life
... No, I never felt like this before ..." I just can't do
it. I really need my sleep and so *Dirty Dancing*
will forever remain unseen, and Baby will remain
forever in the corner.

■■■■■■■■■■■■■■■■■■■■■■■■■■■■■■■■■

Life Lessons from Prince and Suzanne Vega

Okay, so if you are still with me and still consider me your friend,
then come with me through this perfect segue into the music of
1987. As I have mentioned before, the eclectic and experimental
nature of music in the '80s provided us with massive variety
when it came to the Top 40, and 1987 was no different. Let's take
the week of June 6th and see what Casey Kasem was spinning for
us after saying, "And now on with the countdown." Poison was
representing glam rockers around the country with their hit "Talk
Dirty to Me" while Kenny G was providing every freshman college
dorm room with what they thought was smooth and mature
makeout music via "Songbird." U2 was continuing their transition
from alternative to pop with their sing-in-the-shower song "With
or Without You," while Lisa Lisa & Cult Jam and Expose kept the
under-21 club dance floors full with "Head to Toe" and "Point of
No Return," respectively. Rock-and-Roll Hall of Famers Tom Petty
and The Heartbreakers and Bob Seger kept the Top 40 classic
and respectable with "Jammin' Me" and "Shakedown" (the latter
of which appeared on the *Beverly Hills Cop II* soundtrack). And
talking about massive variety, the Top 40 this week also included
the timeless and classy Motown legend Smokey Robinson with
"Just to See Her," which landed just a few spots in front of the
rebel rocker Billy Idol with "Sweet Sixteen."

But it was the song that debuted at #93 that prompted Prince to do something super freakin' rad that provides us the basis for this chapter and the lessons that will follow. Suzanne Vega was an alternative singer who was most known for her song "Left of Center," which appeared on the *Pretty in Pink* movie soundtrack. Now as mentioned before, if you loved John Hughes movies and/or listened to college radio, you would have likely heard of her, but she was not necessarily a household name. Her song that debuted at #93 was one you may remember — *"My Name Is Luka"* — which is an anthem for survivors of childhood abuse. Eventually it would work its way up to #3 and would be her biggest US hit by far.

Prior to climbing the charts, "My Name Is Luka" caught the eye and ear of the magical and wondrous Prince. Just as a reminder, by the time 1987 rolled around, Prince had been nominated for seven Grammys (and he won four), won an Academy Award for the *Purple Rain* movie original score, and had multiple hit songs (including "Little Red Corvette," "Delirious," "1999," "When Doves Cry," "Let's Go Crazy," "Purple Rain," "I Would Die 4 U," "Raspberry Beret," "Kiss," and "U Got the Look." Two of his songs — "Manic Monday" and "I Feel for You" — became huge hits when they were covered by The Bangles and Chaka Khan, respectively. *"I Feel for You"* went on to win a Grammy for Best R&B song in 1985. By 1987, Prince had also formed a band called The Time (with Morris Day), had released nine albums, starred in two movies (*Purple Rain* and *Under the Cherry Moon*), and directed a movie (*Under the Cherry Moon*).[15] A hell of a resume.

I'm sure I am missing a few things here and remember that he still had almost 30 more years of accomplishments ahead of him before he left us way too soon in 2016. We often hear that Michael Jackson was the King of Pop. He can absolutely have that moniker. Prince was the King of Music, and it isn't even close!

---

15 https://en.wikipedia.org/wiki/Prince_(musician), https://en.wikipedia.org/wiki/I_Feel_for_You_(album), and https://en.wikipedia.org/wiki/Manic_Monday

On April 21, 2016, Prince — the King of Music — passed away and it will go down as one of the days in history that "the music died" as Don McLean sang in his classic 1972 hit "American Pie." Prince was a legend who was a combination of the musical brilliance of Mozart, the eclecticism of Van Gogh, the entertaining genius of Sammy Davis, Jr., the determined work ethic of Jimi Hendrix, and the exponential curiosity of Elon Musk. Yeah, you could say I'm a fan.

■■■■■■■■■■■■■■■■■■■■■■■■■■■■■■■■

FUN FACT: Yes. I am a pop culture fanatic with a particular affinity for '80s pop culture, if you couldn't tell. But there have only been five celebrity deaths that really had an impact on me — mostly because they were taken way too early from us and had so much more to offer. Robin Williams, Chris Farley, John Candy, Patrick Swayze, and Prince. Someone once said that the world absolutely missed out on a father/son movie with John Candy and Chris Farley. Yes, we most certainly did. And to take a lesson from the *Vision Quest* chapter, all five of these icons *made their mark* rather than marking the time.

■■■■■■■■■■■■■■■■■■■■■■■■■■■■■■■■

Like so many icons, inventors, and innovators, we learned more about Prince on the day he passed away then we had ever known previously when the spotlight was shining brightest. Lost in the accolades that poured in across the entertainment industry and the mainstream media was a social media post from Suzanne Vega. In the post, she included a photo of handwritten note that Prince penned and sent to her after he heard her song "My Name Is Luka."

The handwritten note said:

Dearest Suzanne,

Luka is the most compelling piece of music I've heard in a long time.

There are no words 2 tell u all the things I feel when I hear it. I thank God 4 u.

— Prince

Man, did he have a way with words. Tell me that it isn't one of the coolest things you've ever read, particularly when you know who wrote it. Pretty damn awesome. I mean, the shock she must have felt when she received and read this. Like New Order "Shellshock" shock, which ironically was also one of the songs on the *Pretty in Pink* soundtrack along with Vega's "Left of Center". While she was opening her mailbox to find a love letter to her song from Prince, the rest of us were waiting for our 8 cassette tapes for a penny from Columbia House or the prize from the secret decoder ring we found in our Captain Crunch cereal box to come in our mail delivery. Good times.

Imagine getting a handwritten note thanking you for something you created or accomplished from the person who is at the very top of the industry you are working in! Add on to it that they are known globally and by one name. And if you go online to see the note, you'll notice that he was using numbers and single letters for words well before text messaging made it a normal part of conversation? Who knows — maybe he was a time traveler as well. Just add that to the resume.

As I mentioned, to really get a full appreciation for the note, you really must go use the Google machine and see it. His hand-writing is as magical as you would expect and he even included a few little drawings of a bird, a flower, and a cross. Its perfection and improbability make it quite literally the handwritten-note equivalent of the Thornton Melon "Triple Lindy" dive, which was pulled off by another genius of entertainment, Rodney Dangerfield, in the 1986 comedy *Back to School.*

So, what did Prince teach us when he penned this handwritten note for Suzanne Vega? He taught us the difference between rulers and leaders:

 **Leaders share the stage of success.**

So to set the stage here — no pun intended — *Webster's Dictionary* defines a leader as "someone who leads or guides" while a ruler is defined as "one who exercises dominion or controlling power over others." Big difference, and that difference is sometimes a big problem in workplaces and in society.

How many of you have been in a job where the person who was supposed to be the leader was a ruler? I suspect most of us have been in that position. Unfortunately, a lot of people who should never end up in leadership of any kind ultimately find their way to positions of power. It's an age-old problem and it happens pretty much everywhere.

I've been there and, although at the time it was pretty horrific, I'd actually go back and thank that person (who shall remain nameless just like "he who walked behind the rows," as Sarah said in the terrifying 1984 horror movie, *Children of the Corn).* Thank him? Yes. He taught me what not to do as a leader in almost every situation. I suffered but I learned. If he handled something a certain way, I just applied the opposite thinking when I became a leader myself. The *complete* opposite. I think we sometimes learn more from negative situations then we do from positive ones. I know I do.

Okay, before we move on with our lessons from the magical Prince, let's go back to *Children of the Corn* for a minute. Terrifying isn't a good enough adjective for a movie about a bunch of kids in a small town who sacrifice all the adults to the devil. For many people like me, *Children of the Corn* did for non-descript cornfields the same thing that *Jaws* did for the ocean or *Psycho* did for showers. I can't unsee it and any time I pass by a cornfield, I look to make sure that Malaki isn't standing there with a sickle. Stupid, demonic Malaki. Yes, indeed — leaders who act and "lead" like rulers can be analogous to the killers in '80s horror movies. How so?

- ➤ They slash through everything and everyone with reckless abandon.

- ➤ In their narcissistic and insane minds, rules and laws don't apply to them.

- ➤ They're petty. I mean, look, Jason killed people in *Friday the 13th* for smoking a doobie or hooking up. So yeah, petty.

- ➤ They believe the more blood, the better — as long as it isn't theirs.

- ➤ No matter how fast you run or how well you hide, they find you. They prey on perceived weakness.

- ➤ They never ever fight fair. When they do, they lose.

- ➤ They get their power through fear.

- ➤ They can't be reasoned with in any way, shape, or form.

There's a reason that people talk about rulers leading with "an iron fist." Rulers are ruthless. So, if we know this and we even have sayings to support it that we quote from centuries ago, why does this continue to happen? Why haven't we learned from it? There are several reasons why we continue to see rulers in positions of leadership:

1. **Nepotism.** Lots and lots of it. We all know it's alive and well and may be the number one contributing factor to rulers in leadership positions. For some, when they inherit their job from Daddy or Mommy, their qualifications and character are rarely even considered.

2. **Lack of accountability.** If you allow rulers to take leadership positions or leave leaders unchecked, accountability is likely at the very back of your workplace culture book.

3. **Fear and unfortunate realities.** The birth of the great resignation, due in large part to COVID, has changed the landscape but there are still hundreds of millions of people around the world who absolutely depend on the job they have and aren't in a position to make a change, so both fear and unfortunate realities will keep them working for a ruler. And without any mass exodus, the ruler will continue to rule.

4. **Politics.** No, not red and blue or left and right. We don't do that conversation in my books, thankfully. Company politics. To this day it is amazing to see people climb the company ladder with no real accomplishments at all except for the ability to throw anyone and everyone under the bus on their way to leadership. The ability to do absolutely nothing beyond point out the faults — real or fictious — in others (usually others who are attempting to do their jobs well) and then getting rewarded with advancement for that nonsense, is quite incredible. This 100% creates rulers and it happens every single day.

5. **Lack of true and active leadership.** A company or orga-
    nization with true and active leadership would never
    allow rulers to find themselves in positions of power, let
    alone allow them to stay in those positions. Sadly, this
    type of leadership has become a rarity in a world where
    leadership is becoming more and more isolated from
    the workers/employees/humans who are truly respon-
    sible for the success of the company. Leadership that is
    heard but not seen and does not have their finger on the
    pulse of their workplace culture will create an environ-
    ment that is ripe for rulers.

So now we've just spent a chunk of this chapter focusing on the
negative and that makes me a very unhappy author. Let's get
back to what that musician who loved the color purple taught us
about leadership.

With a simple handwritten note, Prince taught us the difference
between rulers and leaders. While rulers keep everyone below
the stage they stand on, leaders share the stage of success. Prince
gracefully showed us how leadership works through the simple
lens of acknowledgment and encouragement.

And speaking of acknowledgment, the only reason that we know
about this note is due to a social media posting by Suzanne Vega.
In 2016, when Prince passed away, Suzanne Vega posted the
handwritten note she received from Prince on her social media
for the world to see. My belief is that she wanted us to see the
kind of guy Prince was behind the scenes. Twenty-nine years had
passed since he wrote that note. (And if that line sounds familiar,
well then you are most definitely a pretty hardcore fan of *The
Police,* whose song "Message in a Bottle" had the lyric, "a year had
passed since I wrote that note.")

■■■■■■■■■■■■■■■■■■■■■■■■■■■■■■■■

FUN FACT: The earliest known message in
a bottle was sent in 310 B.C. by the Greek philoso-
pher Theophrastus, one of Aristotle's pupils, as
a way of testing his hypothesis that the Atlantic
Ocean flows into the Mediterranean Sea.[16]

■■■■■■■■■■■■■■■■■■■■■■■■■■■■■■■■

For almost three decades, Vega held onto that note but what
is most impressive is that, as far as we know, Prince never
mentioned it. He wasn't looking for accolades or pats on the back
from the media or fans. That's clearly not why he did it. True leadership — just like true character — is really defined by what you
do when people aren't looking. Prince's public accomplishments
provided the spotlight and he had zero desire to manufacture it
for public relations or goodwill gain. This is not to say that leaders
shouldn't publicize large initiatives that impact communities
in a positive way. Communicating the actions you are taking to
invest in the greater good is incredibly important as it informs,
educates, and inspires others to do the same. But what Prince did
was human to human. One to one. For the recipient, this gift of
encouragement and acknowledgement is wrapped in humility
and authenticity. Any self-promotion of your good deed would
ruin the impact and would most certainly lessen the value to
the recipient.

**True leadership — just like true
character — is really defined by what
you do when people aren't looking.**

---

16 Clara Pinsky, "Sending Out an SOS," *New York Magazine*, July 12, 2013, https://
nymag.com/news/intelligencer/topic/solo-message-in-a-bottle-2013-7/.

What Prince did while standing on the largest stage in the world was so simple — he shared it. He saw greatness in what Suzanne Vega had done with her song "My Name Is Luka" and he let her know. Leaders aren't afraid to share the stage. They look to provide opportunities to others who show that they have the drive, commitment, and talent to be make a bigger impact. They take a little of their spotlight and shine it on others. They don't mind having a little less stage and they don't fear being supplanted, which is usually because they've earned their way into their position and recognize that there is greatness in others that absolutely must be shared with their common audience — whether it be extended family, a small town, a global corporation, or the billions of people who listen to and love music.

Unearned leadership creates pleasers while earned leadership creates believers.

In my 2nd book during a chapter on what we can learn from the classic 1988 comedy *Coming to America,* one of the lessons that revolves around leadership is that *unearned leadership creates pleasers while earned leadership creates believers.* With all the accolades Prince had earned by 1987, he had most definitely earned his leadership position and likely didn't have the self-confidence issues that rulers typically have (because their position is almost always unearned). Beyond having an unearned position, rulers tend to keep everyone below the stage that they stand on. They do so for several reasons:

1. **Lack of confidence.** Because they haven't earned their position, they typically lack confidence and replace it with arrogance. We talked about this in Chapter 1, which was on lessons from *Trading Places.*

2. **They don't want to be challenged.** This is usually because they don't have the answers or solutions that a true leader would have ... and they know it. Or they've been surrounded with "yes people" their entire lives and truly don't believe that they could actually be wrong or that there could be a better way.

3. **They value control.** In their world, the only one allowed to have autonomy and to think independently is the ruler themself. It's difficult to keep everyone "in their place" if you allow them to share the stage with you.

4. **They were picked last on the playground.** Actually, I have no idea if this is accurate, but it sure seems like it would fit.

Another distinct difference between leaders and rulers is that leaders want to provide encouragement to others. With his hand-written note, Prince also taught us that:

 **Encouragement doesn't cost a thing.**

Do you think that Suzanne Vega experienced just a slight confidence boost when she received that note? I would bet all my arcade quarters that I used in the summer of 1983 that she did.

Now let's also remember that when this note was written back in 1987, there was no digital means for Prince to deliver this to her. No email. No social media. No text messages or DMs. No easy way. No shortcut. The closest we had to anything digital was the hip-hop group Digital Underground, which was formed in 1987 and is known best for their timeless and super-fun dance jam, "The Humpty Dance." No, Prince had to either mail it, messenger it (not Facebook Messenger, but a real dude on a bike or in a van!), or hand deliver himself. Just like a lot of things in the '80s — renting a movie, checking your voicemail (answering machine), buying pretty much anything, or hearing your favorite song — there were extra steps that needed to be taken for you to fulfill your mission and it was no different for Prince. Letting Suzanne Vega know that he saw the greatness in her was so important to him that he took the time. My guess is even if she released "My Name Is Luka" in 2014, when multiple digital short-cuts were available to him, he still would have gone the route of the handwritten note because that's what leaders do. When they acknowledge and encourage, they make the investment, and they take extra steps to show that they truly mean it. They make it personal. Prince personalized his message all the way down to the doodles (a flower, a bird, and a cross). Leaders don't cut corners or take the easy route. They don't mass mail with auto-mated signatures and a generic message. You know the type — basically 80% of the mail you receive — both physical and digital.

Lost Arts and Modern-Day Leadership

Just imagine receiving a handwritten note from the person in your industry who is the absolute best at what they do. And not with just any ordinary message, but the perfect message — a message telling you that what you did was the best thing they'd seen or heard in a long time and that there are literally "no words to describe what they felt" when they heard it or saw it. Just thinking about what it must have felt like when Vega opened that note gives me chills. For me, it would be like receiving a handwritten note from Stephen King telling me that he was impressed by my writing or Eddie Murphy complimenting me on one of my open mic routines at a comedy club. The odds of that happening are like winning the lottery. How amazing is it that some people win the "compliments from leaders and icons" lottery? It makes you wonder what you could do in your own life and work to make someone else feel this fortunate. How can you share the stage and offer encouragement?

Prince was magical in so many ways as an entertainer and this simple, yet incredibly thoughtful, gesture that he provided to Suzanne Vega showed us that he was also a magical *human being* with timeless leadership qualities. As a reminder, here is that note one more time:

> *Dearest Suzanne,*
>
> *Luka is the most compelling piece of music I've heard in a long time.*
>
> *There are no words 2 tell u all the things I feel when I hear it. I thank God 4 u.*
>
> *— Prince*

Damn, that is awesome.

Oh, and one more thing: the handwritten note is a lost art. When it comes to a message of encouragement or acknowledgment, take the time to do it right. Don't "Milli Vanilli" it and find the most advantageous shortcut à la email. Be a Chaucer or a Shakespeare or a Mary Shelley, put a real pen to real paper, write something eloquent, and show the recipient how much you truly care about them. Even if your handwriting is illegible muck, just like mine is, you can always follow up with a more legible email.

Remember to **share that stage of success** when you are standing the highest on it. Whether the success comes in your workplace, your personal life, or your community, make sure to recognize and elevate others who are doing great things as well. And remember that **encouragement doesn't cost a thing**. It's free to give and will pay more dividends than shares of Apple or Google ever could.

Okay, with Chapter 4 fully written and in the "books," I need to get dressed up, go out, and have a bourbon — neat, of course. Now, where did I put my Raspberry Beret?

CHAPTER 5

COCKTAIL

"We dazzle him with ice work. We baffle him with bottle work."

— BRIAN COUGHLIN, *COCKTAIL*

If you've ever been to the Caribbean and especially if you've been to the Bahamas, then you most certainly have heard two of the songs from the soundtrack of the 1988 film *Cocktail*. Playing in almost every beach and resort bar practically on a continuous loop are the songs "Kokomo" by The Beach Boys and "Don't Worry Be Happy" by Bobby McFerrin. Both are perfect songs to put you in a day-drinking mood, whether your toes are in the sand or the snow. "Don't Worry Be Happy" is just a fun, easygoing song sure to put a smile on your face, while "Kokomo" falls into the category of '80s songs led by "We Built This City" (Jefferson Starship) that we love to hate but know all the lyrics and will sing loudly with our car windows rolled up or into an air microphone in the privacy of our home. Accurate?

■■■■■■■■■■■■■■■■■■■■■■■■■■■■■■■

⛏ FUN FACT: John Stamos played drums in "Kokomo." Well, he didn't exactly play the drums, but he was in the video "playing" the steel drums. He was starring in an ABC special doing a version of "WipeOut" with The Fat Boys (loved those guys). The Beach Boys were there as well for the opening of the Grand Floridian Disney Resort when Stamos was asked to be part of the video.[17] Apparently, he regrets the fuchsia tank top worn in the video.

■■■■■■■■■■■■■■■■■■■■■■■■■■■■■■■

Now if you just listened to the soundtrack for the movie *Cocktail*, you'd hear even more fun and happy songs like "Tutti Frutti" by Little Richard, "All Shook Up" by Elvis, and a cover of Chan Romero's 1959 hit, "Hippy Hippy Shake" by The Georgia Satellites. And if you've never worked in a bar environment, you may think that the mood of the soundtrack matches the job itself. It's just one big party, night after night, and you are right in the middle of it. Who wouldn't want that job, especially in our youth? A party every night? Yes, please! Well, ask anyone who has worked in the bar industry, including yours truly, and you'll hear a bit of different story. It's a tough job with long hours. Each shift is physically and mentally draining and if you work in a tourist destination like I did, there are no nights off. And if you've ever been 100% sober in a bar on a Saturday night at midnight with a sea of intoxicated people surrounding you, then you've had a taste of the bar employee's life.

---

17 Matthew Trczinski, "What John Stamos Regrets About The Beach Boys' 'Kokomo' Video," April 28, 2021, https://www.cheatsheet.com/entertainment/john-stamos-regrets-appearing-the-beach-boys-kokomo-music-video.html/.

If you work at a "hot" bar or popular club, you can make very good money and if you are financially savvy, you can really set yourself up well for the next stage of your life. But how many of us in our 20s are savvy when it comes to our finances?

Of course, if you work at a "hot" bar or popular club, you can make very good money and if you are financially savvy, you can really set yourself up well for the next stage of your life. But how many of us in our 20s are savvy when it comes to our finances? Which brings us to two of the main characters — Brian Flanagan, a bartender with the soul of an entrepreneur (played by Tom Cruise) and Jordan Mooney, a mysterious artist (played by Elizabeth Shue). Around the middle of the movie, after Brian has left his bartending job and business school in New York City for a bartending job in Jamaica, Brian and Jordan are sitting at a table having a drink when they begin discussing all the products around them — products whose creators are likely now all millionaires. Products like toothpicks, ashtrays, wrappers for the toothpicks, and those plastic pieces for the end of your shoelaces that Jordan names "flugelbinders." Pensively, Brian says, "We sit here and we're surrounded by millionaires." The conversation continues, which we'll get into later, but ends with Jordan saying, "Your flugelbinder is out there, waiting to be discovered." In their discussion of millionaires, they teach us that:

 The difference between *dreaming* the dream and living the dream is the action you're willing to take.

You've likely heard the term "poker face," which is also the title of an awesome Lady Gaga song. Yes, I am fan. Or for those of you who are nostalgic for iconic commercials, how about the "never let them see you sweat" from a Dry Idea campaign back in 1985? So, what do Lady Gaga and Dry Idea have in common? And, most importantly, what do both have in common with the 3rd major character in the movie, Doug Coughlin? Doug (played by Bryan Brown) is a middle-aged lifelong bartender who makes drinks and hustles people with equal proficiency. He has a practiced poker face and he never lets anyone see him sweat. Doug is a mentor to Brian — in life and in business — and lives by his set of Coughlin's Laws, which direct his business and personal life. Some of his so-called laws are funny, some are depressing, and others are downright enlightening.

The Coughlin Law that ties Lady Gaga, Dry Idea, and Doug together — philosophically anyway — is "Never show surprise. Never lose your cool." This is, of course, difficult to do in every life and workplace situation. But:

 Successful negotiating — in life, business, and, most importantly, with yourself — requires patience and a delicate touch.

So, before we see what we can learn from a movie focused on the bar industry, let's jump in the DeLorean and go back to July of 1988.

My Life in July 1988

In the 1986 movie *Highlander*, Connor MacLeod is with Brenda, a forensics expert when he opens a bottle of brandy, sniffs it, and says, "Bottled in 1783," to which she says, "Wow, that's old." He then goes onto say this:

> "1783 was a very good year. Mozart wrote his Great Mass. The Montgolfier brothers went up in their first balloon. And England recognized the Independence of the United States."

So smooth. So refined. I've always wanted to do that on a dinner date with a bottle of wine but because my dating scene has dried up enough to resemble a bag of dehydrated dates in an airport convenience store, what better place than to do it here with all of you! Cue the opening of something from 1988:

> "1988 was a very good year. Andre the Giant defeated Hulk Hogan. Toni Morrison won the Pulitzer Prize for *Beloved*. *Die Hard*, which is a Christmas movie, was released. And I spent a much more refined summer than the previous one in Ocean City, Maryland."

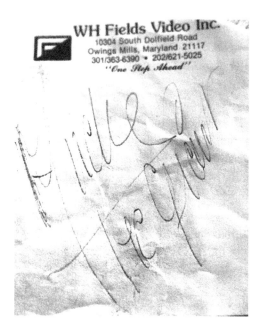

I think it was 1981 when I got Andre the Giant's autograph at a wrestling show.
There is a picture of us and I am determined to find it.

Okay, now I feel all "Fresh" like Kool and the Gang. Maybe I'm a Highlander after all ... nope. So, in July of 1988, I was roughly eight weeks away from starting my college experience and now, as of the writing of this book in 2022, I'm going to my 30th college reunion. If there was ever a time for a "WTF," well this is it. I mean 30th college reunion? That is, well, *Poltergeist* muddy-pool-full-of-skeletons terrifying. Anywhooo (a nod to my Wisconsin-based editor), that July I was working as a bellman at the Holiday Inn Oceanfront on 66th Street, to which I would bike each day from our apartment roughly 50 blocks south. After my shift, I'd go to the gym for two hours and then, with the remaining hours of light, hop in the ocean for some bodyboarding. Yes, I had an Eddy Grant "Electric Avenue" of energy in my youth, as so many of us did.

When you're 18, a job earning tips is usually a pretty good thing and being a bellman was no exception. The job itself was mindless, which was exactly what I needed. But it also involved a lot of people interaction, so you had to be good at conversation. The better the conversation, the better the tip ... usually. An owner of a large and very well-known food company is responsible for the "usually," because the tip I received from him after carrying 30 bags to four separate rooms for his family of 10 were two stickers and a dime-store baseball hat with his company's brand name on them. To this day, I have continued my solo boycott and have not purchased that product and have even refused it when offered. Hey, that's how I "Rick Roll." If you got the whole "Rick Roll" thing, then good on you! If not, Google it. I mean no book about the '80s is complete without at least one Rick Astley mention.

Being a bellman also means you see a *lot* of stuff. Some good, some funny, some weird, and some that just can't be unseen. Whether I had a morning shift or an overnight (those were interesting), I hopped on my bike and pedaled those 50 blocks in my British Knights sneakers, tube socks with colored rings, Oakley frog-skin sunglasses, and my Holiday Inn bellman uniform. Picture me in a light blue button-up shirt and white short shorts. Yeah, you know the ones.

Working at a resort hotel meant that you stayed pretty busy throughout the week, but Saturday mornings were really your opportunity to get "Paid in Full" as Erik B and Rakim rapped in 1987. That was check-in and check-out day, so if you "ran" like Flock of Seagulls told you to, you could leave your shift with a couple hundred dollars in tips. That was a guarantee if you were lucky enough to have most of your clients come from the smoking rooms. (Strange but true that smokers just tended to tip better at hotels and restaurants.) Of course, walking in the gym after my shift smelling like Marlboro Reds didn't exactly expand my dating pool, but at least I could afford more than the Gummy Rats I subsisted on the previous summer.

So, I mentioned the "good, funny, weird, and the things that can't be unseen" that is a bellman's life. I experienced all four of those during one overnight shift. I'm a bit of night owl so having a job that occasionally gave me the opportunity to stay up all night was something pretty cool for me. It's when I do my best thinking and my best writing. (As such, if at the end of this chapter, you think it sucks ... then I probably did most of the writing during the day.) This one particular evening, I started my shift at 11:00 p.m. and things were actually pretty quiet until about 1:30 a.m., when I received a call from my manager.

> **Manager:** "Umm, Chris. We need your help at the indoor pool please."

> **Me:** "Okay. Should I bring my bellcart?"

> **Manager:** "No. Security called out sick and we are hoping that you can handle a situation for us."

Now, by this time, I was a pretty big kid. I was spending a lot of time in the gym and had gotten myself to about 235 pounds. At 6'1", I was definitely bigger than I realized. My dad reminded me of this fact when I shaved my head and he said, "You look a goddamn gorilla." That's my dad. Always ready with a compliment.

Hmmm ... handle a situation. I was jazzed. Bring it on! Maybe there was a fight to break up or something? I thought that could be fun, of course. If only it were that simple.

"Look at the monitors that have the pool cameras and let me know what you think," my manager said with a bit of a chuckle.

I walked around the front desk, stared into the monitor, and saw the beginnings of a nudist colony at the pool. Eight people frolicking, 100% naked, not a care in the world. Unfortunately for me, it was more like an outtake from the movie *Cocoon* than something from the late night '80s Cinemax movie menu. These were not spry spring chickens. On the contrary, they resembled a box of fried chicken skins with Coppertone tans. Eeek!

"Dude. Seriously? Why me? You're the manager," I said with the exaggerated "ugh" of the typical 18-year-old.

"It's in your job description," she said. "Not really, but please help me out here. I can't do this. You can have Saturday mornings for the rest of the summer."

That was a lot of money she was putting on the table, so off I went to break up the Old Man (and woman) River nudist colony. As I was walking down to the pool, I was trying to think of what to say and how to manage this New Order "Bizarre Love Triangle" of really old naked people. When I reached the pool, the reality of the situation set in and what I saw made my eyes burn like the "beds" in Midnight Oil's 1987 smash hit. I will spare you the details, but just imagine all the old people at your childhood Thanksgiving dinners chasing each other around with their twigs, berries, and giblets flying around like Goose, Iceman, and Maverick in their F-14 fighter jets. Yes, it was a sight to behold. I was able to quickly get this rowdy bunch of 80-year-olds under control and convinced them that wrapping themselves in towels would be best for everyone. They all obliged and laughed and, as they were walking out, one of the ladies walked up to me, pinched my cheek, and said, "You should date my granddaughter."

Looking back, I realize that they were having "Nothin' but a good time," Poison style.

I hope I'm like them when I'm 80.

Pop Culture in 1988

Speaking of Poison, time was getting short for the glam rock bands by 1988, but Poison still had a sting with "Nothin' But a Good Time," which sat at #25 but had been as high as #6. DJ Jazzy Jeff and The Fresh Prince rapped their way up to #12 with the youth angst anthem "Parents Just Don't Understand." INXS continued to be one of the coolest and most successful bands of the '80s with another top-5 hit in "New Sensation." And many a slow dance with really bad singing in each other's ears was a result of Cheap Trick's "The Flame" and the #1 song in mid-July 1988, "Hold on to the Nights" by Richard Marx.

In television, the summer of '88 was quite active, which was a pleasant surprise considering the summer season was typically reserved for re-runs. The Discovery Channel brought *Jaws* into every living room with the premiere of *Shark Week*; the World Wrestling Federation (WWF) held its first SummerSlam on Pay Per View; Universal Pictures Debut Network — yes, your guess is as good as mine — broadcasted a two-night special edition with additional footage of the 1984 movie *Dune*; the really fun and quirky hospital drama, *St. Elsewhere,* had its series finale; and Dick Clark hosted his final episode of the game show, *Pyramid*.[18]

18 "1988 in American Television," *Wikipedia*, Last updated July 25, 2022, https://en.wikipedia.org/wiki/1988_in_American_television.

■ ■

🕹 **FUN FACT:** Peter Benchley, who wrote the book *Jaws*, which the legendary movie was based on, felt some regret about how people perceived sharks after the book and the movie. He dedicated a large portion of his life to marine conservation and shark education. He once said, "The shark in an updated *Jaws* could not be the villain. It would have to be written as the victim — for, worldwide, sharks are much more oppressed than the oppressors."[19]

■ ■

At the box office, the summers always delivered with blockbuster movies with big star-power leads, and 1988 was no exception:

➦ Eddie Murphy in the perfect romcom, *Coming to America*

➦ Clint Eastwood reprising Dirty Harry in *Dead Pool*

➦ Bruce Willis "yippie ki yaying" in the Christmas classic, *Die Hard* (which we will get to later)

➦ Tom Hanks getting his wish from Zoltar in *Big*

➦ Sylvester Stallone carving bad guys up again in *Rambo III*, and

➦ Jamie Lee Curtis getting all the laughs in a *Fish Called Wanda*.

But it was a drama — about the life journey of a wannabe entrepreneur attending business school during the day while bartending at night — with a few laughs, great dialogue, and pretty good soundtrack, starring Tom Cruise slinging drinks

---

19 "Peter Benchley," *Wikipedia*, Last updated July 16, 2022, https://en.wikipedia.org/wiki/Peter_Benchley.

from New York City to Jamaica, that will teach us some valuable lessons.

Life Lessons from *Cocktail*

Cocktail tells the story of Brian Flanagan (played by Tom Cruise) who is looking to find his way after returning from the military. He's entrepreneurial and begins studying business at a local city college and takes a job as a bartender — a job he's never performed — under the mentorship of Doug Coughlin (played by Bryan Brown). Doug is a middle-aged bartender and clearly one of the best in the business, attracting crowds of locals and tourists every single night. Doug teaches Brian everything he knows about bartending and life. The two ultimately make an amazing team and discuss opening their own bar — Cocktails and Dreams — but have a falling out, which sends Brian to Jamaica where he masters mixology at a hotel beach bar. It's here where he meets Jordan Mooney (played by Elisabeth Shue), who is an artist on vacation with a friend. Jordan and Brian hit it off and quickly fall in love, but Brian makes a huge mistake when Doug shows up with his wife (played by Kelly Lynch) and bets him that he can't pick up an older wealthy lady sitting at the bar. He does and when Jordan finds out, she immediately goes home to New York City (NYC). Brian ultimately goes back to NYC as a "boy toy" of sorts with the wealthy lady but leaves her and begins his quest to hopefully reunite with Jordan. At one point, the story takes a sad and depressing turn that fuels Brian's newfound zest for life and love. Oh, and you get to sing "Kokomo" a couple times as well!

So, what do a few bartenders and a mysterious artist teach us about our life and workplace?

The difference between *dreaming* the dream and *living* the dream is the action that you are willing to take.

Typically, when I talk about myself in my books, I tend to share stories that are self-deprecating — awkward teenage moments and even more awkward adult moments. This is mainly because there is an endless amount of content for me to choose from and the "Man in the Mirror" (as Michael Jackson sang in 1988) is a really easy target. I know him well and I know all his secrets. So, the saying goes, "If you can't make fun of yourself, who *can* you make fun of?"

But for this lesson, I'm going to take a bit of a different approach. My proudest moment in my life was when I realized that I had officially made the transition from *dreaming* the dream to *living* the dream. It was in the Fort Lauderdale airport when I was waiting to board a flight and the guy next to me struck up a conversation over a funky pair of Vans that I was wearing (which is exactly why I wear them — conversation-starter shoes are the best kind of shoes). Every new person I talk to is a potential opportunity for a speaking gig and because I'm not smooth the way American Light and Fixture's #1 salesperson Del Griffith is smooth when selling shower curtain rings, I don't typically invade people's personal space or take advantage of their valuable time unless there is an outward connection I can see (like someone wearing a sweatshirt from my alma mater Elon University). The conversation that day at FLL went like this:

"Cool shoes," he said.

"Thanks. They're my *stage* shoes," I said back.

"Stage shoes? What do you do for a living?" he asked.

"I'm an author and speaker. I talk about the workplace and life lessons we can learn from '80s pop culture. Mainly the movies. I'm heading to Washington, D.C., to deliver a keynote on leadership lessons from '80s movies."

September 2019 -- Right after moderating a Goonies reunion panel with Sean Astin and Corey Feldman. Check out my stage shoes!

There was a longer-than-normal pause as he looked at me with a mix of surprise, disbelief, and amazement. He laughed and then said, "Excuse my French, but how the fuck did you pull that off? Talking '80s pop culture for a living? Kudos, my man. I can't wait to tell my wife that all my movie-quote knowledge might have a career outlet, after all."

I was officially living the dream. Someone else wanted to do what I did for a living. How many people can say that? When I got to my hotel room after the flight, I reflected on that brief conversation, and I cried. For the previous two years, I had worked

a full-time corporate marketing job that required 50-60 hours
a week in the office as well as some pretty extensive travel. What
little free time I had at night and on weekends, I spent writing
and self-publishing my first book, building a website, creating
my '80s pop culture brand, and developing the content that
would eventually influence the keynotes that I deliver today.
This is the part that no one sees. At some point, you may have
seen the image of the iceberg with only the tip visible above the
water and it says something like "what people see" and then says
something like "success" or "freedom and flexibility." The rest of
the iceberg (around 95% of it) is below the water line and it says
"what you don't see" and it's things like "sacrifice," "risk," "failure,"
"persistence," "disappointment," "fear," and "lack of sleep." It was
a crushing existence that lasted about 20 months with absolutely
no guarantee that anyone would care enough about what I was
building to actually pay me for it. That's the scariest part about
launching an entrepreneurial enterprise — not knowing if anyone
will really care. But when they do, it is exhilarating. And they did!

It was a crushing existence that lasted about 20 months with absolutely no guarantee that anyone would care enough about what I was building to actually pay me for it. That's the scariest part about launching an entrepreneurial enterprise — not knowing if anyone will really care.

I had discovered my flugelbinder. Flugelbinder, you ask?

As I mentioned at the top of this chapter, there's a great 90-second
scene in *Cocktail* in which Jordan and Brian are sitting at a table

at an outside bar. As a quick refresh, their conversation centers around the millionaires "sitting" at their table in the form of the products around them — toothpicks, ashtrays, drink umbrellas, and the plastic tip on his shoelaces, which Jordan refers to as "flugelbinders." The CliffsNotes of the entire conversation are summed up below:

Brian: "We sit here surrounded by millionaires."

That line is followed by possibly the first cinematic reference to what we now call a side hustle:

Brian: "You know, you get a bar job to keep your days free for your real gig. Days get shorter and shorter. The nights get longer and longer. Before you know it, your life is just one long night with a few comatose daylight hours." He chuckles and says, "Stop feeling so sorry for yourself, Flanagan."

Jordan, reaching out and grabbing Brian's hand: "Hey, your flugelbinder is out there just waiting to be discovered."

Brian: "You think so?"

Jordan: "I know so."

It's an absolutely amazing look into the always-on, imaginative-and-confident yet frightened-and-terrified mind of dreamers who seek to take action. In a high school or college business class, they might call them entrepreneurs.

Most of us have probably heard the phrase "If you're going to talk the talk, you've got to walk the walk." Brian was at the talking stage, which is a place where so many people get stuck (and that's totally understandable). Life has a way of getting in the way. It's why, in my interpretation, someone I reference a lot — Henry David Thoreau — said, "The mass of men [people] lead lives of quiet desperation." And he said this all the way back in the 1840s. And during a similar time, Oliver Wendell Holmes said, "Alas for those that never sing, but die with all their music inside them." Getting to the walking stage — that is to say, *doing* what you've been talking about — is not easy and it takes a full-on self-commitment and, more importantly, the loyal support of those around you. (And, yes, this can even mean your dog. My dog Bodhi supports me unconditionally and believe me, it helps tremendously.) Brian does eventually move to the walking stage, with the support of Jordan and a very dark and unfortunate incident that helps him find his way out of his *talking* spiral and into taking *action* on his dream.

So, when we reflect back on that super-simple 90-second "flugelbinder" scene, we learn:

1. **Successful people are all around you.**

2. **You do what you *have* to do to get to what you *want* to do.**

3. **For a dream to become reality, you need to take action.**

4. **Encouragement doesn't cost a thing.** (A lesson we also learned from Prince in Chapter 4!)

5. **Do the thing.** (The essence of a lesson we learned from *Can't Buy Me Love* in Chapter 3.)

Five life and workplace lessons in 90 seconds, which is about the same time it took Eddie Murphy and Nick Nolte to drop 10 F-bombs in the 1982 cop-buddy classic, *48 Hours*.

Now go, dear reader, and discover your flugelbinder! Get yourself a Jordan or Bodhi to encourage and support you along the way. You are going to need it, but when that dream becomes a reality, there is no other feeling like it in the universe. The best way to describe it in '80s terms is from the theme song to the TV show, *The Greatest American Hero*:

"Believe it or not, I'm walking on air.
I never thought I could feel so free.
Flying away on a wing and prayer ...
Who could it be?
Believe it or not, it's just me ..."

It's time to walk the talk, my friends. Get out there. Fly free.

***

One of the first things we all learn when "adulting" — whether we're living our dream or working for the man (or woman) — is that life is full of negotiations. We win some, we lose some, and some feel like a draw. So what can the movie *Cocktail* teach us about the art of negotiation?

Successful negotiating — in life, business, and, most importantly, with yourself — requires patience and a delicate touch.

How many of you have walked into a car dealership to purchase a new car with absolute confidence that you will get the exact deal that you wanted? You likely walked out thinking "Yeah, I got a great deal." No, you didn't. (I didn't either, by the way. Car salesmen are cunning masters of the art of negotiation.) How about a salary negotiation? "This time they are going to pay me what I'm worth or I'll leave this job." How did that one go? Or a negotiation with a higher power after a night out on the town? You know that one — "I swear if you just take away the pain, I will never drink again." Of course, even if the pain was taken away — which it wasn't — you probably did drink again. Enid Strict (the Church Lady of *Saturday Night Live* fame) would be so disappointed in you. Sinner.

As it turns out, there are lessons to be learned about this important life and business skill — negotiating — from *Cocktail*. The main character, Brian, found a mentor for bartending and life in Doug Coughlin, and Doug lives by (and teaches) what he calls Coughlin's Laws. Depending on how you count them, there are 11, including his last one, which instructs us:

> "And as for the rest of Coughlin's Laws, ignore them. The guy was always full of shit."

If Doug actually believed that he was full of shit, it would be impossible to tell. Throughout the movie, we see a guy whose outward appearance is confident in both his actions and his words. Some might say he's more arrogant and crass than confident — particularly when he makes out with the woman who Brian thinks is his girlfriend (played by one of my favorites, Gina Gershon, who also does some really cool art in real life).

Coughlin's Laws are all over the place, touching on different aspects of life and work. For example:

> → "The bartender is the aristocrat of the working class."

> → "There are two kinds of people in this world: the workers and the hustlers. The hustlers never work, and the workers never hustle."

> → "Bury the dead. They stink up the joint."

And one of my favorites:

> → **"Never show surprise. Never lose your cool."**

Easier said than done, right? Unless you are *The Terminator*, who — according to the Kyle Reese character in the 1984 movie — "can't be bargained with or reasoned with and doesn't feel pity, remorse, or fear" or whether you are either Cheech or Chong in the 1983 movie *Still Smokin'* it's a relative impossibility to go through life never showing surprise or losing your cool. And guess what? It's fine; we're human. We aren't perfect and if you think *you* are, then Enid Strict aka The Church Lady is here once again to say, "Well, isn't that special." When Doug makes out with Brian's "girlfriend" in front of him while they are both tending bar at peak-crowd hour, Brian's face is consumed by surprise and he loses his cool just slightly, punching Doug in front of everyone, quitting his job, and moving to Jamaica. (Maybe a bit of an over-reaction there, right?) So yeah, he broke one of Coughlin's Laws right in half, but most would say it was understandable, considering the situation. I mean, really, who *wouldn't* lose their cool?

There is, of course, a time and place for everything and one situation where having that Lady Gaga "Poker Face" and the "never let them see you sweat" Dry Idea philosophy would be at the *negotiating* table. You and I might not spend a lot of time in bars, kissing each other's girlfriends or boyfriends, but I'm sure we do spend a lot of time negotiating — in work and in our personal lives.

Negotiating is not easy. It's a contact sport, particularly when you are the one with less leverage, and we do a lot more negotiating than we realize. Most of us negotiate with ourselves multiple times a day, starting with our approach to the snooze button and how many times we promise that this is really the last time before we get up. My friends who have children are constantly negotiating and I've seen them attempt it firsthand and lose on multiple occasions. I negotiate with my dog Bodhi when he is being stubborn while out for a walk and I need to get back for a meeting (or when he takes up 90% of my king-size bed somehow and I'd just like a little bit of space back). Pretty please, Bodhi? This usually results in him pushing me even further to the edge with his legs, not a care in the world. He does not understand the concept of "give and take."

Beyond snooze buttons, kids eating their vegetables, and dogs taking up more bed space than is necessary, there are more consequential negotiations that occur throughout life. I've already mentioned big-ticket negotiations, like cars and houses, and career-altering ones involving salaries and promotions. But the most important negotiations we have are with ourselves. Those are the negotiations that will drive the choices we make — good, bad, or indifferent — that set us on the different paths that make up our life's journey. The best example of how the negotiation you have with yourself can change the trajectory of your life is from the '80s classic, *Ferris Bueller's Day Off*. It's the scene where Cameron keeps getting into and out of his car after Ferris has demanded that he get out of bed and take the day off with him and his girlfriend, Sloane. We see Cameron in his car and he says this:

> "He'll keep calling me, he'll keep calling me until I come over. He'll make me feel guilty. This is uh ... This is ridiculous, okay I'll go, I'll go, I'll go, I'll go, I'll go. What — I'll go. Shit."

Cameron starts the car and then turns it off and says, "Forget it. That's it. I'm not going." He gets out of the car and goes into his house. We then see him come out of the house, jump around frustrated, and ultimately get back into the car to go meet Ferris and Sloane for the day off. Now he *does* lose his cool a bit but because he took the time to negotiate with himself, he does find himself having an amazing day off, which ends with him realizing that his negative and pessimistic approach to life is driven by his relationship with his father — a relationship that he now seeks to correct. This entire thread in *Ferris Bueller's Day Off* is a pretty cool look into the human psyche.

Believe it or not, it's not easy to find an article on negotiating with yourself, so let's flip this on its head a bit and use an article from *Forbes* on "Ten Tips to Help You Win Every Negotiation."[20]. The

20 Lisa Quast, "10 Tips to Help You Win Every Negotiation," *Forbes*, August 8, 2016, https://www.forbes.com/sites/lisaquast/2016/08/08/10-tips-to-help-you-win-every-negotiation/?sh=60fe1dda436d.

article was designed to help people negotiate at work and within their career, but the tips are perfect for negotiating with yourself:

1. **Do your homework.**

   (Unlike Jeff Spicoli)

2. **See the situation from all angles.**

   (À la the Man in Black during the poison scene in *The Princess Bride*)

September 2019 -- With Cary Elwes, Westley (the Man in Black) in The Princess Bride, at Nostalgiacon, where I moderated Goonies and MTV VJ reunion panels.

3. **Clearly define your goals.**

   (Like Lloyd Dobler: "I don't want to buy, sell, or process anything")

4. **Determine the best timing for your discussion.**

   (Unlike Neal Page at the car rental desk in *Planes, Trains and Automobiles*)

5. **Remain calm and avoid getting emotional.**

   (Coughlin's Law reinterpreted)

6. **Listen, listen, and listen some more.**

   (To that little voice inside of you, just like Magnum P.I.)

7. **Ask for what you want.**
    (À la Human League)

8. **Avoid finger pointing.**
    (Take responsibility, like Ellen Ripley in *Aliens*)

9. **Find a creative solution.**
    (Like an Axel Foley "banana in the tailpipe")

And perhaps most importantly:

10. **Remember that there will always be a tomorrow.**
    (Just like *Annie* loved and I unfortunately sang as a solo in middle school.)

So, if you ever find yourself struggling with that self-negotiation, just remember these words from the wise and wonderful De La Soul in their 1989 hit, "Me, Myself and I":

> *"Proud, I'm proud of what I am.*
> *De La Soul is from the soul.*
> *It's just me, myself, and I."*

Now before I go pour my own cocktail as a thank you to myself for finishing this chapter, I'd like to leave you with one more lesson.

The opening quote to this chapter is Doug talking to Brian about the bar customer when he is in training. He says, "We dazzle him with ice work. We baffle him with bottle work." I'm assuming that it was a take on the memorable W.C. Fields observation, "If you can't dazzle them with brilliance, baffle them with bullshit." I love that line and it is a philosophy that has been used by advertisers and politicians alike since the beginning of time, which prompted me to create a Clews law to close out this chapter:

Clews's Law: "The more it sparkles, the more it should be questioned."

CHAPTER 6

DIE HARD

"Happy Trails, Hans."

— JOHN MCCLANE, *DIE HARD*

Some honesty and transparency here: when originally sketching out the table of contents for this book, this chapter was going to be based on a different movie. I was torn between *Bill and Ted's Excellent Adventure, Three O'Clock High,* and the original *Vacation.* I had lessons chosen for all three films, but then circumstances conspired to change my tact. This was one of the last chapters I wrote because when it came time to put pen to paper for this chapter, the news had just broken about Bruce Willis's health — he was suffering from aphasia, a neurologic condition impacting his ability to communicate and comprehend communication. The actor we all knew and loved for his witty monologues in the television show, *Moonlighting,* and for his epic one-liners in films like *Die Hard* was retiring from acting because he was no longer able to deliver those lines. On a personal level, this was just a heartbreaking thing to hear.

Some more honesty and transparency: I love Bruce Willis. He is a very close second (behind Patrick Swayze) on my "Cool Actors List," which is a very short one. I met Bruce Willis when I was doing security at Planet Hollywood in Orlando during the mid-90s and a buddy and I handled his party for dinner. He was as nice, humble, approachable, and cool as you would hope that he would be. He's that rare human in the most talented of humans who really seemed to have his feet securely on the ground.

I really wanted to find a way to thank him for his years of entertaining us (and *entertain* us, he did) — thus, this chapter in his honor. Most of us know Bruce Willis for his roles on *Moonlighting* and *Friends* and his characters in movies like *Pulp Fiction, The Sixth Sense, Armageddon* (which, in my humble opinion, is the perfect action movie), *12 Monkeys, The Fifth Element, Unbreakable,* and — of course — the *Die Hard* series. But his best roles may have also been his most underrated. If you haven't seen them already, make sure to check out *Bandits, Tears of the Sun,* and *16 Blocks* with co-star Mos Def (who is a groundbreaking rapper and an incredibly talented actor who I wish we'd see more often).

Bruce Willis is so much more than John McClane, but the *Die Hard* series is fantastic and McClane is one of the greatest action heroes in cinematic history. With my thanks to a man who has entertained us for more than 40 years, I give you my take on life lessons from *Die Hard.*

Unlike most of the movies and musicians I choose for my books, *Die Hard* was a difficult movie in which to find dialogue that would provide a foundation for some concrete lessons. After all, action movies don't typically have the type of one-liners that make you think a little deeper — unless we're talking the original *Rambo* and "They drew first blood. Not me." Believe it or not, there is some really introspective and deep dialogue in that movie.

One of the most memorable, famous, and often-parodied scenes in *Die Hard* is when John McClane (played by Bruce Willis) is crawling through the air ducts in the Nakatomi Towers building with nothing but a Bic lighter to light his path forward. Anyone who has any kind of claustrophobia, if forced to crawl through air ducts, would have probably given up and told Hans Gruber (the leader of the terrorists and McClane's main nemesis) that he and his team of terrorists had won. I would have given up for sure, if the vent was home to any number of spiders. That's my red line, as you now know. Spiders. Ugh. McClane is in a tough situation. He is:

➜ Trying to maneuver within a very tight space

➜ Trying to find his way with little visibility

➜ Hiding from a terrorist who is hunting him

➜ Manufacturing a plan to defeat the rest of the terrorists and save the hostages and his wife.

Talk about a challenging set of circumstances and that's just the tip of the iceberg, as you will read later. Like most of us who spend a lot of time alone or at least like yours truly, McClane talks to himself throughout this tightly spaced ordeal. Thankfully for me, I live alone with my dog Bodhi, so if I am talking to myself — and particularly if I'm talking "in my sleep" as The Romantics sang back in 1984 — no one hears "the secrets that I keep" except for Bodhi Boy (and he is a very good secret keeper).

Talking to ourselves — in real life and in the movies — can help us process difficult or surprising situations. At one point while in the air duct, McClane is presumably rehashing a portion of a conversation with his wife, Holly (who is a bad ass in her own right in how she deals with Hans, the head of the terrorist group). Holly had invited McClane out from New York to her company's Christmas party in Los Angeles. While in the vent, he replays her invitation, in a very sarcastic tone: "Come out to the coast, we'll get together, have a few laughs."

The humorous conversation he has with himself during what is a very challenging and difficult moment teaches us that:

Oftentimes, the best way to face a tough or challenging situation is with levity and humor.

I have a simple, hard-and-fast rule in my personal life: If you don't like dogs and you don't swear, then I don't trust you. I've been known to swear like an '80s Eddie Murphy stand-up comedy special but, having said that, I do try to limit the hardcore swearing in my books. However, the John McClane dialogue for our next lesson is best left uncensored. It just doesn't work otherwise. Ever tried to watch the 2007 comedy classic *SuperBad* on regular TV? Then you know. No bueno.

When was the last time that you felt so confident that your actions would result in a positive outcome that you didn't hesitate? Or maybe it wasn't the confidence in a positive outcome as much as it was a confidence in *yourself* regardless of how crazy it seemed. And I don't mean your last libations-induced karaoke night, when you were convinced that if someone from a music label was in the audience, they'd definitely sign you after your perfect rendition of Young MC's "Bust a Move" or Bon Jovi's "Wanted Dead or Alive." Take a moment to think about a scenario in your life or work when you were truly confident. Maybe you were facing an unexpected challenge or a very real and major shift in your life or career. You were dealing with something that — from the outside, at least — offered outcomes that were unknown, at best, and substantially less-than-desirable, at worst. But you knew you were in control. "I've got this," you thought.

That kind of confidence is what we see when *Die Hard*'s John McClane is having a conversation over walkie talkies with the head terrorist, Hans Gruber. They are feeling each other out, verbally sparring, and it's a pretty awesome 90 seconds of dialogue. There are still a lot of unknowns about each other when Hans begins poking McClane a bit about being a renegade American raised on a broken hero-worship culture of people like John Wayne and Rambo. Hans asks: "Do you really think you have a chance against us, cowboy?" To which McClane responds: *"Yippie-ki-yay, Motherfucker."* McClane then disconnects from the walkie talkie and the conversation, leaving Hans mystified and a bit concerned for the well-being of his team. A man with that kind of confidence is either really crazy or really capable.

When McClane says "Yippie-ki-yay, Motherfucker," he teaches us:

 Embrace the insult. Don't take the bait.

If you haven't figured it out by now, I am a creature of habit when it comes to traveling back in time in this book so let's hop in that Bill and Ted's time-traveling phone booth once again and go back to July of 1988, which is a date that we visit twice in this book. It was a pretty good month and year for movies.

My Life in July 1988

In the chapter dedicated to *Cocktail*, which also premiered in July of 1988, we established that I was a bellman at a hotel in Ocean City, Maryland. I was also being exposed to some out-of-my-control, awkward-but-entertaining situations that I am thoroughly thankful for experiencing. But during this era of my life, I also brought on some problematic situations myself. No way! A 17-year-old boy getting ready for his freshman year of college and finding himself in self-induced dilemmas? Never! Or as the totally awesome punk-rock band Agent Orange sang in 1981, "There's no such thing." Of course there is, though.

Do you remember what it was like when you were with a group of your teenage friends, and you were left to your own devices? There are plenty of '80s movies whose plots centered around unsupervised latch-key kids and almost always involved some sort of disaster that: (a) resulted in a kid who had to hide said disaster from their parents, who were typically coming home from a vacation or a business trip, or (b) involved a confrontation and discussion between teens and parents that ultimately led us to a lesson around understanding, growing up, or the consequences from the choices we make. Those second set of scenarios were usually reserved for after-school specials with titles like *Reading, Writing, and Reefer*; *High School Narc*; and *The Day My Kid Went Punk*. Yes, those are real.

My story from the summer of 1988 is a combination of (a) and (b), with the discussion coming almost 25 years later and, just like *Die Hard*, my story also includes a Bic lighter. However, the difference in how they were used is like Schwarzenegger in *Terminator* and Schwarzenegger in *Twins*. John McClane used his lighter in the pursuit of killing terrorists and saving lives, while I used mine in the pursuit of abject stupidity. Jackass before Johnny Knoxville's *Jackass*.

For me and my friends in the summer of 1988 in Ocean City, Maryland, evenings typically consisted of either a house party — usually on 28th Street — or cruising the boardwalk. Yes, I said cruising. That word always reminds of the scene in the 1981 comedy classic, *Stripes,* when they are all introducing themselves in the barracks.

> **Howard J. Turkster (Cruiser):** "I like fast cars and fast women. That's why the guys in the car club call me The Cruiser."

> **John Winger (played by Bill Murray):** "They should have called you the dork."

Yes, looking back, I can concede that we were dorks. One particularly dorky evening, it was also pretty stormy. If you've ever seen a storm come in over the ocean, then you know what type of weather I'm talking about — the growling, flashing, rumbling, beautiful, lights-on-and-off type of storm. This was about the only thing that could keep a bunch of 17-and-18-year-olds cooped up inside at night, but just because we were staying home didn't mean that we were suddenly mature or civilized. We didn't exactly break out a chess board or play some parcheesi. No, we still illegally partook in several libations, which altered our minds just enough to do some really, well, teenage boy stuff.

After a few hours of consumption, I decided to do a science experiment, and this is where the lighter comes into play. I should tell you that I had very similar challenges with science as I did with math. Too many variables and words that had quadruple the number of consonants than vowels. Somewhere in the deep recesses of my little teenage bird brain, I became curious as to what would happen if you took a glass bottle with a small opening (like a Coke bottle), put the top of the lighter into the bottle and pressed down on the lighter, allowing the jar to fill up with the flammable compressed gas, before flicking the lighter to create the intended flame. Yeah, I know. It's a miracle I'm alive to tell this story.

When I flicked the lighter, flames shot out like the pyrotechnics at a Debbie Gibson concert. Wait, that doesn't sound right. Let's try that again. When I flicked the lighter, flames shot out like the pyrotechnics at a Motley Crue concert. Much better. Okay, I'm pretty sure the flames weren't that impressive, but they did what any basic physics class would have taught you if you were paying attention. Flash point or back draft, or something. When gas builds up — no, not that kind of gas, you juveniles — in a vacuum and then a spark is created and sent down into the vacuum, fire is quickly created and quickly spreads. Intense fire looks for a way out of the vacuum, to feed on more oxygen. The only way out for that hungry flame in this scenario was through the top of the Coke bottle, where my hand was still positioned with the lighter full of fluid. And just like *Rock Master Scott and The Dynamic Three* rapped back in 1985, "The hand. The hand. The hand was on fire. We don't need no water, let the motherfucker burn. Burn. motherfucker, burn." Okay, they said the roof, but you get the idea. There's that word again in this chapter.

My hand was on fire and because of my inebriation and immaturity, it took me several seconds to realize what was happening. Once it was established that I had severe burns, a buddy who was not under the influence drove me to the hospital's emergency department. It was midnight and like most teenagers, I didn't really know how health insurance worked and if I even had any, so I did what any good son would do — I called my mom. I told her what happened. Sort of. What she knew was that I burned my hand while cooking eggs for everyone in the apartment. I told her that I needed a credit card to pay for the hospital bill, which she provided, and I promised that I would pay her back with my tips from my bellman job (which I absolutely did). I wasn't a *total* juvenile delinquent. She bought it — hook, line and sinker — or at least I thought she did. I'm pretty sure she knew something else was up, considering I didn't cook anything unless it was in a hot pot.

Fast forward 26 years. At this point, I'm 43 and I have a small scar on my hand from this little Bic-lighter mishap. I'm home for Christmas, which was always a big holiday for our little family, and I'm at Mom's house. We're sitting around the tree, opening gifts, when it comes around to me again. For some reason, I decided that this was the perfect time to tell my mom the real story about my burn. I shared with her that it wasn't actually from cooking but a burn from a Cousin Eddie "I don't know why they call this Hamburger Helper, it just does fine by itself" moment of stupidity. She didn't flinch, but she did laugh and it was in that moment that I knew she knew all along that my cooking story from 26 years ago was a big fat lie.

Christmas 2019. Me, Mom, Jimmy (Step-Dad),
and sister Ashleigh at my childhood home.

All she did was look at my sister and say, "At least I always knew
that *one* of my kids wasn't a complete idiot."

"Ha!" I said. "You have no idea, Mom. There was this one
time when Ash ..."

My sister Ashleigh cut me off and said, "Shut it. Just no." And
then turned to our mom and said, "Don't listen to him. He is just
deflecting." She turned back to me and whispered, "I swear to
God, I will take your Christmas presents away right now." Even as
adults, we are still kids and especially on Christmas morning.

Oh, and you'll have to get my 4th book to find out what it was that
my sister did.

Pop Culture in July 1988

Speaking of parents and kids and the stories we all hide from
each other, DJ Jazzy Jeff and The Fresh Prince had a top-10 hit
on the music charts in the summer of 1988 with "Parents Just

Don't Understand" while our parents got to share a bit of their own music with us when The Fat Boys teamed up with Chubby Checkers in 1988 to do a cover of "The Twist," a 1958 song by Hank Ballard and the Midnighters, which Chubby made famous in 1960.

■■■■■■■■■■■■■■■■■■■■■■■■■■■■■■■■■■

🕹 KIND OF FUN, KIND OF NOT FUN FACT:

Two of the three Fat Boys, all of whom were born after Chubby Checkers exploded onto the music scene in 1960 with "The Twist," have passed away while Chubby is still touring at the young age of 81. Just a reminder that tomorrow isn't promised but if you do get more tomorrows than others, live each one of them as if there won't be another. Chubby is definitely doing that.

■■■■■■■■■■■■■■■■■■■■■■■■■■■■■■■■

Continuing with the music charts and just once again to reiterate the diversity in music genres and their popularity during the '80s, the top three songs were Richard Marx with "Hold onto the Nights," Def Leppard's "Pour Some Sugar on Me," and INXS with "New Sensation." Oh, and just for good measure, let's throw in Pebbles, who was at #8 with "Mercedes Boy." Four very different genres and sounds all in the Top 10. So awesome and never to be seen again, unfortunately.

On television, the Sunday-night lineup was a dream come true for fans of alliteration. *Mission Impossible, MacGyver, Murder She Wrote,* and our favorite for this chapter, *Moonlighting,* were all competing for eyeballs throughout the year. Sunday nights also included other titles with an M including *The Magical World of Disney, America's Most Wanted,* and *Married with Children.* So interesting for us grammar and language nerds. Mmmm ... well played, 1988.

At the box office, superstars ruled the day once again. Eddie Murphy was staring in perhaps the most perfect romantic comedy in cinematic history with *Coming to America,* which earned itself a chapter in my 2nd book. Yet another shameless plug, which is beginning to sound like a great name for an '80s alt band — The Shameless Plugs. Okay, anyway ... back to the superstars. Tom Hanks was everybody's favorite kid in a grown man's body in *Big* while Clint Eastwood was doing Dirty Harry things in *The Dead Pool.* Kevin Costner, Susan Sarandon and Tim Robbins, hit it out of the park in the baseball movie classic, *Bull Durham,* while Pee Wee Herman was biking his way through another adventure in *Big Top Pee Wee.* But it was an action movie set in Nakatomi Towers on Christmas Eve with an unheralded action star that is the basis for our learnings in this chapter.

Life Lessons from *Die Hard*

Die Hard launched Bruce Willis into the stratosphere and immediately put him on the same action-hero level as Sylvester Stallone, Arnold Schwarzenegger, Wesley Snipes, Chuck Norris, and Bruce Lee. Willis starred as a New York City police officer named John McClane, who is invited by his wife, Holly, (played by Bonnie Bedelia) to her company Christmas party in Los Angeles at — you guessed it — Nakatomi Towers. Before he really has a chance to enjoy the celebration, terrorists — not really terrorists, but more like an international crime gang — led by Hans Gruber (played magnificently by the late great Alan Rickman) take over the building and the party. The bad guys have their eyes on a very lucrative heist of $600 million in bonds from the vault in the building and McClane is thrust into the unenviable position of having to try to stop them with minimal resources. McClane's team is composed of his wife, who takes a leadership role with the hostages after her boss is executed, and Al Powell (played by the super-underrated Reginald VelJohnson), a Los

Angeles police sergeant on the ground, who McClane only knows through a walkie talkie.

Again, because it was an '80s movie, it did have a happy ending and eventually this trio take Oingo Boingo's 1986 hit song seriously and turn the company Christmas party into a "Dead Man's Party" via the killing and dismantling of all the terrorists/ international crime gang members. Throughout it all, McClane keeps his sense of humor and the banter between him and Sgt. Powell is all world. It's just a super-fun, action-packed, entertaining film that had (and continues to have) a huge impact on popular culture. It spawned one of the great action heroes of all time and will go down in the cinematic history annals as one of the best action and Christmas movies. Yes, I'm on the side of "*Die Hard* is a Christmas movie." More on that later.

So, what did John and Holly McClane, Sgt. Al Powell, and a bunch of international crime-gang terrorist-type guys (but mainly John McClane) teach us?

 Oftentimes, the best way to face a tough or challenging situation is with levity and humor.

Humor helps in nearly any situation — not just when you're facing off with a bunch of terrorists. Just think about how humor has helped in your own life and work — when a sense of humor saved the day during a crisis, or when a well-placed giggle broke the ice at a funeral or other high-stress moment. We need humor. In fact, we also need comedians more than most people realize. I think a lot of my friends whose marriages ended in divorce might still be together if they would have had a comedian as a marriage counselor instead of going the traditional counselor route. Humor and comedy can be the best medicine in the most difficult of times. Many comedians talk about how some of their best humor came from individual life challenges.

Even when someone is facing imminent death, humor is still prevalent and often instigated by the patient who is terminal. A study done at Kent State and reported in the *American Journal of Hospice and Palliative Care* revealed that humor was present in 85 percent of 132 observed nurse-based visits. Amazingly, they found that 70 percent of the humor was initiated by the patient themselves — the person who has the most reason to be sad or angry.[21] So why wouldn't a cop trapped in a building with limited resources and a bunch of criminals hellbent on destroying everything and everyone in their path *also* resort to a little humor?

Have you ever found yourself laughing somewhat awkwardly or maybe cracking a joke in a difficult or challenging situation? With business challenges, we are taught to buckle down, get serious, and come together to solve the problem. "Our widget sales are down, and this is no laughing matter," someone says with firmness at the management meeting. I don't have any studies on this, of course, but I would imagine that if business leaders brought a little levity and humor to the toughest of meetings, they might find that when everyone loosens up a bit, they also think more clearly and with more open minds. I would also imagine that it might lead to faster, more unique, and ultimately smarter solutions to their problems.

As we discussed earlier, when John McClane is traversing through the building's HVAC ducts, he is having a conversation with himself to lighten up the mood a bit. Beyond his sarcastic shot at his wife, Holly, for inviting him to the party by saying, "Come out to the coast, we'll get together, have a few laughs," he also says this

---

21 Marilyn A. Mendoza, PhD, "The Healing Power of Laughter in Death and Grief," *Psychology Today*, November 7, 2016, https://www.psychologytoday. com/us/blog/understanding-grief/201611/the-healing-power-laughter-in-death-and-grief.

as he flicks the lighter, producing a flame within the metal vent: "Now I know what a TV dinner feels like."

Sidenote here: If you were born after 1990, you may not have had the pleasure of eating a TV dinner, complete with what was surely a very safe silver aluminum covering that looked like metal siding.

McClane finds himself in what feels like an impossible situation, but rather than make it worse by dwelling on all the challenges he's facing, he makes his situation a lot more tenable by cracking a few jokes. Let's take a quick look at the list of challenges McClane is facing:

1. Lack of intel. He initially has no knowledge of the enemy, their capabilities, and numbers.

2. Severely outnumbered by the enemy. Something like 13 to 1.

3. Severely outgunned and under-resourced. He only has a standard-issue sidepiece and a lighter. The enemy has an arsenal of weapons as well as an IT/tech genius capable of equal disruption and destruction.

4. He does not have shoes. He had taken them off in his wife's office to relax after his flight just as the enemy struck and he had to take off without them. Lots of bullets flying around means lots of broken glass, which doesn't bode well for bare feet.

5. The only person who he can communicate with is Sgt. Powell via walkie talkie, and Powell is outside of the building with zero-to-little visibility into the terrorists' movements.

6. Perhaps his biggest challenge was that he was unprepared to be in this situation. He flew across country from New York City to Los Angeles for his

wife's company Christmas party and some rest and relaxation. He was not in a "singlehandedly take on and destroy an international terrorist gang" mindset, but here he was having to do exactly that.

McClane is in a tough spot for sure and, even though this is an '80s action movie, he doesn't have the benefit of unlimited hand grenades and machine guns à la Schwarzenegger in the 1985 shoot 'em up, *Commando,* in which he racked up a then-record 81 kills. McClane does, however, have his sense of humor and it shows up again after he kills one of the terrorists, puts a Santa hat on him and writes on his sweatshirt, "Now I have a machine gun. Ho-Ho-Ho," which I have on a t-shirt in my closet. See ... it's a Christmas movie.

Throughout all his challenges, uncertainty, fear, and a few near-death experiences, there is one constant in McClane's Nakatomi Towers world — humor. It gets him through. It helps him keep his mind clear. It keeps him level and sane. It saves his life and the lives of the hostages including his wife. Had he gone negative and allowed his head to be filled with despair, he would have likely given up, as so many do when faced with what feels like insurmountable challenges.

When we see others refusing to give up when the going gets tough, it emboldens us all. I am reminded of Jim Valvano, who was the college basketball coach at North Carolina State in the '80s, an era in which he and his team won the 1983 college basketball championship. Valvano was diagnosed with meta-static cancer in 1992 and delivered one of the greatest and most moving speeches of the modern era during the 1st Annual ESPY Awards (ESPN Sports Awards) at Madison Square Garden on March 4, 1993. At this point, his body had been ravaged with tumors and his best friend, Dick Vitale (or Dickie V., as we college basketball sports fans call him), helped him onto the stage. Once Valvano reached the podium, he accepted the inaugural Arthur

Ashe Courage Award named after the professional tennis player who valiantly and publicly fought an AIDS diagnosis that likely stemmed from a blood transfusion during a 1983 coronary artery bypass surgery. Before his untimely death, Ashe started the Arthur Ashe Foundation for the Defeat of AIDS and worked to educate others about HIV and AIDS. After accepting the award, Valvano announced the creation of The V Foundation for Cancer Research, which — the last time I checked — had raised more than $290 million that has been distributed in the form of cancer research grants. In Valvano's acceptance speech at the ESPYs, he said this:

> "To me, there are three things we all should do every day. We should do this every day of our lives. **Number one is laugh. You should laugh every day.** Number two is think. You should spend some time in thought. And number three is you should have your emotions moved to tears, could be happiness or joy. But think about it. *If you laugh*, you think, and you cry, that's a full day. That's a heck of a day. You do that seven days a week, you're going to have something special."

At this point, they were running short on time, and Valvano was flashed a 30-second warning to him on the teleprompter, to which he replied:

> "That screen up there is flashing 30 seconds, like I care about that screen right now, huh? I got tumors all over my body and I'm worried about some guy in the back going '30 seconds.'"

The audience laughed (and cried and thought). Valvano embraced humor and levity in the face of a terminal cancer battle that he was losing quickly. As he said at the end of his speech, which is now the motto for the Jimmy V Foundation, "Don't give up. Don't ever give up."

You don't have to be a famous basketball coach or a celebrity to find ways to use humor to help you through the tough times.

Humor most certainly got me through the most difficult stretch of my life. I had quite a run of challenges in 2021. My then-girlfriend struck out on her own, chasing a life journey that needed to be filled, leaving in her RV in March of 2021 after a whirlwind romance that changed us both and you can read about in my short-story memoir, *Coffee. Love. And a Cross-Country Road Trip.* My stepmom was diagnosed with and passed away from pancreatic cancer all within a three-week period during April of 2021. My mom passed away from Alzheimer's in July of 2021. And we moved my dad into independent living in February of 2022. Yeah, my life was a country song. There were three things that kept me afloat during this time:

1. My sister. We kept each other afloat.

2. My rescue dog and best friend, Bodhi.

3. Humor and laughter.

Throughout it all, we kept our sense of humor and, more importantly, so did our mom, stepmom, dad, and stepdad. Collectively, we joked with our mom about our love for Neil Diamond and her equal disdain for him, up until the very end. My stepmom blamed my dad's cooking for her weight loss even in the face of certain death. We laughed with my stepdad about how even when my mom's eyes were closed and she couldn't move, she would know if you were touching her stuff and, without opening her eyes, would say, "Why are you touching my stuff? Stop touching my stuff!" And we learned to laugh when she would say his name and my sister's name over and over again for them to come to her even when I was standing right there. She would say, "Jimmy, Jimmy, Jimmy jim jim" (my stepdad's name) and I would say "Mom, he's downstairs. I'm right here if you need something." She would respond with, "Stop it, Christopher. Just stop it," and then would call for my sister, "Ashleigh, Ashleigh, Ashleigh." We just laughed together when it happened and still laugh about it to this day.

When we moved my dad into an independent living community, like a lot of people in his situation, he was concerned about outliving his finances. My sister and I reminded him that we watch a lot of "true crime" shows and if he gets close to running out of money for the independent living facility, that we know how to "take care of things" for him painlessly, quietly, and without leaving a trace of evidence.

Through it all, I just try to keep laughing. And reminiscing. Surely, my love for '80s comedies has kept my funny bone intact. Humor works — for me, for you, for all of us. My sister and I fought multiple life challenges with humor, Jim Valvano fought terminal cancer with humor, and John McClane fought terrorists with humor. Maybe there is something to this "laugh every day" thing.

It's, of course, important to face your challenges — in the workplace and in life — with determination, positivity, grit, and a belief in self. Just don't forget to throw in a side of humor and take some time to laugh.

What else can we learn from the memorable characters and implausible plot lines of *Die Hard*?

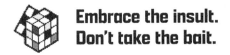

Embrace the insult. Don't take the bait.

The first night of my first job as a bar bouncer, the head bouncer (or "cooler," as you learned in the *Road House* chapter) told me that there would be a lot of intoxicated individuals who would try to bait me into a physical confrontation. "Don't take the bait," he said. "It's not worth it. 99% of the guys won't even remember what they said or did when they wake up the next morning. They won't remember you or any part of their interaction with you. Just don't take the bait." It was good advice, of course, and I took it to

heart. I only took the bait once, but it would take multiple bourbons for that story to come out so thankfully you and I are separated by the kind of time and space that even David Copperfield
couldn't overcome with his best illusion.

My stepbrother, Todd, is an avid fisherman. I would imagine
that it ranks as 2nd or 3rd in his life behind his daughter and
weight training, which is also a component of his job as
a personal trainer and nutritionist. He's loved fishing ever since
I met him when he was five years old, and he has always been
a catch-and-release guy, which is really cool. No matter the size
of the fish, he always releases it back to its rightful place to live
and fight for another day. Now to catch a fish, you're counting
on the fish to take the bait enough to get caught on the hook so
you can reel it in. You've likely heard the phrase "the one that got
away" and besides being something married people say about
the boyfriend or girlfriend that they really wish they would have
married, this expression refers to a fish — usually the biggest fish
ever, if you ask the fisherman — that took the bait with authority
and swam away ever so confidently.

Circa 1976: My now stepbrother, Todd, and me, skipping and holding
hands in my backyard while wearing some fresh plaid slacks!

When John McClane and Hans Gruber first communicate, it's after McClane has established himself as a legit bad ass capable of really screwing up Hans's plan to heist the $600 million in bonds. They go back and forth for a minute, feeling each other out and seeing if one might slip up to give away their position or important information about themselves. When Hans realizes that McClane knows his name and is not an average building-security guard run amok and in way over his head, he has this little exchange with him:

> **Hans:** "You have me at a loss. You know my name but who are you? Just another American who saw too many movies as a child. Another orphan of a bankrupt culture who thinks he's John Wayne, Rambo, or Marshall Dillon?"

Hans is doing his best to bait McClane and get him to take that same bait by getting angry and raising his voice, which would give his position away or, at the very least, allow him to occupy some space inside his head. McClane doesn't take the bait and comes back with this:

> **McClane:** "I was always partial to Roy Rogers, actually. I really like those sequin shirts."

In the movie, we can see the frustration on Hans's face as he realizes McClane is not taking the bait. As good bad guys tend to, he doubles down:

> **Hans:** "Do you really think you have a chance against us, Mr. Cowboy?"

After a few seconds of silence, McClane smirks, smoothly leans back into a door as it swings open and then says into his walkie talkie:

> **McClane:** "Yippee-Ki-Yay, Motherfucker!"

He embraced the insult. He didn't take the bait. So, what do
I mean by this? Let me explain so I don't confuse you like the
song lyrics to the 1988 song "What I Am" by Edie Brickel and The
New Bohemians:

> *"I'm not aware of too many things. I know what I know if*
> *you know what I mean.*
> *Philosophy is a walk on the slippery rocks,*
> *Religion is a light in the fog.*
> *What I am is what I am, are you what you are or what …"*

I love that song and Edie Brickell, but ummm … these lyrics
went over my head like that movie *Arrival* in 2016 that everyone
thought was so great, intellectual, and introspective. I gave it an
'80s Roger Ebert "thumbs down."

Anyway, back to the whole "Embrace the insult and don't take the
bait" and what that means exactly. When I got my first marketing
job, my resume was pretty thin. It basically said, "Bouncer, security guard for celebrities, bellman, valet, bartender, busboy, and
dishwasher." Not exactly a murderer's row of corporate brand and
marketing experience but someone gave me a chance and I am
forever indebted to her for believing in me.

Very early on in my career journey, I was put on a project team with
five other people, all of whom had impressive collegiate pedigrees
— including two with Ivy League backgrounds — and all had more
marketing experience than me (which, as you can see from my
resume, would have been the case even if their names were Rusty
Griswold and Dudley "Booger" Dawson). When I first came into
the room and was introduced to the rest of the project team, one
guy in particular was clearly not going to be a fan of mine. While
everyone else greeted me with the pleasantries typically afforded
the new person, he stayed seated and nodded his head with a bit of
a smug look when we were introduced. I reached my hand out and
said, "nice to meet you" and he turned to the team and said, "so

should we get started?" No handshake, no acknowledgment. I got
dissed. I mean, he did have the whole '80s high-school villain look
that we discussed before — sweater around the neck, perfect hair,
privileged, etc. — so I wasn't entirely surprised.

Because this was my first day on the project and the team was
already a week or so into development, my philosophy (as it still
stands today when I'm in a new room) was to listen and learn
and say as little as possible. About an hour into the conversation,
they were at an impasse and really struggling with the messaging
for the product launch. There were also disagreements about the
secondary target audiences and markets. You could say they were
a little discombobulated, which is very typical at stages during the
creative process. Discombobulated. I love that word. Just wanted
to find a way to get it in.

With all this discombobulation, one team member turned to the
new guy — that's me — and asked if I had any ideas or sugges-
tions. She mentioned that maybe a fresh set of eyes could help.
Now before I go further, I do need to let you know that, at this
time, I was 25 years old and one of the most important things
in my life was lifting the heaviest weights possible in the gym.
I'm 6'1" and at the time I weighed about 235-240 pounds, hence
the bouncing at bars and security jobs. Just to be clear, this is not
my Ron Burgundy *Anchorman* looking-in-the-mirror moment
when he said "Hey everyone! Come see how good I look!" Okay,
not an '80s movie but so good and definitely flows and feels like
an '80s comedy. I tell you this because, just as this team member
reached out to me for some feedback and potential ideas, our
sweater-around-the-neck guy leaned over to the person next to
him and said — under his breath but loud enough for me to hear:
"Why is she asking him? Look at him. He's just a dumb jock."

Yes, he said that. And I do think he intended for me to hear it, but
when he realized that I *had* indeed heard it and the consequences
of his words were a bit unknown at that point, he slumped down

a bit and you could see the sweater get a bit tighter around his neck. There were a lot of options for me here, but I just took a deep breath, looked at him, smiled, and said: "Maybe I am, but I score a lot and my end-zone celebrations are pretty sweet."

That, my friends, is what I mean by: **Embrace the insult. Don't take the bait.**

And before we go any further, let me just clarify that I didn't mean "score" in the sense that you are thinking, you filthy animals. What I meant with the word score was victories over smarmy sweater-around-the-neck guys. Actually, what it really meant was that I considered both small and large accomplishments victories and I embraced and acknowledged each one of them in the same positive way. Big victories like packing up my car at 22 and driving 1,800 miles away from home to start my life on my own terms. Big victories like getting my first marketing job after taking jobs bussing tables and bouncing at bars. Small victories like learning how to cook something without a hot pot. Small victories like it sticking it to you, sweater-around-the-neck guy, by embracing the insult and not taking the bait. Well, also throwing it back at him as well but that's part of the embracing of the insult sometimes.

There was an awkward silence before everyone started laughing — everyone except sweater-around-the-neck guy, who had a look on his face that was a mix of relief that I didn't "do a Rambo" on him as Oran' Juice Jones rapped in his 1986 hit, "The Rain," and the embarrassment that Neil Page had on his face when Del Griffith embraced the insult and threw it back a little bit in one of the most moving scenes in '80s cinema from *Planes, Trains and Automobiles*. This scene is one of the best examples of this lesson. When Neil finally shows his true colors after being around Del for a few days, they have this exchange:

> **Neil:** "You're no saint. You got a free cab, you got a free room, and someone who'll listen to your boring stories. I mean, didn't you notice on the plane when you started talking,

eventually I started reading the vomit bag? Didn't that give you some sort of clue, like, hey, maybe this guy's not enjoying it? You know, everything isn't an anecdote. You have to discriminate. You choose things that are funny or mildly amusing or interesting. You're a miracle! Your stories have none of that. They're not even amusing accidentally! 'Honey, I'd like you to meet Del Griffith, he's got some amusing anecdotes for you. Oh, and here's a gun so you can blow your brains out. You'll thank me for it.' I could tolerate any insurance seminar. For days, I could sit there and listen to them go on and on with a big smile on my face. They'd say, 'How can you stand it?' I'd say, 'Because I've been with Del Griffith. I can take anything.' You know what they'd say? They'd say, 'I know what you mean. The shower-curtain-ring guy. Whoa.' It's like going on a date with a Chatty Cathy doll. I expect you to have a little string on your chest, you know, that I pull out and have to snap back. Except I wouldn't pull it out and snap it back. You would. Agh! Agh! Agh! Agh! And by the way, you know, when you're telling these little stories? Here's a good idea — have a point. It makes it so much more interesting for the listener!"

Del: "You wanna hurt me? Go right ahead if it makes you feel any better. I'm an easy target. Yeah, you're right, I talk too much. I also listen too much. I could be a cold-hearted cynic like you ... but I don't like to hurt people's feelings. Well, you think what you want about me. I'm not changing. I like ... I like me. My wife likes me. My customers like me. 'Cause I'm the real article. What you see is what you get."

When someone's first instinct is to insult you or to find a way to poke you a little bit, it's usually due to either their own insecurities (in the case of Neil Page) or (as in the case of Hans Gruber) it's a bit of gamesmanship hoping to throw you off your game and get into your head. Athletes do this all the time with their opponents and sometimes we are lucky enough to hear it if the on-field mic picks it up. With combat sports like boxing and mixed martial arts, the gamesmanship of insults starts well before the fight during press conferences and weigh-ins.

Embrace the insult. Don't take the bait. That's exactly what they want. They want you take the bait. So instead, embrace it, turn it around on them and take the conversation and most importantly, the power back.

Hans's face after McClane embraces the insult and says "Yippee-Ki-Yay, Motherfucker" was one of defeat, frustration, and despair. McClane won by not taking the bait. He took the conversation and the situation back. Ultimately, it was Hans who got frustrated and impatient and made the mistakes that allowed McClane to be victorious and save everyone while Hans perished without ever getting his hands on the $600 billion in bonds. Sorry, another spoiler, but if you haven't seen *Die Hard*, I don't think we can be friends ... so I don't feel bad at all.

And just to settle the debate once and for all, *Die Hard* is a Christmas movie. How else can you explain this scene?

Argyle turns on the radio in the limo and Run DMC's "Christmas in Hollis" plays ...

> **Argyle:** "Hey, that'll work."
>
> **McClane:** "Don't you got any Christmas music?"
>
> **Argyle:** "This *is* Christmas music!"

"Christmas in Hollis" by Run DMC is a Christmas classic up there with "White Christmas," "Rudolph," "Jingle Bell Rock," "Rockin' Around the Christmas Tree," and "Fairytale of New York."

Not enough evidence? Okay, how about the last scene?

> **McClane:** "Merry Christmas, Argyle."

Argyle: "Merry Christmas." [Under his breath as he closes the limo door] "Man, if this is their idea of Christmas, I gotta be here for New Year's!"

As Bill Murray's character John Winger said in the 1981 comedy classic, *Stripes*, "That's the fact, Jack!" I just deal in facts and *Die Hard* is awesome and a Christmas movie.

CHAPTER 7

FIELD OF DREAMS

"People will come, Ray. People will most definitely come."

— TERRANCE MANN, *FIELD OF DREAMS*

However and whenever you tell the story of America, there should always be two institutions included — Hollywood and Baseball. Movies and America's favorite pastime have both had massive impacts on our culture and the everyday life of the average American. And when Hollywood has a chance to tell a baseball story, the result can be magical. Case in point: *Field of Dreams*. Hollywood "built it" in a cornfield and "they" (the public) came. But more on that later.

In Chapter 4, we talked a little bit about cornfields. Terrifying, possessed cornfields where demonic children with names like Malachai hid, waiting for their next adult victims who would be

sacrificed to the devil, who was talking to them through the cornfields. Thankfully, these are not *those* cornfields. These cornfields
in *Field of Dreams* are the exact opposite. More heaven than hell,
and they also had a voice that spoke to the movie's main character, Ray Kinsella.

2005: Me playing baseball at Comerica Park, where the Detroit Tigers play.

Seems like a lot of people heard voices in the '80s. The aforementioned Malachai and his little demon crew in *Children of
the Corn*; Carol Anne in *Poltergeist*, who heard them through her
TV; Magnum P.I. heard them in every episode through his "little
voice inside;" and Ray Kinsella and eventually his wife, Annie,
the heroes in *Field of Dreams*, heard them coming from their
cornfields in Iowa. The voices that Ray heard were so convincing
that he removed a large portion of the corn on his farm (a crop
that served as the primary source of income for his family) and

replaced it with a baseball diamond, complete with lights for night games.

As Ray looked over the completed project, he said, "I have just created something totally illogical." And he was right. A baseball diamond in the middle of a privately owned cornfield in Iowa. But it turns out that some of the most "illogical" inventions and ideas often give us our best success stories and ultimately spur advances and progress on this little illogical blue marble where we all reside. When Ray builds the baseball field, he teaches us the difference between logical and illogical:

 Logical equals safe. Illogical equals crazy. From crazy comes innovation, creativity, and advancement.

In the movies and in our lives, it sometimes happens that someone we think is insignificant in the shaping of the story is found to be a key player. Without that character or person, the story — in the form of a script or our life — cannot move forward and ceases to exist. Surely, there is someone in your life who you initially thought would be a bit player in your journey but — for a specific reason you couldn't initially see — that person became someone who must be mentioned in your life story for it to be wholly complete.

Such is the case for Dr. Archibald "Moonlight" Graham, who is a supporting but integral character in *Field of Dreams,* who when reflecting on his life says:

> "We just don't recognize life's most significant moments while they're happening. Back then I thought, 'Well, there'll be other days.' I didn't realize that was the only day."

He's reminiscing on a youth that has long since passed him by and he's realizing that the moments he considered insignificant were actually quite profound; some moments seem insignificant in real time but were clearly formative when we look back on them. And with that quote, he teaches us that:

 The moments in our life are like snowflakes. None are the same. Embrace each one. You'll look back one day and realize that they were all significant in their own way.

So, before we "go deep" (to use a baseball term) into these lessons from *Field of Dreams*, let's *Time Bandits* this thing, fall into the empty void at the end of the hallway, and take a trip back to the '80s once again.

My Life in May 1989

It was May of 1989, and I was finishing my freshman year at Elon College, now Elon University. University has a much more mature and "higher learning" tone to it, doesn't it? I guess that's what happens when you stop letting in students with mediocre SAT scores and a proclivity for fireworks battles that set dorms on fire. Besides, the dorm fire technically happened in September of 1988. I mean, from what I've heard anyway, and I'm pretty sure that by the time the story came back around to me, it had been exaggerated a bit. Sort of like the rumors that swirled around Ferris Bueller's actual day off:

> "My best friend's sister's boyfriend's brother's girlfriend heard from this guy who knows this kid who's going with a girl who saw Ferris pass-out at 31 Flavors last night. I guess it's pretty serious."

Okay, okay. The story was about me, and we did catch our dorm on fire. And when I say "we," I mean a few of my very close friends from college who I had just met three weeks prior to our epic fireworks battle and who shall remain nameless because they have wives and kids and real jobs and all that mature adult kind of stuff.

Back to May of 1989, and although I'd had almost nine months to mature from the days of firework-battles lore, I was still living by the lyric "Hey teacher, don't you fill me up with no rules ..." in Motley Crue's 1989 cover of Brownsville Station's "Smokin' in the Boys Room". This time, however, I was incorporating a different one of the four elements of nature — water. I don't actually recall how it came into our possession, but my friends and I were able to procure a water-balloon slingshot — which is exactly what it sounds like, only much larger and more powerful than you think. To use it properly required a team of three, with one person on each side holding the "arms" on the left and right, and the gunner in the back. The gunner loaded the water balloon and pulled back the slingshot as far as humanly possible to maximize the projectile distance. I was the gunner (I know that doesn't surprise you!) and I'd read on the product box that the slingshot could shoot up to 100 yards, which is the length of a football field! So, of course, that became our goal.

I don't actually recall how it came into our possession, but my friends and I were able to procure a water-balloon slingshot — which is exactly what it sounds like, only much larger and more powerful than you think.

Now to properly handle a water-balloon slingshot, you first need to consume a few libations. Being 19, underage, and broke, our options were limited, so we went with a few mysteriously acquired bottles of Mad Dog 20/20 and Night Train. Quite possibly the worst-tasting and god-awful alcohol you could find to consume on planet Earth.

■■■■■■■■■■■■■■■■■■■■■■■■■■■■■■■■■

🍸 **FUN FACT:** Both Mad Dog 20/20 and Night Train are considered Fortified Flavored Wines, which is a category that rose to popularity during the Great Depression.[22] Night Train (Night Train Express) appeared in the 1980 movie classic, *The Blues Brothers*, when Joliet Jake (John Belushi) consumed a full bottle. It is also the subject of the song "Night Train" by *Guns N' Roses*, which appeared on their 1987 debut album, "Appetite for Destruction."

Me with Dan Akroyd and Jim Belushi before
a Blues Brothers concert in Chicago, 2013.

■■■■■■■■■■■■■■■■■■■■■■■■■■■■■■■■■

On the day in question in May of 1989, my two friends and I consumed a full bottle of Night Train à la Joliet Jake, which absolutely gave us an appetite for destruction. So going out to an empty football field and slinging water-balloon shots would be way too boring for 19-year-olds jacked up on fortified flavored wines. No, we aimed a bit higher. We targeted the dorm across the street from ours. I mean, what better way to get a date than firing water balloons at the girls' dorm, where those you adored from afar lived? Ever wonder where the term "pea brain" came from? There you go.

---

22 "Flavored fortified Wine," *Wikipedia*, Last Edited September 8, 2022, https://en.wikipedia.org/wiki/Flavored_fortified_wine

We set up shop on the sidewalk across from the dorm and as we prepared the slingshot for the first launch, a few girls on the 2nd floor saw what we were doing, opened their windows, and dared us to try to hit their room. Challenge accepted. With a man on each arm of the slingshot, I placed the water balloon in the holder and pulled back as the two guys in the front planted their feet and held firm. I could feel and hear the stretching of the slingshot as I continued to pull it back further and further (far further than I would assume the instructions would have recommended, if there were any included in the box).

I yelled, "Ready. Aim. Fire!" as I let go of the slingshot and watched as the water balloon flew with the accuracy of Ralphie's "official Red Ryder carbine-action 200-shot range model air rifle," which is to say it flew inaccurately in the hands of an amateur. As the girls cheered for the water balloon to come their way, it took an unfortunate path to their right and straight into the resident assistant's open window. The balloon exploded with so much force when it hit the back wall of the dorm room that we could see water flying back out of the window. At the time, the RA was taking a nap, so she was awoken drenched in chilled balloon water. It was clear from her first words as she leaned out of the window that she was not happy with us at all. Everyone scattered, leaving me "holding the bag" in the form of the slingshot. I eventually ran as well and the three of us were on the lam from campus security for about two days before our deeds finally caught up to us. We were each given 40 hours of community service and a stern talking-to by the Dean of Discipline, who I got to know very well over the next several years.

Pop Culture in May 1989

Oddly enough, the Top 40 plus a few during that week in May of 1989 had some songs that tied nicely into our two days on the run from campus security. "Like a Prayer" from Madonna was sitting at #2, while "Second Chance" from one of the most underrated '80s bands, .38 Special, was holding down the #7 spot. Deon Estus, the bass player from that eightiest of '80s pop groups, Wham!, was having some success of his own with his hit "Heaven Help Me" at #21, while "Coming Home" from glam band Cinderella was at #43 and rising.

On TV, May of 1989 was one for the small-screen history books. While only one show made its debut — *Think Fast* on Nickelodeon — some of the most popular shows to ever enter the living rooms of Americans came to an end. May brought us the finales for *Family Ties, Dynasty, Moonlighting, The Gong Show,* and perhaps the show that had the most influence on all aspects of pop culture in the '80s from music to fashion, *Miami Vice.* How much influence? Well, Don Johnson released his debut album, *Heartbeat,* in 1986, which included the single — yes, you guessed it, "Heartbeat" — which went all the way to #5 on the Billboard charts. Unfortunately, May 1989 also brought us one of the most heartbreaking Hollywood deaths to date when the comedic genius Gilda Radner passed away from breast cancer on May 20, 1989, at the incredibly young age of 42.

At the box office, my man — Patrick Swayze — was protecting the patrons of the Double Deuce bar in *Road House* (Chapter 8 of this book — keep reading, it'll knock you out!) while Lloyd Dobler, played by John Cusack, was showing us how romantic a boombox can be in *Say Anything (*a movie featured in my 1st book). That's got to be my 4th or 5th shameless plug. Need more superstars? How about Dustin Hoffman and Tom Cruise in the "Best Picture" Oscar winner, *Rainman,* and Harrison Ford and Sean Connery foiling the Nazis once again in *Indiana Jones and The Last Crusade.* There were also two baseball movies, albeit very different, that were sitting in the top five at the box office. We had *Major League,* which is one of the greatest sports comedies of all time, and the subject for this chapter, *Field of Dreams,* which is one of the greatest all-around sports movies in cinematic history.

Life Lessons from *Field of Dreams*

Field of Dreams tells the story of an Iowa farmer named Ray Kinsella (played by Kevin Costner), who hears a voice coming from his cornfields that says, "If you build it, he will come," and "Ease his pain" — both references to Ray's father, a former minor-league player. At the time that this is happening, Ray's farm is close to going into foreclosure and he knows that he should be focusing on the work at hand, but the voice keeps beckoning him. His wife, Annie (played by Amy Madigan), is very into following your heart and the vibes that you feel. When Ray confides in her about the voices and that he thinks they are telling him to build a baseball diamond in the middle of the cornfield, she encourages him to go for it even though it could break them. In the hopes that building the baseball field would beckon players, they moved forward, hoping whoever it is would come." And come they do, in the form of Shoeless Joe Jackson (played by Ray Liotta) and seven other White Sox players who were banned from baseball for throwing the 1919 World Series (although it is a bit more complicated than that historically and there are still a lot of questions around the story). At the point when Shoeless Joe comes out of the cornfield and onto the baseball diamond, he asks, "Is this heaven?" to which Ray says, "No, this is Iowa." Just a great moment in the movie.

■■■■■■■■■■■■■■■■■■■■■■■■■■■■■■■■

FUN FACT: There are hundreds of songs with the word "heaven" in the title and 43 that are named simply "Heaven."[23] My favorite is the 1989 ballad by the glam-rock band, Warrant, which went all the way up to #2 on the billboard charts. It just gives me the nostalgia feels every time I hear it. The opening stanza goes like this:

---

23 "Song Title 15 — Heaven," TSORT, https://tsort.info/music/57ppnp.htm.

"Got a picture of your house
And you're standin' by the door.
It's black and white and faded
And it's lookin' pretty worn."

■■■■■■■■■■■■■■■■■■■■■■■■■■■■■■■■■■■

The voice in *Field of Dreams* continues to talk to Ray Kinsella and it sends him on a journey to pick up Terrance Mann (played by James Earl Jones), who is a famous author who spoke to a generation of youth in the '60s. Kinsella convinces Mann to come to Iowa with him to the baseball field, and there in that field — that stunning, quiet place full of profound potential — the story really reveals itself in multiple ways through heartbreak, frustration, patience, understanding, sacrifice, and redemption.

Any movie that has James Earl Jones will always be worth the price of admission and more, but this one is special. There's something chill-worthy about a movie featuring a voice coming from a cornfield — a voice telling a farmer to build a baseball diamond so that "he will come" (along with the ghosts of a 1919 World Series team). *Field of Dreams* would become a classic for generations to come, reminding us how important it is for our culture and society to have great storytellers. *Field of Dreams* is a magical sports fantasy movie that finds a way (in less than two hours!) to tell us about America, family, baseball, and the importance of believing in something bigger than yourself.

Field of Dreams is a magical sports-fantasy movie that finds a way (in less than two hours!) to tell us about America, family, baseball, and the importance of believing in something bigger than yourself.

■■■■■■■■■■■■■■■■■■■■■■■■■■■■■■■■■

FUN FACT: James Earl Jones is a cinematic giant, known by most of us for his TV, stage, and movie roles that date all the way back to his debut on the soap opera *Guiding Light* in 1952. And, of course, he is known for that booming and commanding voice of his, which gave life to characters like Darth Vader in *Star Wars* and Mufasa in *The Lion King*.[24] But his most amazing voice work may be his least known. In 1927, James Weldon Johnson, who was an African-American poet, novelist, and civil rights activist, wrote a collection of poetry called *God's Trombones,*[25] which contained seven poems. One is called "The Creation" and it retells the story of the creation of humans, as told in the Christian Bible. James Earl Jones narrates it for the audio book and let me tell you that if someone ever had to cast the voice of God, they need look no further.

■■■■■■■■■■■■■■■■■■■■■■■■■■■■■■■■■

So, what does this movie about a crazy farmer who builds a baseball diamond in his corn fields teach us about life and the workplace?

Logical equals safe. Illogical equals crazy. From crazy comes innovation, creativity, and advancement.

When Ray Kinsella finally succumbs to the voice coming from his cornfield and bulldozes his prized crops — along with his main

---

24 "James Earl Jones," *Wikipedia*, Last Edited September 19, 2022, https://en.wikipedia.org/wiki/James_Earl_Jones

25 "God's Trombones: A Trilogy of African-American Poems," IMDB, https://www.imdb.com/title/tt2459356/.

source of income for his family — to build the baseball diamond the voice craves for, he looks out over his creation and says: "I have just created something totally illogical."

Yes, yes, he had ... but the best part is that he said it and smiled the happiest smile that we've seen from his character at that point in the movie. The exchange between Kinsella and his wife — as they look over the baseball diamond the first night under the lights — is an exercise in partnership, teamwork, and support:

> **Ray:** "I have just created something totally illogical."
>
> **Annie:** "That's what I like about it."
>
> **Ray:** "Am I completely nuts?"
>
> **Annie:** "Not completely ... it's a good baseball field, Ray."

How many of us have just wanted to do something radically different — with our lives or our careers — when, from the outside, it looked like we had a pretty good life and seemed to have everything under control? How many of us acted on that impulse? How many people have had an idea that seemed totally illogical to those around them and rather than following their passion, illogical as it may have seemed, listened to those around them who projected their own fears of the unknown onto them, thus keeping them in their safe and logical place?

When creating or doing something "totally illogical" that you 100% believe in, it's always good to have the support of the people closest to you. Ray had Annie. I had my family and friends. Support matters. But it isn't always the case that people wanting to do something revolutionary have supporters and believers all around them. In fact, it's more likely that many a dream has died before they even had a chance to get started. Not everyone has an Annie in their life. There's a reason why, in the 1800s, we had two authors/poets who were already recognizing this and writing about it: Henry David Thoreau said, "The mass of men [people] lead lives of quiet desperation" and Oliver Wendell Holmes said, "Alas for those that never sing, but die with all their music in them."

Sigh. Alas, indeed. And yes, that's like the 93rd time you've heard these quotes in my book. Maybe a tattoo of one on each of my arms is in order. Hmmm.

Before the industrial revolution, before people toiled for a lifetime in jobs they didn't like, and before many of us sat hunched over in cubicle farms, there were already people who were recognizing the ease with which individuality and the human spirit can be traded for logic and safety. Thankfully for all of us, there are just enough "totally illogical" and "good crazy" people in each generation who make us think, laugh, wonder, and advance as a civilization.

Before the industrial revolution, before people toiled for a lifetime in jobs they didn't like, and before many of us sat hunched over in cubicle farms, there were already people who were recognizing the ease with which individuality and the human spirit can be traded for logic and safety.

Fortunately for me, the people closest to me totally supported my illogical act of leaving the corporate marketing world after 20+ years and at the age of 47 to pursue my writing and speaking career. My roommate from my late 20s and very good friend said, "It's about time, man. You've been talking about writing books and speaking for years!" I didn't even realize how much I talked about it (and for how long) until he mentioned it.

Of course, there were others who said it was a bad idea and were focused on the possibility that it would be a failed dream. "You have a plan B, right?" "Who is going to care about workplace and life lessons from '80s pop culture and who are you to think you can make a living at it?" "You are in such a good place right now with your career, why would you do this?" It was hard not to take those assessments and comments personally, but I realized later that they were just projecting their own fears of change and the unknown on me. And many of them were in their own "quiet desperation" and didn't really have a way out at the time. Entrepreneurship is a risk, and a lot of people are pretty risk averse.

My illogical moment was really about making sure that my tombstone didn't just say "he was a pretty good marketing guy" and that's about it. In some ways, I'd been doing the "easy" thing by working hard for someone else and collecting a paycheck every two weeks. It's what most "logical" people do. Hell, it's what most people do regardless of where they fall on the logic scale. My first experience with the idea of chasing something totally *illogical* happened in the early '80s. (The '80s? Shocking, I know.) Although I was a pretty good athlete, I was what is called a "late bloomer" physically, so my size left me vulnerable to bullies until the age of 14. (Of course, wearing a mock turtleneck in the school choir and singing an alto-soprano solo of "Send in the Clowns" by Judy Collins didn't help either.) At one point, I was challenged to a one-on-one basketball game at a set of courts not too far from my house. I accepted the challenge and beat my challenger easily. He was not happy at all and took a swing at me. When I retaliated, his two friends jumped in and the three of them gave me a pretty good "whooping," as they say in the American South. At that point, if I wanted to be able to protect myself in the future, I had one of two options: (a) wait for my growth spurt, which wasn't a guarantee or (b) join a gym and start lifting weights. I chose the latter and never looked back.

It was at this time that my dad gave me a VHS tape titled *Richard Simmons: The Stomach Formula — Seven Minutes a Day, Seven Days a Week to Great Abs*. As a newbie to the lifting and physical fitness world, I looked to the most popular exercise and fitness icons in the early '80s for boys: Arnold Schwarzenegger, Bruce Lee, and the fictional threesome of Rocky Balboa, Apollo Creed, and Clubber Lang (Mr. T) from the *Rocky* movies. Oh, and any number of massively large NFL players. So here I was, looking at the cover of this VHS tape and I see someone who does *not* look like any of these characters. In fact, he doesn't even look muscular at all. He's got a large and wild permed hairstyle, and he's wearing little shorts and a tank top complete with crystals or sequins, and he has an average body.

Me: "Dad. Seriously?"

My dad: "Give it a shot. Let's see if you can do it."

Me: "C'mon. Seven minutes of abs? No problem. If he can do it, then it will be easy. He doesn't even have abs!"

My dad just smiled that "dad smile" — you know the one, when they know something you don't. I popped the tape into the VCR, got down on the floor, and waited. In came Richard Simmons with a few people in the background, all dressed for some serious 1980s aerobics. He had a headband on with a unitard of sorts and his signature tank top. "This is going to be a cakewalk," I thought to myself.

"You gotta be tough on yourself and do all of the exercises all seven days," he said. And then the camera panned out to show all of them sitting on the floor in a semi-split position. "Inhale, exhale, inhale, exhale, and to the right," he said as they reached for their feet to stretch. I laughed out loud — a hearty laugh

— and my dad just looked at me with that dad smile. About two minutes into the seven minutes of ab exercises, I tapped out with the same vigor as Roberto Duran in his 1980 boxing match with Sugar Ray Leonard when he supposedly said "No mas" (or "no more") to the referee in the 8th round and gave up. I couldn't believe that I gave up so quickly! And this was my official introduction to the illogical, completely unexpected Richard Simmons.

Richard Simmons as a brand and a phenomenon is most certainly an illogical creation that was born from chaos. In his early years, he was an overeater and became obese and there is a decades-long conversation about whether he was a background character in several Fellini films. Standing just 5'7", he weighed in at 268 pounds during this time in the late 1960s before his transformation into the person we know and love today. He was a far cry from the bulging biceps, ripped abs, and "we want to pump you up" training mentality of the early '80s. Now I would be remiss not to mention that there was an alternative market for physical training with the explosion of at-home aerobics via VHS tapes, led by the likes of Jane Fonda and Denise Austin, but they too were ripped, in incredible shape, and "camera ready" as they say in the industry.

Richard Simmons was not ripped, did not have bulging biceps and was not what most would consider to be camera-ready, but he built a fitness empire that includes books, DVDs, television shows, movies, and exercise studios. He's been featured in commercials for major brands like Sprint, Yoplait, and Herbal Essences Shampoo and guest starred in shows from *CHiPs* to *Arrested Development*. He was the star of an ESPN commercial for Sportscenter, won an Emmy for his show, *The Richard Simmons Show,* and had a radio show on Sirius for two years called *Lighten Up with Richard Simmons.* And he gave us five minutes of comedy gold when he guest-starred on an episode of the improv comedy sketch show *Whose Line Is It Anyway.*[26]

His fitness career spanned almost 40 years and he claimed to have helped humanity lose almost 12 million pounds,[27] which is probably pretty close to the truth. His charisma, energy, and genuine nature brought an entirely new audience to the fitness world: a massive group of people who were barraged with images of unrealistic body shapes and gyms that didn't cater to the average person. He helped them believe in themselves and helped them find their self-confidence through fitness, nutrition, and exercise. Richard Simmons changed people's lives for the better and, more importantly, changed people's perceptions when it comes to what a spokesperson and leader should look like and not just in the fitness world. He opened doors of acceptance through his grace, honesty, and ultimately his ability to deliver on his message of making people healthier. And he did all of this in the world of "no pain, no gain" '80s fitness, while wearing red-and-white pinstriped short-shorts, a bedazzled tank top, an average body, and a perm that was only rivaled by Bob Ross and his "happy little trees."

When I think of Richard Simmons, I think of John Candy's character Del Griffith in *Planes, Trains and Automobiles,* when he said this during a very moving monologue: "I'm not changing. I like me. My wife likes me. My customers like me. 'Cause I'm the real article. What you see is what you get." Richard Simmons is totally illogical and that makes him totally awesome.

Fast forward to today and a guy who *doesn't* wear bedazzled tank tops but isn't afraid to fire up a doobie and get stoned on a podcast is leading the way in creating from illogical chaos: Elon Musk. Hate him, love him, or somewhere in-between, the

---

26 "Richard Simmons," *Wikipedia*, Last updated August 22, 2022, https://en.wikipedia.org/wiki/Richard_Simmons.

27 "Richard Simmons's Story, Part 2," *The Dr. Oz Show*, https://www.drozshow.com/videos/richard-simmons-personal-story-pt-2.

irrefutable fact is that Elon Musk is an innovator. He's as close to mad genius as we currently have in the world. Full stop. As you already know, I have no interest in discussing anything political, so I'll let others opine about Musk and Twitter. But just swap the Delorean with a Tesla and he is a modern-day Doc Brown from *Back to the Future*. Just to give you an idea of my maturity level, if I could ask him one question, it would be, "Could you please just say '1.21 gigawatts! Great Scott!'" That's all I would need from him.

Today we see Elon Musk the billionaire but what we don't see is the "awkward and introverted kid" as he is described in the biography by Ashlee Vance, *Elon Musk: Tesla, SpaceX, and the Quest for a Fantastic Future*. I imagine him to have been similar to Corey Haim's character in the incredibly underrated 1986 film, *Lucas,* which is about the trials and tribulations of a socially awkward, super brilliant, and inept 14-year-old who spends his days catching insects with his butterfly net so he can look at them and then let them go. At one point, Lucas (played by Corey Haim) is hoping to win over his crush, who is a football cheerleader, by suggesting the following for a date: "We can collect tadpoles tomorrow." That just feels so teenage Musk.

■■■■■■■■■■■■■■■■■■■■■■■■■■■■■■

⚓ FUN FACT: Lucas was the film debut for Winona Ryder, Courtney Thorne-Smith, and Jeremy Piven. All three went on to have successful careers but '80s movies would not have been as totally awesome without Ryder as she added her talents to two '80s classics — *Heathers* and *Beetlejuice* – as well as two early '90s movies that most definitely feel '80s with *Reality Bites* and *Edward Scissorhands*. I love all four of these movies. Oh, and for those who may not have known her from the '80s/'90s, then you just might know her as Joyce Byers in a little-known TV series *set* in the '80s — *Stranger Things*.

■■■■■■■■■■■■■■■■■■■■■■■■■■■■■■

Surely, I don't know a lot about teenage Musk or modern-day Musk, beyond what we read in the news. But I do know that he's created revolutionary change in two industries that have lacked major innovation for a long time: automobiles and space travel. Musk has invited us to ask questions that we'd before considered, like "Why do cars and trucks only work with fossil fuels? And why do we just use our rockets once when we send them to space?" Fast forward to 2021 and Tesla, the electric car company chaired by Musk, has sold over 2,000,000 electric cars, which makes it the global leader. Ford is 117 years old, Chevrolet is 110 years old, and Honda is 75 years old, and it took Tesla and Elon Musk less than 20 years to move the industry forward.[28] In October 2021, Tesla also reached a $1 trillion market capitalization and is only the sixth company to do so in U.S. history.[29]

When it comes to space exploration, Musk has found a way to create reusable rockets that come back from space, landing where they were launched and has put us on the cusp of civilian space travel to Mars. He's also begun digging tunnels for underground hyperloop travel in major cities that may have started with a simple tweet in 2016 that said, "Traffic is driving me nuts. Am going to build a tunnel-boring machine and just start digging" — thus proving that being illogical (and maybe frustrated) is the real mother of invention.

And the "creativity from the craziness of the illogical" comes in so many forms and from all walks of life. Lady Gaga started life as Stefani Joanne Angelina Germanotta. She dropped out of music school, couldn't get a second look at any acting auditions in New York and finally got a bit part on an MTV reality prank show called *Boiling Points*, which she parlayed into her current status as quite possibly the biggest star on planet Earth. And I think we

---

28 Mark Kane, "Tesla Sold 2 Million Electric Cars: First Automaker To Reach Milestone," *Inside EVs*, October 21, 2021, https://insideevs.com/news/542197/tesla-sold-2000000-electric-cars/.

29 "Tesla, Inc.," *Wikipedia*, Last Edited September 8, 2022, https://en.wikipedia.org/wiki/Tesla,_Inc.

can all agree that much of her creation comes from craziness or chaos. Now we do need to separate the voice from the character. Her voice is majestic and magical. Some of the notes she hits literally leave me breathless. Her voice just cements the fact that having to create a character — the Lady Gaga character — to be noticed and find fame is definitely Illogical. Oh, and my mom loved her, so she was going to be in my 3rd book somewhere no matter what.[30]

Now I am certainly not advocating for anyone to try and replicate this feat and it may not link up with all of the other examples here, but it is most definitely illogical. Dock Ellis, a major league baseball pitcher for over a decade, threw a no hitter while tripping on LSD. Just to put it in perspective there have been just 341 no hitters in the history of baseball dating all the way back to the inaugural year in 1869. During that time there have been 234,095 games played which means a no hitter occurs .00145 of the time. And Dock Ellis threw one while tripping on Acid. Illogical.[31]

The Wright Brothers had their first flight with an aircraft in 1903. I fly a lot and it still seems incredibly illogical to me so I can only imagine what people thought on that beach near Kitty Hawk, NC, watching those kooky and very unsafe brothers attempt to put that mechanical machine in the air.

Every small business owner is illogical. Ask them. They will tell you. It is absolutely illogical to lay your head on the pillow each night wondering if the next day will bring the business necessary to pay your bills and keep a roof over your head. It's mental chaos, but from it comes creativity and every small business owner will tell you that they wouldn't have it any other way.

---

30 "Lady Gaga," *Wikipedia*, Last Edited September 7, 2022, https://en.wikipedia.org/wiki/Lady_Gaga.

31 https://en.wikipedia.org/wiki/Dock_Ellis and https://www.baseball-reference.com/leagues/index.shtml

Every small business owner is illogical. Ask them. They will tell you.

And the earth is illogical and most certainly chaotic. I mean think about it. Trillions of rocks floating around in space and ours has intelligent life. Maybe there's another rock like ours but at the moment there's no factual proof unless, of course, you go down the *Ancient Aliens* rabbit hole, which I do not recommend. I've been there. It's fascinating but about as unbelievable as the fact that parachute pants, Members Only jackets and Drakkar Noir cologne were paired together as a legitimate outfit in the '80s.

So much about our lives are prescribed, rigid, boring, "logical." And I contend that the logical path isn't always the best path. So go ahead — do that illogical thing you've been thinking about. Logical is Cameron Frye. *Illogical* is Ferris Bueller. Which one sounds more fun to you?

***

Now, what else can we learn from a Hollywood hit about base-ball? Oh, so much! *Field of Dreams* is about magical moments. It reminds us that:

The moments in our life are like snowflakes. None are the same. Embrace each one. You'll look back one day and realize that they were all significant in their own way.

He may not have been the mainest (my made-up word) of main characters in *Field of Dreams* but he did have a totally awesome nickname — Dr. Archibald "Moonlight" Graham — and he did deliver some of the most inspirational lines in the movie. One of my favorites that's worthy of repeating: "We just don't recognize life's most significant moments while they're happening. Back then I thought, 'Well, there'll be other days.' I didn't realize that was the only day."

Graham was a real person (not just a movie character) and his nickname Moonlight was given to him because he was supposedly "fast as a flash." He played two innings of professional baseball and never had an at-bat, as he was on deck when the player at-bat made the 3rd out, ending the inning. He went on to become a medical doctor for 44 years in Chisholm, Minnesota, and was known for his generosity, including giving away eyeglasses to children in need and free medical care to families who could not afford to pay. In real life, he was actually a pretty incredible person — totally awesome, in '80s terms.[32]

"We don't recognize life's most significant moments while they're happening," the Hollywood version of Dr. Graham said. And he was right. So, let's talk about moments. Fair warning: This portion of the book is going to be the most personal for me, and I'm imagining that it will be cathartic for me to write about it. I know you're accustomed to my personal stories being pure shenanigans and lots of fun. My significant moments of late — my unique snowflakes in time — have been bittersweet. You see, 2021 was the most difficult year for me personally and, unlike most people, those difficulties had nothing to do with the COVID. In March of 2021, my stepmom, a healthy and active 78-year-old, was diagnosed with pancreatic cancer. Just weeks later, on April 16, 2021, she died. We barely had time to say goodbye.

---

32 Jimmy Keenan, "Moonlight Graham," Society for American Baseball Research, Last revised August 13, 2022, https://sabr.org/bioproj/person/moonlight-graham/.

And then on July 5, 2021, my mom passed away after battling Alzheimer's disease for several years. With my mom in Baltimore and me in South Florida, I was fortunate to be able to drive up on several occasions to spend a few weeks at a time with her. I chose to drive, rather than fly, so I could bring my rescue pitbull mix, Bodhi, with me. My mom was a huge animal advocate and lover of dogs, and I wanted her to meet my dog before she passed. And because neither I nor my sister have kids, Bodhi was my mom's only grandkid. The first time she met him, my mom was heading downhill rapidly and he sensed it, as dogs often do. We walked up to her bed, I put my hand on hers, and he put his head on both of our hands. Even though her eyes were closed, she smiled slightly, and asked if that was Bodhi on her hand. He licked her hand, she touched his nose, and then she went back to sleep. I left her bedroom for a few minutes and when I came back in, he was laying on the floor next to her bed, keeping watch over her. When I walked up, he sat up and put his head on the side of her bed. These were significant moments.

Bodhi meeting my mom for the first time, shortly before she passed.
Walked into her room and put his head on her hand.

Although I wasn't there for my stepmom's passing in April, I was able to fly home to spend the last day and evening with my mom in July. The backdrop was surreal, as it was the evening of the 4th of July and the skyline was lit up beautifully with every conceivable color — fireworks raining down across her neighborhood and the nation. People were laughing in their backyards, music playing, enjoying family. My stepdad, my sister, and I could smell hamburgers, hot dogs, and patriotic American BBQ cuisine. A red, white, and blue smorgasbord of Americana filled every one of our senses and, under normal circumstances, we would have partaken in all of it. But our mom was dying. Her breathing was becoming more shallow. We told her that it was okay to let go as we talked to her about all the significant moments that we had shared together throughout her wonderful life. The lights and the sounds of the fireworks came bursting through her bedroom windows — greens, reds, blues, yellows — and you could sense that she could see and feel them. We told her that there was a huge celebration in her honor all over the neighborhood and even though she wasn't communicating any longer, I could hear her laughing and saying, "Stop it, Christopher. You are so ridiculous sometimes." And then at 4:00 a.m., she was gone. That was it. No more significant moments. No more other days. Our mom had passed.

I'm no stranger to loss. Before losing my mom and my stepmom, I lost my two best friends — one at 23 and one at 38. These were the guys who I was going to grow old with. The guys who would share rocking chairs with me on a porch somewhere in the middle of nowhere. But that isn't going to happen. (Unless they want to scare the hell out of me and rock the empty chairs to either side of me on that porch. I wouldn't put it past them, actually, and I kind of hope they do.)

What I'm thankful for is that I did have a lot of significant moments with my mom, my stepmom, and my two best friends — Chris and Dexter. Unfortunately, with the latter three, they were taken from us so quickly and without warning, I didn't realize that my recent moments with them were as significant as they were until much later. I assumed there would be more moments. With my mom, I was able to reminisce while she was still with us and reach into that catalogue of significant moments so we could share them together one last time.

Disney World with my mom, circa 1976.

Significant moments don't have to be life changing events, like graduations, births, marriages, career accomplishments, or wrecking your mom's car trying to jump railroad tracks with your aforementioned best friends. (That last one wasn't life changing, but it was significant because we did get airborne for a second or two.) In actuality, the most significant moments are sometimes the ones that wouldn't necessarily end up in a scrapbook of life highlights. Moments like when my sister and I made a bumper sticker with Neil Diamond on it that said "Honk if you love Neil." My sister and I love Neil Diamond, and Mom loathed him. We put the bumper sticker on her car, and it was there for over a month before she found it. She kept calling us saying, "People are so rude. They keep honking at me for no reason. I stop at a red light and people keep honking at me. I'm parking and they are honking at me. I'm stuck in traffic and they are honking at me. I'm a good driver. Why do they keep honking at me? So rude." I'm laughing as I write this because my mom was such a patient and gentle soul, but she was so frustrated at the honking. I don't think she talked to me or my sister for a few weeks after she found the sticker.

There's so much to say about my mom. I could write a whole book on her life. So many significant moments and she was such an interesting character. She loved being a teacher and spent years teaching English as a second language (ESL); she loved all animals and taught us the importance of rescuing and saving as many as possible; she loved March Madness and how the kids played their hearts out; she loved the movie *Sixteen Candles* and was convinced that I was just like Farmer Ted in high school; she loved *The Big Bang Theory* and the character Stuart; she was fascinated by space and the size of the universe; one of her favorite songs was "Insane in the Membrane" by Cypress Hill ... yes, you read that correctly; and she loved Lady Gaga. We never got a chance to take her to a Lady Gaga concert, but Mom will always be a Little Monster, which is how Lady Gaga refers to her hardcore fans. We had a graveside service, and we recited these lyrics from Lady Gaga's, "Born this Way":

> *"I'm beautiful in my way*
> *'Cause God makes no mistakes.*
> *I'm on the right track, baby.*
> *I was born this way."*

That was her.

One of my favorite life quotes comes from an '80s movie. (Shocking, I know.) Ferris Bueller says, "Life moves pretty fast. If you don't stop to look around once in a while, you could miss it." It really does. The significant moments may not seem significant at the time, but there are no other days or moments that will be the same as the one that is happening right now. They really are like snowflakes. None are the same. Embrace them, particularly with the ones you love. Memories are great, but moments are better. Memories can't replace the present. Make sure to recognize the significant moments while they are happening. They won't happen again.

Field of Dreams is a masterclass in what it means to take a risk, consequences be damned. For a life to be truly lived, it needs to have a bit of risk. And it needs to be full of beautiful moments, precious and unique and fleeting as snowflakes. I'll leave you with these words from James Earl Jones's character, Terrance Mann, when he is contemplating accepting the invitation to go into the cornfield with the ballplayers as they disappear for the evening: "There is something out there, Ray, and if I have the courage to go through with this, what a story it'll make."

Be courageous. Your story is most certainly out there.

CHAPTER 8

ROAD HOUSE

"Nobody ever wins a fight."

— DALTON, *ROAD HOUSE*

F or those of you who don't know, *Road House* stars Patrick Swayze. I love Patrick Swayze, as you already know. I even have a St. Patrick's Day shirt that says *Happy St. Patrick Swayze Day* with an illustration of Swayze pointing forward and saying, "Ditto." Yes, you need one too.

Now, how many of you reading this book have seen the television series *Cobra Kai*? If you haven't, and you are a fan of the '80s, you need to put it on your binge-watching list. After you've read *this* book, of course. The reason I mention *Cobra Kai* at the beginning of the chapter for *Road House* is because I believe one of the reasons that '80s pop culture continues to resonate is that it wasn't always perfectly polished and packaged before it was released to the public. Today's pop culture — and, in particular, the movies — is beautifully packaged to eliminate any potential flaw. Everything is perfect and while that makes for an enhanced viewing experience, it also doesn't allow the room for authenticity, realness, and the raw nature of old-school storytelling. And, of course, if I am being honest and not totally '80s biased, it also doesn't have that little bit of after-school special and/or cheesy feel that some '80s movies were known for a little more than others.

Cobra Kai is the perfect balance of authenticity and cheesy. It has totally awesome and grody-to-the-max '80s oozing out of every conceivable pore and so does *Road House*. Of course, as we do with every chapter, we will get much deeper into the movie as we move forward. And no genuine '80s-movie time capsule would be complete without a copy of *Road House*. Not for anything groundbreaking in its storytelling or special effects and certainly not for the awards that it won (it didn't win any). It owns a place in that time capsule because it was so perfectly and authentically "raw and cheesy '80s" in every aspect — from the characters to the fashion to the story and dialogue. Oh, and it starred Patrick Swayze in the main role as a nightclub bouncer named Dalton. "Swayze" equals "spot in the time capsule."

I believe that the best lessons for life and the workplace come from the most unexpected of places.

In my books, I try to find lessons from characters, quotes, and sometimes movies that are unexpected. I believe that the best lessons for life and the workplace come from the most unexpected of places. A nightclub bouncer with a degree from NYU

in philosophy (!) who makes a living throwing people out of
a roadside bar in Jasper, Missouri, is the definition of an unexpected character to learn from ... but learn we most certainly do.

■■■■■■■■■■■■■■■■■■■■■■■■■■■■■■■■

FUN FACT: Jasper is a real town in Missouri with
a population of just under 1,000 people. Although
the Double Deuce is not a real bar in Jasper and the
film was shot in California, the Jasper Chamber of
Commerce members were invited to the premiere
of the film in St. Louis, MO.

■■■■■■■■■■■■■■■■■■■■■■■■■■■■■■■■

Our life and our workplace can both be complex at times. Some of
it is out of our control while other times we create the complexities through overthinking and our desire to thread the proverbial needle perfectly. If we could just remember one of the first
acronyms most of us were taught in elementary school — K.I.S.S.
— "keep it simple, stupid." Not sure they use that anymore, but it
works for our purposes here today.

Dalton is hired to be the head of the bouncers, which in bar
talk is called the "cooler" (and that sounds much cooler). Head
bouncers are incredibly level-headed and look first to cool things
off or cool people down but make no mistake — they are always
the most bad-ass guy on the staff and usually in the entire bar.
One cooler who I worked with when I was bouncing was a Navy
Seal named Brian. He'd pretty much seen everything, and he was
the nicest and calmest guy you could ever meet. Every so often,
someone with what we called "beer muscles" would ignore his
multiple warnings, probably because his approach was so calm,
understanding, and gentle. But when it came time for Mr. Beer
Muscles to leave and they still refused, it was a sight to behold.
They knew they were in trouble after the first move, but it was
already too late. Kind of like when Bruce Lee or Chuck Norris
took their fighting stance and their opponent in the movie quickly

realized that this was not going to end well. Brian never hurt anyone too badly. He just did what he needed to do to get them away from the person they were harassing and out of the bar into the hands of the cops, who were usually outside on the street somewhere in the downtown area. And then he would stroll back in and take his place at the bar where he could continue to calmly observe the ridiculousness that would most surely ensue.

The Double Deuce in *Road House* had a cooler-than-a-cucumber "cooler" too. Now when Dalton introduces himself to the team, he has three simple rules. He says:

> "All you have to do is follow three simple rules. One, never underestimate your opponent. Expect the unexpected. Two, take it outside. Never start anything inside the bar unless it is absolutely necessary. And three, be nice."

Depending on their self-perceived strengths or weaknesses, each of the bouncers may have focused on different aspects of Dalton's leadership chat with the group, but the main lesson that we should all take away is this:

Simplicity rules.

The Double Deuce has hit rock bottom and is an absolute disaster of a bar. And by "disaster," I don't mean those disgustingly sticky floors and overflowing-bathroom type bars that many of us frequented in our 20s. Cody, the blind musician for the house band (played by Jeff Healey) says to Dalton when he first arrives, "Oh, man. It's a mean scene around here, man. There's blood on the floor of this joint every night." After observing a few nights first hand, Dalton calls it a "slaughterhouse" — and this from a guy who has seen his share of rowdy joints.

After one of Dalton's first official nights running the bouncer team (as "the cooler"), Frank Tilghman — the guy who hired him to clean up the mess — says: "Well, it was a good night.

Nobody died." To which Dalton replies: "It will get worse before it gets better."

Frank nods in agreement, letting Dalton know that he understands the rebuilding process that they have ahead of them. It's also an acknowledgment of the trust he has in Dalton to "right the ship." Dalton saying it will get worse is his way of letting Frank know that rebuilds are never easy and that trusting the process requires trusting the person, which is true in life and in the workplace. Let me say that again, in bite-sized "lesson" format:

Trusting the process requires trusting the person.

■■■■■■■■■■■■■■■■■■■■■■■■■■■■■■■■■

⌨ FUN FACT: Musician Jeff Healey didn't just play a blind musician — he was blind in real life. He lost his sight at the age of one due to retinoblastoma. He began playing guitar at three and formed his first band at age 15. He went on to lead The Jeff Healey Band, whose biggest hit was "Angel Eyes" off the album *See the Light*, which also included his Grammy-nominated song "Hideaway." Throughout his career, he toured with everyone from BB King to ZZ Top to The Allman Brothers.[33]

■■■■■■■■■■■■■■■■■■■■■■■■■■■■■■■■■

Before we learn how to really handle ourselves in a bar fight (with words, of course!), let's jump in this time-traveling phone booth à la Bill and Ted and travel back in time to May of 1989 one more time.

---

33 "Jeff Healey," *Wikipedia*, Last Edited August 23, 2022, https://en.wikipedia.org/wiki/Jeff_Healey.

My Life in May 1989

If you read the preceding chapter about *Field of Dreams*, you
know that I was finishing up my freshman year of college in 1989
and had a little incident with a water-balloon slingshot. While
I was on the lam from campus security, I was also preparing to
spend another summer living in Ocean City, MD, with friends in
what was — in the words of the band Warrant at the beginning
of their 1989 smash hit "Cherry Pie" — a "dirty, rotten, filthy,
stinkin'" dump of a beach place.

My three summer roommates had finished school about
two weeks before me and planned to head down early to get
a jumpstart on the summer. Because we were college students
and the summer months were prime rental months, we were
required to pay two of the three months upfront. This was standard in Ocean City, MD, at the time and, looking back as an
adult and property owner, I can certainly understand why they
structured the contracts this way. College-age kids aren't exactly
known to be the most responsible tenants and most of us were
not known for our tidiness. Just the thought of what my bedroom
looked like that summer makes me want to vomit, like the *Stand
by Me* blueberry pie barf-o-rama scene vomit. That was so gross
and so was my room. But this story isn't about my no-good,
horrible, disgusting bedroom during my 19th year on this planet.
Because of my three knucklehead friends, I almost didn't even get
the chance to sleep in that stink-bomb of a room.

■■■■■■■■■■■■■■■■■■■■■■■■■■■■■■■■

🕹 **FUN FACT:** During my junior year
of high school, I acquired a handful of
super-strong-smelling stink-bombs. The liquid
came in a little glass container and when you
broke the glass — or whatever it was — the liquid
dissolved, leaving no trace of said stink-bomb. On
the package, they promised that it would clear

out a room with a "horrible rotten-egg smell" and boy did it deliver on that promise. I broke one open in the cafeteria during lunch and hundreds of students and faculty cleared out as fast as the Cabbage Patch kids on shelves at toy stores during that crazy 1983 Christmas. I was ratted out, but that's a story for another day.

■ ■

Brian White, 20, of Baltimore, above, listens to tapes in the O.C. apartment he shares with fellow Baltimoreans Chris Clews, 20, foreground at left, and Mark Mitchell, 20, background.

Summer 1989 (which was a whole lot like the summer of 1988). Me with two of my Ocean City roommates, featured in a newspaper article about kids living at the beach for the summer.

The rent for the summer was $1,800 a person so each of us had to pony up $1,200 (two of the three months) before we could move in. That was a lot of money for 19-year-old college kids in 1989 and none of us came from wealthy families. Since OnlyFans didn't exist yet, we had to get creative. My approach was to convince my mom to lay out the deposit for me with an agreement that I would pay her back each week from my tips that

I would make as a bellman. She agreed because, well, my mom was awesome. And just like that, my spot was secure in the "dirty, rotten, filthy, stinkin'" dump of a beach place.

So, with my spot secure, I continued my time on the lam from campus security while my buddies moved into our place on 4th Street in Ocean City, Maryland. They arrived and settled in two weeks before I was scheduled to get there. Now, OC (as we called Ocean City), was known for its parties. Really big, *huge* parties. I'd been to plenty over the previous two summers and saw how hundreds of kids would find a way to cram them-selves into a 1,200-square-foot apartment with a balcony big enough to hold five or six people. It was pretty spectacular, and so was the damage to the apartment that was typically visible by morning.

Fast forward a week later and my discipline had been doled out for the water-balloon slingshot incident on campus. My room-mate yelled down the hall, "Clews, phone call for you."

Me: "Hello."

Mom: "Christopher, it's your mom." *The full first name. This was not good.*

Me: "Hey Mom, what's up?" I was trying to sound noncha-lant, knowing the school must have called her about the water-balloon slingshot.

Mom: "Your friends threw a party at the Ocean City apart-ment. A big party. The landlord called me and apparently there was damage, and the police were called. They are keeping the deposit that I paid and kicking you all out." She said it matter-of-factly.

My first thought was "Why didn't they wait for *me* to throw the party?" and my second thought was "Those idiots." If there was one thing about my friends, they didn't do anything small, and I was pretty sure there was no coming back from this one.

> **Me:** "Mom, I didn't know they were going to throw a party. Honestly, I didn't. Let me make a few calls and see what is going on."

> **Mom:** "Okay, and I know that you didn't know. But that's a lot of money wasted. I hope it was worth it. And *you're* the one who none of the other parents trust. Ha!"

> **Me:** "What? What do you mean by that?"

> **Mom:** "Christopher, you know. Mr. Water-Balloon Hotshot, slingshot, whatever, I love you regardless."

> **Me:** "I have no idea what you are talking about. Water balloon what? Love you too." I hung up the phone quickly.

So, yes, my friends did throw a party. A huge *Weird Science*-style house party in an apartment minus the nuclear missile, grandparents catatonic in the closet, and the killer mutants on motorcycles (at least I *think* so, but I wasn't there!). Ultimately, we did get everything worked out with the landlord and we were able to spend our summer in the "dirty, rotten, filthy, stinkin'" dump of a beach place and I did pay my mom back for the deposit. The other guys had to do a little handyperson work on the apartment as part of the agreement with the landlord and, for the rest of the summer, we just *attended* parties rather than throwing them. It wasn't the "Summer of '69." It was the Summer of '89 but as Bryan Adams sang:

> *"Oh, when I look back now,*
> *The summer seemed to last forever.*
> *And if had the choice,*
> *Yeah, I'd always wanna be there.*
> *Those were the best days of my life ..."*

I could not agree more, Mr. Adams.

Pop Culture in the Summer of '89

The beginning of that summer, the Top 40 music charts were delivering songs for dancing, air guitar, and rapping by yourself in your shower or car. Living Colour, Guns N' Roses, Warrant, and The Cult (one of my all-time favorites) all delivered on the air guitar front with "Cult of Personality," "Patience," "Down Boys," and "Fire Woman," respectively. Bobby Brown, Paula Abdul, Madonna, and Stevie B got people out on the dance floor (for better or worse in the '80s) with "Every Little Step," "Forever Your Girl," "Like a Prayer," and "In Your Eyes." Oh, and even a group that won Grammys without even singing, Milli Vanilli, got people cabbage-patching with "Baby Don't Forget My Number." I mean, honestly, their music was fun and catchy, you have to admit. And LL Cool J, Tone Loc, De La Soul, and the super-underrated Neneh Cherry had us all thinking we had a rap career ahead of us (we didn't) with "I'm That Type of Guy," "Funky Cold Medina," "Me, Myself and I," and "Buffalo Stance." Oh, and this little flash-in-the-pan group, Beastie Boys (insert sarcasm), dropped their classic hip-hop album, *Paul's Boutique*, toward the end of July. I'd also be remiss if I didn't mention that one of my favorite songs from the '80s, "Send Me an Angel" by Real Life, was on the charts for a short time that summer. It was a remix of the same song they released originally in 1983, which was also on the soundtrack of the totally awesome 1986 BMX movie, *Rad*.

On July 5th in the summer of '89, television gave us the pilot episode of what would go down as one of the greatest sitcoms in history with the launch of *Seinfeld*. That alone would pretty much be enough to make it one of the great summers in television but on August 20th, we also saw a show grace our screens that was previously called *Good Morning Miss Bliss* relaunch as *Saved by the Bell*. CBS aired a pilot of a proposed adaption of the 1988 comedy classic *Coming to America,* which, if you are wondering, has some great leadership lessons from Prince Akeem. And even though *Miami Vice* ended its magnificent run on May 21st, NBC broadcast three "lost episodes" throughout the month of June.

For me and my knuckleheaded friends, that summer was full of events that shall not be mentioned so it was appropriate that at the box office, two comedic giants, Richard Pryor and Gene Wilder, were sitting in the top five with *See No Evil, Hear No Evil.* Sequels were all the rage with *Karate Kid III, Lethal Weapon 2, Ghostbusters 2,* and *Friday the 13th Part VIII,* all hoping for another bite at the box office apple. One of the most important movies of the decade, *Do the Right Thing,* was doing its thing at the box office across the country. And a romantic comedy famous for its "I'll have what she's having" scene inside of a diner, *When Harry Met Sally,* was wildly popular with moviegoers.

But it was a movie about a bouncer that debuted on May 19, 1989, that is the premise for this chapter. *Road House* — starring Patrick Swayze, Kelly Lynch, Ben Gazzara, and Sam Elliott (who has not aged and has the 2nd-best mustache in Hollywood behind Mr. Magnum P.I. himself, Tom Selleck) — tells the story of a bouncer hired to clean up a rough-and-tumble bar, The Double Deuce, purchased by an entrepreneur in Jasper, Missouri.

Life Lessons from *Road House*

First, the movie's hero isn't just an ordinary bouncer. Dalton (played by Patrick Swayze) is a hired gun with a mysterious past and a reputation for being able to clean up the rowdiest of places, helping to turn them into legitimate, violence-free watering holes. He meets the Doc (played by Kelly Lynch) when he goes to the hospital to close a knife wound that needs staples after a bar fight and promptly waves off the numbing agent with a classic line — "Pain don't hurt." Only the '80s would give us a line like that and only Patrick Swayze could deliver it. Doc's connections in the little town of Jasper run deep but you'll have to watch the movie to find out more. Brad Wesley (played by Ben Gazzara) is the ultimate '80s wealthy bad guy with his own helicopter and who dresses like Crockett and Tubbs from *Miami Vice*. He doesn't want any competition from "outsiders" and wants the town to remain the same, so he can continue to lord over everyone. To bring order to The Double Deuce — both with the bouncers and the patrons — Dalton brings in an old bouncer friend named Wade Garrett (played by Sam Elliott).

As I mentioned in the intro, *Road House* is the perfect '80s movie and well worth every single re-watch on AMC. So, what can a few bouncers tasked with cleaning up a "slaughterhouse" of a bar in Jasper, Missouri, teach us about our life and our workplace?

 ## Simplicity rules.

How many times in your life or in your workplace have you said to yourself or others, "Why do things have to be so complicated?" If you're like me, then you've said it more than once. So, what was your answer? Hmmm ... I'll bet in all the times you've asked it, you haven't really answered that question and if you did, it was a frustrating rant instead of a productive epiphany. I mean let's be honest, when things are unnecessarily complicated, it will make anyone frustrated; yet we do it all the time — choosing to create or build or perpetuate systems and rules that are unnecessarily complicated. And sometimes it's out of our control, like when we receive our 150-page new employee manual or pretty much anytime we call customer service and have to navigate through an unending tree of "press 1 for this and 4 for that and, oh, 5 for that." With those automated phone systems, the worst is when you think you can skip it by pressing zero but it's not an option and the kind generic voice says, "Sorry that's not an option. Thanks for calling." Click. Or you say "representative" at the beginning, but it keeps insisting "I just need a bit more information to get you to the right person" or, worse yet, the ones that say, "Sorry, I don't understand. Please call back again later." Okay, now I'm getting frustrated just thinking about it and I imagine you are as well. See what complicated can do when you just *think* about something that is complicated? You don't even have to be involved in the action at the time. Just getting in your head-space is enough.

How many times in your life or in your workplace have you said to yourself or others, "Why do things have to be so complicated?"

Tips for dealing with life's complications can come from anywhere, but I love it when they come from a movie like *Road House*. When Dalton comes to town and takes over the bouncer crew, he calls a team meeting and says this:

> "All you have to do is follow three simple rules. One, never underestimate your opponent. Expect the unexpected. Two, take it outside. Never start anything inside the bar unless it is absolutely necessary. And three, be nice."

Seems simple enough, right? Not a lot of room for misunderstanding. He's clear, concise, and straightforward.

Now bouncers being bouncers, they of course like to challenge anything and anyone. I should know because I spent several stints as a bouncer at bars in Orlando and Fort Lauderdale. Again, a story for another day. (Many stories, actually!) One of Dalton's bouncers challenges him on one of his rules, which prompts this exchange:

"I want you to be nice until it's time *not* to be
nice," says Dalton

"Well, how do we know when that time is?" one of the
bouncers asks.

"I'll let you know," Dalton answers.

Simple question. Simple answer. For those of you who
have been in the workforce for any amount of time, the
simple-question-begets-simple answer scenario is as rare as the
DJ not talking over the first 20 seconds of the song you wanted
to record, back in the day, for a very important mix tape. Why
did they do that?! I don't want to hear the radio-smooth voice of
Vinnie "Vibes" on "your station for today's hits." I want to hear
the entirety of "Nite and Day" by Al B. Sure! and so does my crush
who I'm making the mix tape for — at least I hope she does. Sigh.
Automated phone systems in the 2020s and chatty DJs in the
1980s. Am I right?

Okay, because we can all use the peace and productivity that
happens when you slay the complications, let's breakdown
Dalton's simple rules for life and the workplace outside of the bar
scene. Rule #1:

Never underestimate your opponent. Expect the unexpected.

Can you think of a time in your life when you underestimated
someone or something and were proved wrong in a very real way?
Maybe you had a pre-judgement based on something silly like
someone's appearance or perceived lack of experience. Maybe
you didn't work hard enough beforehand. Or maybe, like so many
before you who were surprised and defeated by a "lesser" challenger or challenge, you allowed your confidence to be overtaken
by arrogance.

A life truly lived will be rife with mistakes — and hopefully *growth*
through those mistakes. Oh wait, you've never made a mistake?

Oh, well, then in the words of Enid Strict, better known as the Church Lady from SNL, "Well, isn't that special." The rest of us mere mortals have made plenty of mistakes, and some have been self-inflicted mistakes like choosing to underestimate someone or something.

A life truly lived will be rife with mistakes — and hopefully growth through those mistakes.

A common theme in '80s movies was the character in a "better position" (more wealth, more popularity, etc.) underestimating their opponent and ultimately paying the price — whether it was the loss of a job, status, power, or their life. Dozens of movies — including *Revenge of the Nerds*, *The Lost Boys*, *9 to 5*, *Working Girl*, *Rocky III*, and *Red Dawn* had this as a direct theme or one that was underlying within the overall story. I don't want to start any "Blasphemous Rumors" (as Depeche Mode sang in 1984) and I know this may feel like sacrilege to us '80s kids, but one of the best scenes for representing this message came from an early '90s classic: *White Men Can't Jump,* starring Woody Harrelson and Wesley Snipes as two great basketball players who make their living hustling guys out of their money on basketball courts around their city. At one point in the movie, Wesley Snipes's character, Sidney, bets two guys $500 that he can beat them — with the kicker being that they get to choose his teammate. Woody Harrelson's character, Billy, stands out quite a bit, sitting on the bleachers watching the guys play as he is dressed in a tie-dyed hologram hat that looks like Marty McFly's from *Back to the Future,* combined with a cut-off sweatshirt and what looks like swim trunks with palm-tree patterns. The exchange goes like this:

Sidney: "$500, baby, and you can pick my teammate."

Opponent: (Pointing at Billy) "Give him the chump."

Billy: "You mean play basketball?"

Sidney and Billy win their $500 easily, much to the chagrin of the guys who have been hustled. It's a quick study in underestimating your opponent and a very good one at that.

One of the most widely circulated business stories around underestimating your opponent is Bill Gates and IBM. Because the story is a complicated web of fact, fiction, hearsay, and tech-speak and because this lesson is about simplicity, let me just point out that the ease with which IBM gave a young Gates the keys to the kingdom is quite remarkable. In essence, they asked him to build an operating system (OS) for them, which he had never done. He referred them to a friend who couldn't come to an agreement with IBM, so they came back to Gates — who then purchased an OS from Seattle Computers for $50,000 and subsequently told IBM that if they want it, they must agree to a non-exclusive royalty agreement. Well, they did ... and the rest is history. IBM was holding all the cards. Gates had absolutely no leverage. They could have said that the agreement had to be exclusive, or they could have offered him a very big check for the OS; but they didn't, and the history of their companies — and the world — were changed forever. They totally underestimated him and let their confidence turn to arrogance and it almost buried them as a company.[34]

We've already talked about two tech tycoons now in this book and because this lesson is from a movie whose main characters are brawlers (and not techies), let's shift our focus now to two boxers and their match in Tokyo on February 11, 1990. Billed as *Tyson*

---

34 Chris Hladczuk, "When Bill Gates 'got lucky' with IBM deal: The hidden story," October 11, 2021, https://nextbigwhat.com/when-bill-gates-got-lucky-with-ibm-deal-the-hidden-story/.

is Back!, the match between Mike Tyson and Buster Douglas was expected to be — as HBO boxing analysts, Larry Merchant, and Jim Lampley said, "a 90-second annihilation." Of course, they could back that up with the fact that Buster Douglas was a 42-1 underdog. The odds were *not* "ever in his favor."[35]

For the purposes of this lesson, we are going to focus on Tyson the champion fighter and not Tyson the man (which would be a very different conversation). Mike Tyson was the undisputed, undefeated heavyweight champion of the world and held all three belts — World Boxing Council (WBC), World Boxing Association (WBA) and International Boxing Federation (IBF). He was 37-0 with 33 knockouts and his most recent fight against Carl "The Truth" Williams lasted all of 93 seconds before Tyson knocked him out. He was, as he said himself, "The baddest man on the planet" and is arguably the greatest boxer of all time, although if you walked into the My-T-Sharp barbershop from *Coming to America*, a few guys in there may counter you with Joe Louis, Muhammad Ali, or Rocky Marciano. It's a fun debate but it's not why we are here today. Tyson won 19 of his first 22 fights by knockout with 12 of them coming in the first round. That is just unheard of. And he was the youngest boxer to ever claim a heavyweight belt at age 20 years, 4 months, and 22 days.[36] He even made great fighters retire, as was the case with Michael Spinks, who he fought in a heavyweight championship bout in 1987 and knocked out in 91 seconds. Spinks walked away from boxing with a record of 31-1. He was undefeated before meeting Tyson.

On the other hand, although Buster Douglas was ranked as the #7 heavyweight, he was a journeyman of sorts. A journeyman is a boxer who makes the rounds (no pun intended) taking fights

---

35 "Mike Tyson vs. Buster Douglas," *Wikipedia*, Last Edited September 5, 2022, https://en.wikipedia.org/wiki/Mike_Tyson_vs._Buster_Douglas.

36 "Mike Tyson," Wikipedia, Last Edited August 30, 2022, https://en.wikipedia.org/wiki/Mike_Tyson.

as needed and as asked. They typically have an above-average win/loss record that keeps them in the game, but they are not normally a threat to upend the top fighters — which is why they are often chosen as warm-up fights for contenders or champions before they have a legitimate match later in the year. *Rocky III* took a look at this real-life scenario when Clubber Lang, one my favorite characters from '80s movies, heckled Rocky in front of a crowd of people watching the city of Philadelphia dedicate a statue to Rocky. He points out that Rocky as the champ was dodging Lang, the #1 contender, by fighting "the easy matches, fighting other bums." Douglas was Tyson's warm-up for the ultimate prize, which was a fight with the #1 contender, Evander Holyfield. Buster Douglas had already lost a handful of fights and his best opportunity to make an impression ended in a 10th round TKO (Technical Knock Out) during a title fight against Tony Tucker. But Douglas had now won six straight fights and was presented with the opportunity to fight Mike Tyson — a fight that he would *surely* lose but would provide a nice payday along the way and, little did he know, ultimately etch his name in the annals of sports history.

Douglas was contending with some serious personal issues leading up to the fight, as the mother of his son was battling a severe kidney ailment, his own mom passed away several weeks before the fight, and he came down with the flu the day before he was to step in the ring with Tyson.

When Tyson and Douglas were preparing to square off in Tokyo back in 1990, we had about a 1/1000th of the content options that we have today. Any time that Tyson fought, it was a global event that was reported on from every possible angle. So "set" was Douglas's fate by those in the know that they resorted to talking about the differences in the dogs that they had in their family. Tyson's dog was a white pitbull (my boy Bodhi is a pit mix and he is awesome) named Duran after his idol Roberto Duran, who was a former lightweight, middleweight, light middleweight and welterweight boxing champion. Douglas had a beagle named Shakespeare who was named as such because Douglas loved the play *Romeo and Juliet*. It's likely that the only thing that Tyson and Douglas had in common was that they were professional boxers.

When the two boxers finally stepped in the ring, it was obvious that Douglas had prepared and did not have the fear that so many before him did when they stood in front of Tyson. He had clearly studied Tyson's fighting style and employed a strategy that allowed him to pepper Tyson with jabs over the first few rounds, ultimately causing Tyson's left eye to swell up considerably. Tyson was known for his devastating uppercut and Douglas took that away by keeping Tyson at arm's length with that barrage of jabs.

While Douglas had done his homework (and his training), Tyson seemed incredibly ill-prepared for Douglas's approach. He seemed slow, even timid at times and clearly surprised by the way Douglas had set up his attack. By the third round, it was obvious that the biggest difference between the two was preparation. Tyson's corner and Tyson himself were so confident that he would overpower Douglas quickly and win without any issues that they didn't even bring ice packs or any of the standard tools to alleviate swelling. This would be like a mechanic going to work without a wrench or a cop heading out to their beat without handcuffs or even a business leader trying to do their job without an email address. Having the right tools for the job is absolutely essential. So, when Tyson's eye began to swell shut, they had to resort to filling a rubber glove with ice water between rounds.[37]

Meanwhile, Douglas continued to outfight and outwit Tyson through eight rounds. I can remember watching with a group of friends at a house on our college campus and we were all in disbelief at what was happening. It didn't seem real. For most sports fans, Tyson was immortal and unbeatable and here he was being

---

37 "Mike Tyson vs. Buster Douglas," *Wikipedia*, Last Edited September 5, 2022, https://en.wikipedia.org/wiki/Mike_Tyson_vs._Buster_Douglas.

dismantled before our very eyes by a guy who was a 42-1 longshot. But then Tyson caught Douglas with his signature uppercut and put him on the canvas with about 10 seconds to go in the 8th round. This was it. Balance in the universe was restored and Tyson would escape with a well-earned victory. But to the shock of everyone, Douglas got up and beat the count. The bell rang to end the round and both fighters went to their respective corners.

For most sports fans, Tyson was immortal and unbeatable and here he was being dismantled before our very eyes by a guy who was a 42-1 longshot.

Looking back, those gatherings with my friends are a phenomenon of youth that I really miss. What was on TV didn't matter. When I close my eyes and visualize that Saturday evening, I see 25 guys and girls all hanging out on ratty couches, some sitting on the arms of the couches while others were lying on thin carpet or hardwood floors propping up their heads with their hands. Pretty much everyone had a beer in hand or in front of them. We were all yelling at the television, going crazy with each punch that landed. We had not a care in the world and even after the fight was over, there would be something else to do. I never married and never had kids and, as I sit here writing this chapter at midnight on a Friday with my dog Bodhi sleeping across my feet and no other humans in sight, I really miss that time in my life. Someone was always around to do something with — whether it was 3:00 p.m. or 3:00 a.m.

Okay, before I go too far down that road, let's get back to the fight and our lesson. Douglas survived the 9th round after hitting the canvas in the 8th. And in the 10th round, he dominated Tyson. You could feel the energy from the crowd through the television as he continued to move forward on Tyson, landing every punch he threw. And then it happened. He connected with an uppercut that put Tyson on his back. You could hear the collective screams and the collective silence at the same time all around the globe. It was the modern-day version of Mighty Casey striking out. Tyson had been put into a deep enough sleep that Freddie Krueger was on standby ready to invade his dreams.

■■■■■■■■■■■■■■■■■■■■■■■■■■■■■■■■

FUN FACT: If you've ever seen a movie produced by New Line Cinema — and you probably have (*Lord of the Rings* is just one example) — then you have Freddy Krueger and the 1984 horror classic, *A Nightmare on Elm Street,* to thank. New Line was broke in the early '80s and this was the last film they were going to be able to finance before closing their doors. The budget was a measly $1.1 million and the movie broke even its third day in release, ultimately going on to make more than $57 million at the box office. Since its release in 1984, it has spawned six sequels, a television series, and tons of merchandise.[38] Who knows — maybe Broadway is next?

■■■■■■■■■■■■■■■■■■■■■■■■■■■■■■■■

And then we saw one of the most famous sports images of all time. Tyson trying to stand up, while he searched for his mouthpiece, ultimately finding it on the mat and then putting it back in sideways with one end sticking out of his mouth. Yes, it is cliché, but David had slain Goliath and not because he was the better fighter. Tyson was the greatest fighter on the planet and Douglas was a journeyman, but Douglas was prepared, and Tyson had seriously underestimated him. Douglas brought a solid strategy to

---

38 "A Nightmare on Elm Street," *Wikipedia,* Last Edited September 14, 2022, https://en.wikipedia.org/wiki/A_Nightmare_on_Elm_Street

the fight from the very first ring of the bell. He wasn't the least bit fearful, and Tyson wasn't expecting that. The lesson is so powerful for us all — preparation is everything.

If you really want to know how much Tyson underestimated Douglas, you need look no further than the autobiography of New Edition founding member and '80s solo R&B artist, Bobby Brown. In his autobiography, *Every Little Step: My Story*, he says that he partied with Tyson the night before the fight and that Tyson stayed out super late, ignoring calls for him to go to bed early and get rested for Douglas. He said Douglas was "an amateur that he could beat even if he didn't sleep for five weeks."[39]

It's pretty clear that Tyson didn't see *Road House* before his fight or he may have just heeded Dalton's first rule — "Never underestimate your opponent. Expect the unexpected."

One of the coolest things I got to do while working in corporate marketing was sponsor Ultimate Fighting Championship (UFC) fighters. I really enjoyed my time with them and look back on that experience very fondly. I keep in touch with several of them and four of them became champions — Chris Weidman, Luke Rockhold, Robbie Lawler, and Ryan Bader (who has held both Light Heavyweight and Heavyweight titles in Bellator MMA). They are all incredibly disciplined individuals, extremely approachable, and very unassuming. They don't wear UFC fighter on their sleeve. In my experience, they're just really good dudes and really awesome role models for the kids who look up to them. One freezing night in Chicago, I was out with a few guys, including a UFC fighter at the time. This was pre-Uber, so we were waiting for a cab. It was so cold that it reminded me of the scene in the 1987 classic film, *Planes, Trains and Automobiles*, when Del and Neal are in the back of a pick-up truck, driving through very cold weather when they have this exchange:

39 Bobby Brown and Nick Chiles, *Every Little Step: My Story*, 1ˢᵗ Edition, New York: Dey Street Books, 2016.

Neal: "What do you figure the temperature is?"

Del: "One."

We came out to the cab that pulled up and the passenger in the back was really taking his time paying the cabbie. He was a larger guy, probably 80 to 100 pounds more than the fighter we were with. After literally three minutes of waiting for this guy to pay (while we froze our butts off), our fighter friend knocked on the window. The passenger rolled it down and this exchange ensued:

Passenger: "What!?"

Fighter: "Ah, its' freezing out here and we were hoping that you might be able to finish up so we can get in."

Passenger: "I'll finish when I finish." [He then began to roll up on the window.]

Fighter: [Putting his hand on the window to keep it from rolling up.] "It would be great if you could help us out here, man."

Passenger: "You better move your hand before I move it for you. What are you, some kind of tough guy or something?"

Me: "Well, yeah. He's a UFC fighter so he's kind of tough."

Passenger: [Tone completely changing.] "I knew I recognized you. Man, I'm sorry. Let me get out so you guys can get in. It's so cool to meet you. Get in, get in."

He put his hand out and our fighter friend shook it, gave him a smile, and got in the cab. The guy waved to us as the cabbie drove off.

"Bet he didn't expect that answer to his 'tough guy' question," he said to me.

"No, I think sarcastically calling a UFC fighter a 'tough guy' was definitely an unexpected moment for him this evening," I said.

In life, in sport, and in business, it helps to expect the unexpected (and it helps *you* if your opponent underestimates you). The stories about Bill Gates and Buster Douglas are good reminders. If one of the most successful companies in the world can be gamed by a no-name 20-something computer nerd and if "the baddest man on the planet" can be knocked out by a journeyman with 42-1 odds, any company and anyone can be bested by someone or something that — at face value — doesn't look like a threat. Whether it is in your personal life, your business, or your career, never underestimate your opponent and always expect the unexpected.

Dalton's second rule for his bouncers is our second lesson for this chapter:

Take it outside. Never start anything inside the bar unless it is absolutely necessary.

How many of you have said something in "the heat of the moment?" You knew that you should have either walked away from the situation or taken the conversation to an area that was a little less public. (*Quick sidenote: For our purposes in this lesson, we are going to define "take it outside" in the verbal-confrontation sense rather than the physical one.*) If you know what I'm talking about, then chances are you're currently reflecting on one of those situations and turning just a little red or shaking your head in disbelief at what you said or did in front of witnesses who didn't need to be involved and/or in a way that was too knee-jerk or entirely out of proportion to the situation. Congratulations — you're human. De-escalation is an art form and we're not born artists. Just taking the time to pause long enough during a passionate discussion to ask the other party to move somewhere less public is not something that is easy to do, particularly when you're defending yourself, your stakeholders, or your position on an issue that you're passionate about.

▪▪▪▪▪▪▪▪▪▪▪▪▪▪▪▪▪▪▪▪▪▪▪▪▪▪▪▪▪▪▪▪

FUN FACT: Of course, not all of us get to write a hit song about our "moment," as is the case with John Wetton. "Heat of the Moment" was the first single released by the '80s rock supergroup Asia and it peaked at #4 on the Hot 100.[40] It was written by their singer, John Wetton, who said it was about an apology — his apology. "So certainly 'Heat of the Moment,' the whole song is just an apology. It's just saying I fucked up. I hold my hand out and I got it wrong. I never meant it to be like that. I didn't want it to be like that. And so I'm sorry. That's basically what 'Heat of the Moment' is."[41]

▪▪▪▪▪▪▪▪▪▪▪▪▪▪▪▪▪▪▪▪▪▪▪▪▪▪▪▪▪▪▪▪

Getting riled up and losing control is human. But there is also a more nefarious reason why some people don't "take it outside" — power, control, and arrogance. I happen to think these are the three main traits of a coward. Toxic workplaces and personal relationships thrive on berating and belittling the party that is perceived to be in a "lesser position." When it comes to melt-downs by toxic people, the public display is purposeful and designed to make a scene. It makes sense, if you really think about it. When they aren't in their position of power at work, nobody sees them or gives them a second thought. I would imagine that the vast majority of people who act this way were probably chosen last on the playground throughout their youth,

---

40 "Heat of the Moment (Asia Song)," *Wikipedia*, Last Edited August 22, 2022, https://en.wikipedia.org/wiki/Heat_of_the_Moment_(Asia_song).

41 Greg Prato, "John Wetton of Asia (ex-King Crimson)," Song Facts, September 16, 2014, https://www.songfacts.com/blog/interviews/john-wetton-of-asia-ex-king-crimson.

but I'm not a psychologist so I'll just stop there. When it comes to hot-headed people who refuse to "take it outside," I am not a fan and I've seen way too many of these individuals.

Road House delivers scene after scene with folks who can't or won't "take it outside." Dalton knows that to clean up the bar, you have to first start with the way the staff handles things. The patrons will take their cues on how to act by watching the staff. Sound familiar? Just insert leader for staff and employees for patrons or parent and child or, in my case, dad and dog.

When Dalton first arrives at The Double Deuce, he just observes from afar and what he sees is essentially anarchy. There are fights everywhere. It's so bad that the band has a chicken-wire cage built around them to avoid being hit by flying beer bottles. The energy in the bar was aggressive, to say the least, and as he looked around, he quickly realized that the bouncing staff was more to blame than the patrons themselves. If tempers flared and a fight was ready to start, the bouncers didn't look to de-escalate the situation. Quite the contrary — they were also ready for a fight and more than happy to get physical in front of the patrons, which of course caused even more fights across the bar.

It's because of this violent and toxic dynamic that Dalton delivers Rule #2 during his leadership meeting with the bouncers: "Take it outside. Don't ever start anything in the bar unless it is absolutely necessary."

We often hear sports teams talk about "keeping it in house." What they mean is that if there is a problem between two players, two coaches, or a player and a coach, that it stays with them. No public airing of disputes and nothing that could split the team into two separate factions, especially when it comes to the coaches. The players will emulate how the coaches act. And if it is a professional sports team, there are the added complexities of the media and the fans.

Now in sports, there are times where we see a "dressing down" of sorts on the sidelines during the heat of battle from coach to player or player to player. Passions and emotions run high during high-level competition and the passion often serves a purpose. This is where the "unless it is absolutely necessary" comes into play. In sports, there are a finite number of minutes in which the battle is either won or lost on that particular day. Decisions and strategic changes need to be made quickly, and praise for accomplishments and critique of mistakes must be delivered in a matter of seconds. In these instances — in the heat of battle – it is oftentimes necessary to "start it in the bar." But only a tiny percentage of people play sports at a competitive collegiate level and only a minuscule amount of those end up playing at a professional level, so for 99.9% of the population, the rule still holds: take it outside.

If you've worked in an office, then you've likely seen or even been part of a situation where two people raised their voices at each other in disagreement. Human emotions happen. We are not, contrary to the arena-rock band, Styx, designed to be an emotion-less "Mr. Roboto." Good luck getting "Domo arigato, Mr. Roboto. Domo. Domo." out of your head for the next day or so. Although professionalism would tell us that we should always find ways to have difficult office conversations in private, it is imperative that anyone in a leadership position learn to consciously "take it outside" before engaging in a difficult conversation with a team member or any discussion that may lead to a disagreement or a misunderstanding. There's just no excuse for it. Take it from someone who knows.

Unfortunately, I've been on both sides and although I had no control over the dressing down from a manager that I experienced in front of an entire office full of my team members, I'm embarrassed to admit that I'm guilty of having a public disagreement with a fellow leader years ago that I still regret. Both of us had very strong opinions about the appropriateness of a record investment in a marketing project. Our working relationship at the time was one of basic tolerance for each other but that was about it. Although we disagreed often on strategy, we always did so in a professional manner that is expected of two colleagues. At one point, there was a lack of communication between both of us over a period of several weeks that was leading up to an all-hands marketing meeting. During this time, one of our major initiatives had gone a little, shall we say, sideways and much of that was due to our professional immaturity via our communication breakdown. During the meeting, our executive vice president asked specifically about said "sideways" project and both of us put on a good face and reassured her that we would prioritize resolving the issues. When the meeting broke and we began walking down the hallway toward our offices, we both realized that the project was, as Expose sang in their 1987 hit, at the "Point of No Return." This realization led to fervent and loud disagreement, complete with finger pointing, blaming, and a fairly substantial amount of four-letter words. The hurling of insults would have made even Gunny Sgt. Hartman from 1987's classic *Full Metal Jacket* both blush and make green with envy. All of this in a hallway that was surrounded by a cubicle farm (don't you love those things) with no less than 150 people within earshot. Just visualizing it as I write this makes me cringe. I imagine that it looked like the Geico meerkat commercial where the woman is in her cubicle on the phone talking to her boyfriend who is breaking up with her and all these meerkats (representing office workers) are popping their heads up over the cubicle walls to see what is going on. We were creating a scene, in every sense of the word.

It was not my best moment and I assume not his as well — at least I hope not. What seemed like 30 minutes was about 30 *seconds*, but it was raucous enough for several people to get up from their chairs and inquire about what was going on. We finally got our wits about us and went our separate ways, but there is no doubt that the damage had been done. Several years of earned credibility and leadership was likely diminished all because we didn't "take it outside" — which is such a simple thing to do. Simplicity rules.

De-escalation is, no doubt, an art form and so is the ability to "start something inside" without causing a disruption and without losing credibility, face, and most importantly the belief in you as a leader. A great example of how to wield power in a room full of colleagues is through the nickname that Condoleezza Rice was given when she was the National Security Advisor (2001-2005). They called her the Velvet Hammer because of her ability to provide a public dressing down of sorts using an approach that was professional and gentle, but firm. When she was done and left the room or meeting, it was often noted that the person or team didn't even realize that they had been proverbially bludgeoned over the head multiple times, hence the velvet hammer moniker.[42]

Very few have the acumen, intelligence, poise, and resume of Condoleezza Rice, so we are all better off heeding Dalton's 2nd simple rule — "Take it outside. Don't ever start anything inside the bar unless it is absolutely necessary."

And ...

Be nice.

As I mentioned earlier in the chapter, one of the bouncers challenges Dalton on his final rule, "be nice," which prompts this exchange:

> "I want you to be nice until it's time not to be nice," says Dalton.

> "Well, how do we know when that time is?" one of the bouncers asks.

"I'll let you know," Dalton answers.

Simple rule. Simple question. Simple answer.

I heard the words "be nice" a lot when I was a kid. Before the age of five, any time we were in a situation where something might be confusing to me or there could be a misunderstanding between, say, two four-year-olds — which we know never happens — my mom would look at me and say "be nice." It's also something people say to their dog if it happens to be a bit temperamental when meeting other dogs. They'll say something like, "Now Buttercup, be nice."

■■■■■■■■■■■■■■■■■■■■■■■■■■■■■■■■■■

🕹 **FUN FACT:** Princess ButterCup, also known as
The Princess Bride, in the 1987 classic, *The Princess
Bride*, is also a farm girl and the true love of Westley,
also known as The Man in Black. Princess ButterCup
was also the name of my friend's dog, who was
named by his female roommate. When he moved
out with Princess Buttercup, he shortened her
name to BC. She was an awesome dog who loved
everyone, and we loved her back.

■■■■■■■■■■■■■■■■■■■■■■■■■■■■■■■■■

When we become adults, we aren't often told to "be nice" because it is assumed that we've matured enough to figure that one out on our own. Ah, the assumption. One of the worst nouns in the English language. Not because it did anything wrong. It's just that the assumption is kind of the lazy way out. You can assume and then you don't have to ask any questions. In all honesty, when we become adults, the "be nice" is generally replaced with "don't be a dick" or "don't be an asshole." So, essentially, we have to be told not to be mean. Well, that's just great. We've matured just wonderfully, haven't we?

To just be nice, you don't have to be John Candy's character in pretty much every movie or *Say Anything*'s Llyod Dobler or even Chris Farley's *TommyBoy*. Gasp, there's another '90s movie reference. Okay, look — if I was to make a list of '90s movies that feel '80s, the two I've mentioned so far — *TommyBoy* and *White Men Can't Jump* — would be on the list, so at least give me that. To be nice, you just need to pay attention. It's really that simple. You don't need to walk around with an awkward smile on your face all day telling everyone its's a B-E-A-utiful day (damn 2000s movie references) or say hello to every single person you pass by on a given day, although it would be funny once in a while when someone says hello to you to channel the great Lionel Richie and say "Hello ... Is it me you're looking for?"

To be nice, you just need to pay attention.

Just pay attention. The opportunities to be nice are all around you.

Of course, as Dalton said, there are times "to be nice until it's time not to be nice." For me, the time to no longer be nice is when it's in defense or protection of friends, family, and animals but I'll leave that consideration to you. And remember that, contrary to what Dalton said, the "pain does hurt" so if you decide not to be nice, prepare for it.

Life, work, relationships — they are full of complexities and, unfortunately, we spend an inordinate amount of time assessing and analyzing the details of those complexities. But if a bouncer in Jasper, Missouri, who everyone thought would "be bigger" can find a way to simplify things, so can you. Simplicity rules.

One last lesson before we say farewell to Patrick Swayze and to *Road House*:

Trusting the process requires trusting the person.

How many of you have heard the term "trust the process?" You've likely heard it or said it in your workplace and in multiple situations throughout your life. Learning is a process; grieving is a process; maturing is a process. I've heard it from a variety of golf teachers throughout the years, regarding my swing. "Trust the process," they say and yet I still have a swing that only a mother could love. Sure, I have my moments but damn that stupid, aggravating, good-for-nothing process! It has been said that golf is just "a good walk spoiled" and if you can't tell, I most certainly agree. Ugh, so frustrating. Okay, Christopher, stop thinking about your golf swing and get back to writing.

My golf swing aside, when people talk about trusting the process, they are generally talking about the unique steps that one needs to take to get to a solution or result. The "process" is generally born out of experience with a lot of experimentation, disappointment, frustration, and multiple failures that resulted in a deep, dark "rock bottom" that would make most people give up. But we have processes to follow because, somewhere along the way, someone didn't give up. Someone pushed through. And they developed a roadmap or "process" for the rest of us. A few years ago, a buddy of mine had his bachelor party on the Bourbon Trail in and around Louisville, Kentucky. It was an awesome trip, as bachelor parties tend to be, but it was also the first bachelor party I had attended that had an element of education.

■■■■■■■■■■■■■■■■■■■■■■■■■■■■■■■■

⚒ **FUN FACT:** The 1984 comedy movie *Bachelor Party* — with the tagline "He will get married in the morning ... if he makes it through the night" — starred Tom Hanks and Tawny Kitaen. If Tawny's name sounds familiar, then you were likely an '80s MTV junkie and saw her in one of the most famous music videos of all time: "Here I Go Again" by Whitesnake, where she danced on the hood of two Jaguar cars. Sadly, we lost Tawny in 2021 at age 59 and a piece of my MTV youth went with her.

■ ■

In our visits to the different distilleries, we learned the definition of a Kentucky hug (that warm feeling you get in your throat and lungs when you drink a real Kentucky bourbon); we also learned that 95% of the world's bourbon is made in Kentucky; and we were told that the sweet spot for aging bourbon in barrels is between 5 and 12 years (to be considered straight bourbon whiskey, it must be aged at least two years). This all got me thinking about the *process* back in the day. It's one thing to develop a process for something you produce over the course of a few days but *years*? How many times did the original makers of bourbon have to start over after spending years on a process that didn't work, and who was the lucky person who got to taste the abominations that came out of the barrel? How did they even know what it was *supposed* to taste like and how did they know that the process was even correct? Someone had to trust the *person* who said, "trust the process" and, eventually, they got to the end result. In the case of world-class bourbon, it was a result that — throughout multiple generations — has been the common denominator for many, shall we say, "interesting stories" (including a few that involved yours truly, but that is most definitely for another book ... unless, of course, you get a bourbon or two in me sometime).

How many times did the original makers of bourbon have to start over after spending years on a process that didn't work, and who was the lucky person that got to taste the abominations that came out of the barrel?

Now this idea of trusting the person responsible for the process is especially true for organizational rebuilds. As a refresher, after Dalton's first official night as the cooler running the bouncer team, Frank Tilghman, who had hired Dalton to clean up the "road house" bar known as The Double Deuce, says:

> "Well, it was a good night. Nobody died."

> To which Dalton replies: "It will get worse before it gets better."

And worse it most definitely got. To turn around the bar, Dalton needed to take actions that he knew would result in much bigger issues, including vengeance and violence:

1. He cut loose several of the bouncers who had short fuses or were consuming alcohol and drugs on the job.

2. He fired a waitress who was dealing drugs in the bar.

3. He gave the boot to the head bartender, Pat (who also happened to be the nephew of our antagonist, Brad Wesley) for skimming cash.

4. And, of course, he laid down his three simple rules.

All these actions were necessary for the complete rebuild that Dalton's boss, Frank, needed and all could have potentially caused a little chaos, but it was #3 — firing Brad Wesley's nephew — that triggered the "worse before it gets better." Dalton knows this is coming so he calls his old bouncer friend Wade (played by Sam Elliot) to come help him clean up The Double Deuce and provide a reinforcement if necessary. So how much worse did it get? Well, let's make another numbered list for clarity and simplicity:

1. First and foremost, Brad Wesley pretty much owned everything in town and did as he pleased — including extorting businesses for money each month. The skimming was apparently his extortion fee, so he wasn't happy to see that go away when his nephew Pat got fired.

2. Pat returned with a few goons to rough up the new owner, Frank, and explain to him how it works in Jasper, Missouri. When Dalton sees what is going on, he confronts them, which then turns into a massive brawl with broken windows, broken tables, broken bones, and one knife wound that sends Dalton to the hospital. In this case, it was "absolutely necessary to start — or finish — something inside the bar." The good news here was that he meets Doc (Kelly Lynch), who stitches him up and ends up being his love interest.

3. Unbeknownst to Dalton and Frank, Brad Wesley controls all the alcohol distributors around the area, so he cuts off all deliveries to the Double Deuce, essentially putting them out of business. No booze, no business.

4. Wesley tries to hire Dalton away from the Double Deuce to work with him as an enforcer for his criminal enterprise. "Tell me if I owned a bar and I wanted to clean it up, how much would it take to get you to come work

for me?" Dalton declines quickly, saying, "There's no amount of money."

5. As Dalton expects, things turn personal as well. Doc's uncle, Red Webster, has his store set on fire by Wesley's goons; those same goons blow up the house where Dalton rents a small place above the stable; they then destroy a car dealership owned by a guy who supports the new Double Deuce; but the final straw is when Dalton finds his best friend Wade dead with a knife in his chest and a note from Wesley taunting Dalton.

So yes, things have most certainly gotten worse around this rebuild at the Double Deuce, but they do get better as things seem to do whenever Patrick Swayze is around. Ultimately, Wesley gets his comeuppance in a most deserved way and the Double Deuce becomes the fun, safe, and hip place that Frank knew it could become when he hired Dalton to help clean it up.

If you know that something is going to get worse before it gets better, it takes a very strong mindset and a lot of willpower to then see it through. Preparing to sink deeper before seeing results means that you must trust the person or people with the process that is going to get you there. We've seen this publicly with organizational rebuilds like when Steve Jobs took the reins at Apple when they were losing around $1 billion a year and, as Paul Harvey said, I think we "know the rest of the story." People trusted Jobs, so they were able to trust his processes.

If you know that something is going to get worse before it gets better, it takes a very strong mindset and a lot of willpower to then see it through.

Another dynamic leader whose employees trusted him to lead them through revolutionary changes in process is Hubert Joly, who brought Best Buy back from the brink with "five consecutive years of sales growth, a 263% increase in shareholder return and doubling of online sales."[43] He then passed it on to Corie Barry in 2019 and she has continued to push Best Buy forward in a market where big box had been shrinking.

Cadillac, which was known as the last vehicle you purchase before you age out and leave this Earth, was dying as quickly as their consumer base. They had tried multiple gimmicks to drive down the age of the consumer base, but nothing was working. So in 2002-2003, they completely revamped the design of their cars, licensed a Led Zeppelin song for a massive marketing campaign, and held their collective breath. The result was an immediate 16% increase in sales and typical customer who was under 60 for the first time in decades. There are now several living generations who have a completely different perspective on the brand because Cadillac trusted that the coolness and the singing voice of Robert Plant (lead singer of Led Zeppelin) could transform their brand.

And most recently in 2019, Stephanie Stuckey left the legal profession to become CEO of Stuckey's — the iconic candy company that was started by her grandfather as a roadside pecan stand back in 1937. The company was purchased by a large corporation in the late '70s and went from a peak of 350 locations to just a handful of stores in the early '80s. The Stuckey's brand had all but disappeared. In 1984, Billy Stuckey — the son of the founder — brought it back into the family and began the rebuild process, which has accelerated considerably under Stephanie's leadership. In less than three years under Stephanie's leadership as the CEO, Stuckey's grew to 65 licensed locations with a distribution center, acquired multiple

---

43 Lisa Earle McLeod, "The Best Buy Turnaround: Purpose-Driven Leadership with Hubert Joly," May 3, 2021, https://www.forbes.com/sites/lisaearlem-cleod/2021/05/03/the-best-buy-turnaround-purpose-driven-leadership-with--hubert-joly/?sh=516d24a2469e.

strategic businesses, and positioned Stuckey's pecan snacks and candies in more than 200 retailers.[44] Trusting the process requires trusting the person, and Stuckey's trusts Stephanie.

But if you ask me, the most impressive rebuilds happen out of the spotlight. The ones where it will absolutely, without a doubt, get "worse before it gets better." And those are the rebuilds that happen every day with individuals like you and me from all walks of life and all corners of the globe. Maybe you've even had one yourself — a moment of reinvention, rebirth, growth, comeback, or a rebuilding of your career, life, or personal brand. A lot of people — thanks to the ripple effects of the pandemic —were forced to re-evaluate who they were and where they were going. A lot of people questioned, as my mom often did, "what does this all mean?" and "why are we here?"

April 2022, presenting a keynote on lessons from '80s pop culture
at the EMERGE Conference in Lexington, Kentucky.

When I rebuilt my career at mid-life — moving from the predict-ability of being a corporate marketer to the uncharted and entrepreneurial odyssey of being a speaker, author, and '80s pop culture guy, it required trusting my process and myself. Now my process was based on a quote from Charles De Mar, who was Lane Meyer's best friend in the super awesome '80s dark comedy *Better Off Dead*, which starred John Cusack, Diane Franklin (who wrote the foreword to my 2nd book), and Curtis Armstrong,

44 https://stuckeys.com/letter-from-our-ceo/history/

who played the aforementioned De Mar. When looking down
at the very steep, very high, and very scary K-12 ski slope, Lane
had second thoughts about his attempt to traverse down the
K-12. He stood there, with his skis over the edge, when his best
friend, Charles De Mar, said this, "Just go that way really fast. If
something gets in your way, turn." And that is exactly what I did.
I pointed myself in a career direction, moved fast, and stayed
vigilant about when I might need to turn. Of course, I had no idea
that a global pandemic would be the thing that got in the way.
Just as momentum was building considerably with my speaking
gigs in March of 2020, the world shut down — hard and fast. I lost
eight speaking gigs in a 24-hour period and I'm sure my face
looked like Emmett Fitz-Hume and Austin Millbarge in the 1985
comedy *Spies Like Us* when they walked out of G-Force training.
I was stunned.

One of my very good friends called me to encourage me and
told me that I better not give up on this journey. He said, "Look,
if anyone can caveman it, you can. Be smart with your money,
minimize your expenses, grow your own food, learn to cook,
exercise in your driveway. There are plenty of cost-free ways to
entertain yourself and, most of all, find ways to keep yourself
and your content out front and relevant. This, too, shall pass."
As Dalton said in *Road House*, "It will get worse before it gets
better" and it did. But I took my dear friend's advice — minus the
growing of food thing, which I know would cost me *more* money
because I'm a terrible gardener — and I pushed through. I trusted
the process, which required trusting myself, and sit here today
writing my 3rd book while averaging four speaking gigs per month.
"I'm baaaack!"

Not everything and everyone can be rebuilt or "built on rock and
roll" like the city in Starship's 1985 super-cheesy but unfortunately catchy hit song. Compared to so many others, my rebuild
was easy. Every day, people must rebuild their lives because
of myriad crises and tragedies, like illness, addiction, natural

disasters, business closures, and the death of loved ones. And every day, those same people trust themselves and trust the process — knowing that it will likely get worse before it gets better but also knowing that the reward is rebuilding yourself in a better form than before.

So, in the end, a bouncer at the Double Deuce bar in Jasper, Missouri, taught us that we should never underestimate our opponent, that simplicity rules, and that trusting the process requires trusting the person. We also learned that we should always look to Patrick Swayze for life lessons and personal enlightenment. Because, well, he's Patrick Swayze.

CHAPTER 9

DEAD POETS SOCIETY

"There's a time for daring and
a time for caution and a wise person
understands which is called for."

— JOHN KEATING, *DEAD POETS SOCIETY*

I love poetry. When most people, especially kids, hear the words
"poem" or "poetry," they make a mad dash for the closest
exit. What they often don't realize is that many of our great
modern songwriters would have likely been poets were they born
in a different era. Song lyrics are poetry set to music. From Bob

Dylan, Jimi Hendrix, Janis Joplin and The Grateful Dead to Billy Joel, Prince, U2, Morrisey, Lady Gaga and Chris Stapleton, some of our most iconic musicians also wrote or write many of their own lyrics. The old-school blues guys — like Robert Johnson and Muddy Waters, amongst others — were prolific song writers. One of my favorite songs from the '80s, "Closer to Fine" by The Indigo Girls, was written by Emily Sailers, one of the members of the singing duo. I challenge you to listen to the lyrics of that song and not think that it could be dropped into any *Collections of Great Poetry* books during any era.

My dad's first job out of college was as a university professor of English. He raised us on English and American literature and issued nickel fines for every time we said the word "like" in conversation. He traveled extensively for business, and pretty much any night he was home before I turned five, he would read me three poems: "Mighty Casey at the Bat," "Wynken, Blyken and Nod," and "Annabel Lee" — the last of which was the last complete poem composed by Edgar Allan Poe, which told the story about a guy who continued to lay down each night next to his dead wife ... so that was an interesting choice for toddler poetry night.

I was destined to someday write about poetry — even if it's a review of a *movie* about poetry. Like my dad, Hollywood character John Keating (played by Robin Williams) is also an English professor — albeit at an elite boarding school — in the fantastically dark and inspiring film *Dead Poets Society*. Most of the kids at the school come from wealth and privilege and are taught, from a young age, that their lives and careers will follow the exact path their families have laid out for them. There will be no discussion and no freedom of choice. They are told, in essence: "You will be a doctor or an attorney or you'll run the generational family business, regardless of what you want." They will most certainly not go into any creative endeavor — artist, actor, writer — and any discussion of this path will be met with swift condemnation.

Mr. Keating says nonsense to all of this and teaches the boys to be who they really want to be and to explore their own path and journey. And he does this through poetry.

Even if you haven't seen *Dead Poets Society*, you've likely heard the Latin phrase "carpe diem" or its English translation "seize the day." The phrase has been around since 23 BC, when the Roman poet Horace included it in his *Odes*. Carpe diem — seize the day — was popularized in 1989 because of a great scene in Dead Poets Society when Mr. Keating takes the boys in front of the school trophy case and shows them pictures of boys who went to the school decades before. In describing how those celebrated alumni are no different from the boys today, he ends a fantastic little monologue with:

> "These boys are now fertilizing daffodils. But if you listen real close, you can hear them whisper their legacy to you. Go on, lean in. Listen. You hear it? ... Carpe ... hear it ... Carpe. Carpe diem. Seize the day, boys. Make your life extraordinary."

It's an incredibly inspirational scene but at another point in the movie, he says something even more important to his students: "No matter what anybody tells you, words and ideas *can* change the world." And they really can. But they also require action – "if you're going to talk the talk, you've got to walk the walk." So with Keating's "words and ideas" and a commitment to put those ideas into action, we learn that:

Change starts with dialogue but making a real impact requires action.

Throughout the movie, Keating finds clever ways to make his key points, in the hopes that the boys will find his lessons memorable and retain the information that he is teaching them. Beyond teaching them about poetry, he takes them on little field trips on campus and at one point he stands on top of his desk while teaching the class and says: "I stand upon my desk to remind myself that we must constantly look at things in a different way."

He then invites all the students to stand on their desks, delivers another great monologue (which we will get to later in the chapter), and encourages the boys to look at the classroom from a different perspective. With this exercise, he teaches them and us that:

 Bubbles are only good for wrap, blowing, and baths.

I promise to explain that one. But before we dive deeper into brainstorms and bubbles, let's jump into our wardrobe closet time machine à la *Time Bandits* and go back to June of 1989.

My Life in June 1989

That summer, I once again found myself with a job as a bellman, which is something I would do again at Disney my first year out of college in 1993. This bellman gig in the summer of 1989 was at a hotel just outside my hometown of Baltimore, MD. As I recall, the hotel had a private racquet club attached to it but unfortunately did not come with its own John Cocktolstoy, the Scottish-Romanian tennis-playing alias of Chevy Chase's character *Fletch* in the 1985 movie by the same name.

So because *Dead Poets Society* was a turn toward the dramatic for Robin Williams at the time, this story from the summer of 1989 will also be a turn from the hopefully comedic and definitely self-deprecating stories that I typically share.

That summer, I was home from my freshman year of college and happy to have a good job that would give me *more* than pizza-and-beer money for my sophomore year. The best part was that I was working with my two best friends — Chris and Dexter. They actually got me the job before I was home from college when their manager took them at their word that I was enough of an upstanding citizen and intelligent enough to take luggage to and from rooms, as well as drive the airport shuttle when necessary.

That summer wasn't as "eventful" as some of the others that I've told you about (in this book and in my previous books) but knowing what I do now, this summer and this job would provide me with memories that I will cherish until my last breath. Little could Chris, Dexter, or I imagine that, by 2008, there would only be one of us left alive on this big blue marble of ours.

Just five short years later, in 1994, Chris would die alone late at night in a single-car accident. He was 24 years old. And then in 2008, Dexter would also die alone in his sleep, leaving behind a son who was just turning two years old. Dexter was 37. These were the guys who I was supposed to grow old with, but by my late 30s, they were both gone. I'm so grateful for the summer of '89.

That summer of '89, we spent pretty much every waking hour together. If we weren't at work, slinging luggage around, we were playing on our travel baseball team, shooting hoops in my side yard arguing over called fouls or the lack thereof, or watching the underrated Robert Townsend classic from 1987, *Hollywood Shuffle*. We knew every word in that movie. And we should have, considering we watched it at least 20 times that summer alone. What I remember most about that summer with Dexter and Chris is the amount of laughing that we did. My cheeks hurt from smiling and laughing. Starting in high school, we played this game called "Psych," where you would tell a story to the others and once you had them believing it, you would say "Psych!" — meaning it was fake and I fooled you. It was just a silly nonsensical game that we continued to play on phone calls during and after that summer. I just miss those simple and silly things. In case you were wondering, yes — Chris and Dexter were two of the seven guys I lived with in Ocean City, MD, during the summer of 1987.

Those memories were with me 19 years later, on a cold January morning in my hometown just outside of Baltimore, when I spoke at Dexter's funeral. It was a small predominantly black Methodist church. Around 150-200 people were packed into the space.
I stood at the podium and when I looked down to my left, I saw my best friend Dexter laying in the casket that would be his final resting place. I froze, which is something I never do in front of a group of people. It was all too real at this point. I looked to my left and one of the men who played in the band at the church was looking back at me, holding his guitar. He resembled the legend B.B. King and he saw me struggling with the realization that my best friend was dead. He gave me a nod and said, "God is good." Now for transparency's sake, I am very much a spiritual person, but I am not religious in the traditional sense. In that moment, I found comfort in his eyes, his smile, and his words. I took a deep breath and delivered my eulogy to my best friend.

After the graveside service, there was a lunch at the pastor's house next to the church. For the first time, I met Dexter's extended family from Tennessee. We had a huge group hug and laughed and cried simultaneously. When the group hug was finished, one of his cousins looked at me and said with a smile, "Chris Clews. We didn't even know you were white. You walked up to the podium, and we all looked at each other and said, 'Chris Clews is white?'" We all laughed and then cried again at the pure and beautiful soul who we had lost way too young. Dexter and I had known each other since we were six years old and when he told stories about me to his extended family, he never thought it was important to mention my skin color because, well, it wasn't important. A purer and more beautiful soul you will not find.

Circa 1988: My favorite pic of my best friend, Dex, and me.
He had the greatest smile the world has ever known and
he left us way too soon in 2008. I miss him every day.

One of my favorite lines, in any book or movie, is at the very end of the 1986 classic, *Stand By Me,* when the main character, Gordie, says: "I never had friends like I did when I was twelve. Jesus, does anyone?"

Truer words have rarely been spoken or written. If you are lucky enough to still have your childhood friends alive and well, take a few minutes to reach out and say hello. A simple social media search can often connect you with a childhood friend you've lost touch with for years. It will do their heart and yours some good.

Pop Culture in June 1989

Okay, enough with the real-life stuff. Geez, Clews. This is supposed to be fun. Alrighty, let's get back to talking 1989 and the pop culture that we were enjoying and consuming. The Top 40 charts in June of 1989 included three hair-metal bands, an awesome musical sound and genre that unfortunately Grunge would swallow whole just a few years later. Cinderella clocked in with the ballad "Coming Home" while Warrant continued to tell us that the "Down Boys" were going somewhere but didn't actually tell us where, and Guns N' Roses had a top-10 hit in their ballad, "Patience." We can argue later whether they were truly a hair-metal band. One of my favorites, Neneh Cherry, was sitting at #5 with still one of the best hip-hop songs ever, "Buffalo Stance." Another one of my favorites, "Send Me an Angel" by Real Life was hanging on at #40, and the boy band of boy bands, New Kids on the Block (now often called NKOTB), were at #2 with "I'll Be Loving You Forever." What was it with ballads that summer?

■■■■■■■■■■■■■■■■■■■■■■■■■■■■■■■■■

🕹 **FUN FACT:** Neneh Cherry was born in Stockholm, Sweden, to the son of a tribal chief from Sierra Leone and a Swedish painter and textile artist, but her parents separated when she was very young and she took the last name of Cherry from her stepfather, Don Cherry, a famous American jazz musician who helped raise her from birth. You may have also heard of her half-brother, musician Eagle-Eye Cherry, who had an international smash hit in 1997 with "Save Tonight."[45]

■■■■■■■■■■■■■■■■■■■■■■■■■■■■■■■

In television, *21 Jump Street*, a drama about a group of undercover cops posing as high schoolers, was enjoying a solid second season while a reality show that premiered in 1988 about real cops and criminals, *America's Most Wanted,* was a hit as a 30-minute show that was quickly given a one-hour time slot in 1989. After beginning as a series of specials in 1987, *Unsolved Mysteries* also earned a weekly one-hour time slot in the summer of 1989, while we said goodbye to *The Facts of Life.*

At the box office, well, things were absolutely amazing, as usual. Spike Lee's spot-on commentary on society at the time, *Do the Right Thing,* was finishing a pretty good run; Lloyd Dobler was still being his charismatic kick-boxing self in *Say Anything*; Tom Cruise and Dustin Hoffman were still bringing in the $2.00 movie tickets and soon-to-be awards in *Rain Man* (which was still in the

---

45 "Neneh Cherry," *Wikipedia*, Lasted edited August 13, 2022, https://en.wikipedia.org/wiki/Neneh_Cherry.

top 15 even though it was released on December 16th of 1987!). *Road House* (with my man, Patrick Swayze), *Field of Dreams, Ghostbusters 2,* Michael Keaton as *Batman,* and *Indiana Jones and The Last Crusade* were all in the top ten with the latter sitting at #1 overall. Damn, it was a great time to be alive!

And sitting at #4 was a Robin Williams-led drama called *Dead Poets Society,* which told the story of John Keating (played by Williams), a new English professor at an elite preparatory boys' school, who shuns tradition to teach the boys in a maverick and unorthodox way.

Life Lessons from Dead Poets Society

Four of the main characters are students Todd Anderson (Ethan Hawke), Knox Overstreet (Josh Charles), Neil Perry (Robert Sean Leonard), and Charlie Dalton (Gale Hansen). Todd is shy and introverted but has huge shoes to fill as his older brother was a star at the school and valedictorian. Todd's roommate, Neil, is more extroverted and outgoing but struggles with an incredibly demanding father. Their friend Knox is a budding romantic while Charlie is, shall we say, a challenging teenager. All the boys are expected by their families to be highly successful in traditional fields like medicine, law, and business and they are expected to do what they are told. Professor Keating says, in no uncertain terms, "nonsense boys." He tells them that they are individuals who should pursue their dreams and become who you want to be, even if it is outside of the acceptable lines drawn by those around them. He teaches them through poetry to "carpe diem" or seize the day and choose the path that best represents each of them and who they want to be. This doesn't sit well with many of the parents, as well as the leaders at the school, and ultimately several events unfold that are both inspirational and upsetting. It's an incredible movie about the life journey and it reminds us that challenges exist for every person — regardless of their real or perceived station in life.

So what does an eccentric and unorthodox but brilliant English professor and his classroom of prep school students teach us about the workplace and life?

Change starts with dialogue but to make a real impact requires action.

I wonder how many of you, at some point in your youth, said, "One day I am going to change the world." And I can guess how many of you, now as adults, have said, "Change is hard!" As kids, we have the desire and time but not the savvy or know-how. Then we become adults and we have the savvy or know-how but not always the desire or time. It's quite the conundrum. I'm so glad I found a way to use the word conundrum. I'm a huge fan. Conundrum. I'm surprised that an '80s alternative band didn't have that word in their name — something like Confounding Conundrums. Anyway ... most of us ultimately want to leave the world a little better than we found it. That should be pretty easy to do, especially with the technology that we have at our fingertips in 2022.

When Professor John Keating says to the boys, "No matter what anybody tells you, words and ideas can change the world," he is at the beginning of an incredibly inspirational monologue about why we read and write poetry. (You may have heard that speech again in an Apple iPad commercial in 2014. It's a great commercial. Look it up.) The movie is set in 1959, a time when getting your words and ideas out to the world wasn't so easy. I know this firsthand, well not the growing up in 1950s, although a little six-year-old girl who lives around the corner from me said that I should be careful running so fast with my dog Bodhi through the neighborhood because I might have a heart attack. She probably thinks I'm 91. God, I felt really old in that moment.

When I say firsthand, I mean that growing up in the '80s, if I wanted to get my words and ideas out to the "world," I could try to publish something in *The Community Times* newspaper, which was the weekly paper of record in Reisterstown, MD, where I grew up. If I was lucky, maybe 30 or 40 people would read it. I grew up just outside of Baltimore, MD, so it wasn't a "Small Town," as John Cougar Mellencamp sang back in 1985, but this was back before any kind of digital communication beyond the modem that my friends and I hooked up to my Commodore 64 computer in the hopes that we could hack into Toys R' Us and have all the toys shipped to us. I mean Matthew Broderick hacked into a US Military Supercomputer in the 1983 thriller *WarGames,* so we figured, "Why not us and why not now?" It didn't work, which is probably a good thing for all of us.

If you set aside the fact that conversations can take place with no live social interaction and with only acronyms and emojis, technology has completely changed the way that we communicate in an incredibly positive way. And nowhere was this change more impactful than through our ability to effect change beyond just the street that we lived on. In the palm of our hand, we now can send our words and ideas out to the world. You don't have to be a politician, pro athlete, celebrity, journalist, author, or world leader. The combination of smart phones and social media is the great communication equalizer. Your words, your ideas can now reach anyone in the world the very moment you hit send, submit, publish, tweet, or post and that is pretty awesome.

But there's a second piece to this lesson and a more important one. Remember in Chapter 5 on the movie *Cocktail*, I mentioned "if you're going to talk the talk, you've got to walk the walk." We are going to go back to that proverbial well again and no, not Terence Trent D'arby's "Wishing Well." It's one thing to talk the talk but you must walk the walk to really turn your words and ideas into action and ultimately contribute something that will make a difference.

What is your walk the walk? What cause motivates you to participate in ways where you can make a difference? Are you an Aerosmith/Run-DMC "Walk This Way" or a Bangles "Walk Like an Egyptian"? Just seeing if you are still paying attention. Where is it that you contribute more than a monthly automatic donation or the reposting of a story that resonates with your cause? These, of course, are both very important and noble efforts but causes need real tangible action. They need people to get involved.

Me and my sister spending time with my grandmother while traveling the country in her RV that she loved so much! Insert Cousin Eddie joke here: "Shitter's Full!"

My walk the walk is animal rescue. Saving animals makes the kind of difference in the world that I think Professor Keating was talking about in *Dead Poets Society*. We start with ideas and words, and then choose actions that matter. I was lucky enough to be raised in a household whose only furry family members throughout my youth were rescues. My mom invested time, money, and love into animal rescues of all kinds and saved every animal that she could wherever she went. It started with my grandmother, who was way ahead of her time advocating for rescue animals in the 1940s. At one point, she had four Dobermans, six cats, and a Mynah bird with a 100-word vocabulary. All were rescues and all went on road trips with her in her

RV. My sister rescued one cat in the middle of the night from a crack house, where it was being abused, and saved another from a couple that was using it for target practice. So yeah, she definitely walks the walk. She also dives with sharks without a cage but, of course, no one ever said that intelligence was a pre-requisite to rescue animals.

For years, I lived in a condo that didn't allow dogs and if have any regrets about my adult life, it's that I lived there as long as I did. During this time, I volunteered at the Humane Society as a dog walker and playmate to the shelter dogs. I loved every minute of it, and I hope that my time with each of them brought a little joy to their lives. I was doing my best to "walk the walk." And then two years ago, after I had bought a house and was no longer restricted by condo rules, a totally awesome four-legged knucklehead came into my life. His name was Austin, which I promptly changed to Bodhi, naming him after Patrick Swayze's character in *Point Break*.

■ ■

FUN FACT: I love Patrick Swayze. You know this by now. When filming *Point Break*, he wanted to do the skydiving scenes himself but the insurance company said no way during "principal photography" — otherwise known as the main filming of the movie — so a stunt double was used. During filming, he was sneaking out to get trained and after the film wrapped, he went skydiving with the cameraman and reshot scenes that were eventually used in the film. Man was he awesome.[46]

■ ■

Bodhi (my dog, not the Swayze character) was likely a day away from dying. He was found lying on a street in Miami, just hoping

---

46 Skydive Perris, "Behind the Scenes of *Point Break*," May 15, 2017, https://sky-diveperris.com/blog/point-break-skydive-behind-the-scenes/.

someone would save him. He couldn't walk, he was malnourished, had bugs all over him, couldn't go to the bathroom, and had wounds on different parts of his body. With all of that, it was clear that he just wanted to live. A couple of Miami cops found him and got him to Wonder Paws Rescue in Ft. Lauderdale, FL, who basically brought him back to life. Just amazing.

These days, I can't imagine my life without Bodhi. We've already been through so much together. Just within the first 10 months that we were together, my girlfriend packed up an RV and left (on a journey that she needed, and I 100% supported), my stepmom died suddenly from pancreatic cancer, and my mom died of Alzheimer's disease. All these events happened within a five-month window. Yes, my life was a bit of a country song, and throughout it all, Bodhi provided the loyalty, joy, and unconditional love that I so desperately needed. We most certainly rescued each other. He really does have a heart of gold and he is, without a doubt, my best friend. He loves every human and every dog who he meets. Our walks take twice as long as necessary because he lays down when he sees someone coming and refuses to keep walking until he can say hello. And he gets a sad and confused look on his face if they aren't interested in meeting him. As I sit here typing this, he is wrapped around me on the couch with his head tucked between my leg and the couch cushion.

Now for one more thing about Bodhi before we get back to our lessons from *Dead Poets Society*. Bodhi is a bully-breed mix, which is the group of breeds that includes pit bull terriers. His breed is so incredibly misunderstood and if dogs like Bodhi teach us anything, it is the reinforcement of one of the most important golden rules: "Don't judge a book by its cover." This should be as true for dogs as it is for humans. Adopting him has made me a huge advocate for the bully breeds and there are amazing organizations doing tireless work on their behalf all across this great country of ours. Stand Up for Pits, East Coast Bully Advocates, Forever Bully Love Rescue, and Bark Nation are just four of many groups that work every day on behalf of bully breeds — from actual rescue on the streets to medical care, fostering and adoption services, to organizing for legislative change at the local, state, and federal levels.

Whatever your thing is — whatever the area that needs your words and ideas and actions — there's most definitely a community that supports it at multiple levels. People just like you who are deep in it and walking the walk to effect the change that will make the world a better place.

During the *Dead Poets Society* monologue in which Professor John Keating says, "No matter what anybody tells you, words and ideas can change the world," he also quotes the great American poet Walt Whitman, who said:

> "Oh me! Oh life! of the questions of these recurring,
> Of the endless trains of the faithless, of cities fill'd with
>   the foolish,
> Of myself forever reproaching myself, (for who more foolish
>   than I, and who more faithless?)
> Of eyes that vainly crave the light, of the objects mean, of the
>   struggle ever renew'd,
> Of the poor results of all, of the plodding and sordid crowds
>   I see around me,
> Of the empty and useless years of the rest, with the rest me
>   intertwined,
> The question, O me! so sad, recurring—What good amid
>   these, O me, O life?

Answer.

> That you are here—that life exists and identity,
> That the powerful play goes on, and you may
>   contribute a verse."

Then Keating asked the boys, "What will your verse be?"

If you've been talking the talk, it's time to walk the walk and take action — because the play will most certainly go on and your verse will be your legacy. What is the good that you will leave behind?

Would you believe that something as simple as standing on top of a desk can teach us about bubbles? No, not bath bubbles, Bubble Yum, or bubble wrap, but the kind of bubbles we can end up living within if we choose to isolate ourselves from others who may think, act, or look different from us.

 ## Bubbles are only good for wrap, blowing, and baths.

There were lots of songs about school in the '80s — "Smokin in the Boys Room" by Motley Crue, "Parents Just Don't Understand" by DJ Jazzy Jeff and The Fresh Prince, "Rock n Roll High School" by The Ramones, "Centerfold" by The J. Geils Band, and the one that spawned one of my favorite music videos, "Hot for Teacher" by Van Halen. You'll notice that none of them were about how cool and totally awesome math can be ... because it isn't.

I sucked at math, especially geometry. I was so inept that when I got to college, they put me in a class called finite math, which was supposed to be practical and applicable to real life. The first day, we were challenged with things like understanding the difference between the empty set and the set of zero. The professor put up two visuals on the chalkboard — one that had brackets with nothing in them and one that had brackets with a zero written in the middle. It was likely the first math pop quiz that I'd ever gotten correct. Pat on the back for me. The first day of algebra class in high school, on the other hand, I knew within the first five minutes that it was going to be an abject disaster for me. They had the audacity to introduce the alphabet into math. I was having a hard enough time with long division and now I'm looking at something that says x + 10 + y = 16. Letters with numbers? C'mon. Either this is stupid or I'm stupid. It's the latter, by the way.

But it was geometry that completely threw me off. Letters were one thing, but now math and *shapes*? The only way I got through it was cheating off my dear friend Angie, who was much smarter than me and would consistently slide her paper over to my side of the desk so I could copy her answers. And all the tools we needed — protractors, compasses, spirographs — I'm getting sick just thinking about it.

So why am I bringing math — and specifically geometry — into a lesson about bubbles? Angles. One thing I remember about geometry is that there is a plethora of angles: acute, obtuse, right, straight, reflex, full rotation. And then there are complementary, supplementary, adjacent, and vertical angles as well as something called linear pairs. (Just a note – I didn't remember all this. Thank you to a learning app called BYJU's for the info.[47])

Besides confusing us in geometry, what do angles do? They allow us to look at things from a different perspective, just like Professor Keating did when he jumped up and stood on his desk to teach the class and said:

> "Why do I stand up here? I stand upon my desk to remind myself that we must constantly look at things in a different way. The world looks very different up here. Don't believe me? Come up here and see for yourself. Just when you think you know something, you have to look at it in another way. Even though it may seem silly or wrong, you must try."

---

47 https://byjus.com/maths/types-of-angles/

The boys get in line and, one by one, stand up on the teacher's desk. Most just stand on it for a second and then get down quickly, which prompts Professor Keating to say: "Don't just walk off the ledge like lemmings. Look around you."

The students, at first, weren't comfortable seeing the world in a new way, or breaking free from their ideological bubbles. I love popping bubble wrap, by the way, and when I was kid, I loved blowing bubbles with Bubble Yum or Big League Chew. As an adult, I'm not afraid to admit that I love bubble baths. Chandler in *Friends* helped make it completely acceptable for a grown man to appreciate a long and relaxing bubble bath (even without a toy battleship). One thing I *don't* like about bubbles is that so many people live in them. Experiencing a different perspective (or angle, as we were taught in geometry) is a requirement for growth as a human being. You cannot grow without getting outside of your bubble. That is an absolute truth. It's just not possible. In 2022, when we hear the word bubble, many people think political or geographic which ultimately leads back to political. Maybe you've heard it referred to as an echo chamber. Someone else can handle that conversation. I'm not that guy. Don't want to be. Nope. I'd rather focus on bubbles in terms of perspective, which was what Professor Keating was hoping to accomplish when he stood on the desk in front of the class.

Somehow, my dad keeps popping up in this book. Spending most of his life in the entertainment business has a way of producing some interesting and very cool stories. So as David Coverdale sang in WhiteSnake's huge 1987 smash hit, "Here I Go Again" with another story from my dad's collection.

Back in the early 2000s, my dad had a documentary film project in Africa. At one point, he was in Sierra Leone and spent some time in the capital city of Freetown, though his filming was to take place in an area the locals referred to as "Bone Suffer" (because everyone who lived there suffered to the bone). Bone Suffer was directly across a canal from Freetown and could only be accessed by walking across a makeshift bridge of very unstable fallen trees. If someone from Bone Suffer stole food that was necessary for their survival or needed materials from Freetown and ran across this "bridge," the police would not chase them for fear of falling into the disease-ridden canal. Yes, it was a bad as it sounds. Freetown, on the other hand, was growing along with its economy that centered around the harbor — which is the largest natural harbor in Africa. And although the people are known to be very friendly and inviting, the country was still struggling with civil war throughout, which created an incredibly brutal, violent, and terrifying existence for many of the people who were just trying to provide the mere basics for their families.

After one particularly difficult and emotional day of filming in Bone Suffer, my dad went for a walk to clear his head on the beautiful, unspoiled, and white sand beaches along the peninsula. He noticed a few wooden fishing boats on the shore, waiting silently until morning when the fishermen would arrive to go out once again and catch what they could to sell at market. As he glanced around, one boat caught his attention. It was one of the smaller ones, all wooden like the others but the name of the boat made all the difference. Painted on the side of the boat was one word: Perseverance. My dad would later say that he was impressed immediately — most of the people he had met spoke Krio, and most people with English as their *first* language wouldn't even be able to spell the word perseverance properly (just for reference, I spelled it wrong both times I typed it out and had to rely on spellcheck). But here it was the name of a boat in a war-torn country with so much despair around it.

Photo credit: Allen Schied, my dad's co-worker.

My dad was determined to wait for this person who had named their boat Perseverance, even if he had to sleep on the beach that night. Thankfully, he didn't have to do that as the fisherman saw my dad looking at his boat and walked up to engage him in conversation.

"Hello. I see you are looking at my boat," the fisherman said.

"Yes, I just love the name. Perseverance," my dad replied.

"Ah, yes. The day I named it Perseverance, I caught more fish and have each day since," he said with a smile.

"That's absolutely amazing," my dad said. "Do you mind if I take a picture of the boat? I think there are people at home who could use a little perspective and your boat's name and story may just help them find it."

"Of course. Please. I would be honored. We could all use a little perspective at some point," he said with a smile as he walked back up the beach to the street. "Have a nice evening. I hope the picture helps."

"Thank you," my dad said. "You will be an inspiration to so many and lesson for so many others in how to make the very best of a situation."

The fisherman tipped his hat to my dad and that was it. He was gone, but not without providing a short and powerful lesson on perspective. When I think of that fisherman, the situation in his country at the time, and what he chose to name his boat, I can't help but think of the lyrics from the 1985 song, "Never Surrender" by Corey Hart:

> "With a little perseverance
> You can get things done
> Without the blind adherence
> That has conquered some ..."

■■■■■■■■■■■■■■■■■■■■■■■■■■■■■■■■■■

🕹 **FUN FACT:** Talking about his song, "Never Surrender," Corey Hart said that his influences for the name of the song came from his mom and Winston Churchill, both of whom never gave up.[48]

■■■■■■■■■■■■■■■■■■■■■■■■■■■■■■■■■■

My dad's friend Allen took the picture of the boat and when he returned stateside, he made copies of it and gave a framed copy to every person at his production company. He also gave one to me, my sister, and my stepbrother. To this day, we all display it proudly in our homes and share the story with others.

If you could benefit from seeing things in a fresh way, the good news is that you don't need to travel halfway around the world to get some perspective or look at things from a different angle. And you don't need to teach a class while standing on a desk (although that would probably make you a pretty cool teacher). Gaining a valuable new perspective is pretty simple to do. Just get out of your bubble. It can be as simple as looking through a telescope to appreciate how small we are in the scheme of

---

48 "Never Surrender (Corey Hart Song)," Wikipedia, Last Edited November 28, 2021, https://en.wikipedia.org/wiki/Never_Surrender_(Corey_Hart_song).

things. Ronald Miller from *Can't Buy Me Love* would be proud of you. Live in the city? Go out to the country for a night. Live in the country? Venture into the city for an evening. Take a morning and trade in the Starbucks crowd for the crowd at Dunkin Donuts or Dunkin Donuts for Starbucks. If you are a night owl like me, trade in a sunset for a walk with the people of the sunrise and vice versa for that dreaded morning person. Kidding — you morning people aren't really dreadful. If you are a morning person, stay up until 2:00 or 3:00 a.m. one night and you might feel the energy that we creatives feel when everyone else around us is sleeping.

Gaining a valuable new perspective is pretty simple to do. Just get out of your bubble.

There are so many different angles from which we can look at life and each other. I guess geometry did teach me something, after all. Just not what was originally intended.

CHAPTER 10

THE BREAKFAST CLUB

"Dear Mr. Vernon ..."

— THE BREAKFAST CLUB

John Hughes was a genius. He helped define an entire generation and because he was behind the camera instead of in front, he doesn't always get mentioned with other pop culture generation and decade definers. He was as prolific a writer, producer, and director as we have ever seen and likely will ever see. Just in the '80s alone, he gave us *Mr. Mom*, *Vacation*, *Sixteen Candles*, *European Vacation*, *Weird Science*, *Pretty in Pink*, *Ferris Bueller's Day Off*, *Some Kind of Wonderful*, *Planes, Trains and Automobiles*, *She's Having a Baby*, *The Great Outdoors*, *Uncle Buck*, *Christmas Vacation*, and the movie that defined Generation X, *The Breakfast Club*. And if we sneak 1990 in there, he gave us a little film called *Home Alone*. Prolific indeed.

I talk a lot about the many ways in which '80s pop culture continues to resonate generation after generation. At the time of the writing of this chapter, *Stranger Things* (Season 4) — which is set in the '80s — is the #1 show on Netflix and likely planet earth, and *Top Gun: Maverick* is the #1 movie and destroying every box-office record on the books. Yeah, the '80s aren't going anywhere anytime soon, so for all Gen Xers everywhere, I say "thank you for your support" — as Bartles & Jaymes used to tell us in commercials for their very-affordable-for-high-school-students wine coolers. Of course, the legal age for drinking supposedly precluded us from partaking in high school, but rules were made to be broken, right? Besides it's not like we stood out in front of the gas station asking people of legal age to buy us alcohol. Okay, that rule was broken as well. Damn those rule breakers. The 2015 song "Renegades" by X Ambassadors sums up the rule breakers perfectly and it gives a nod to Spielberg so, yes, I can include it in my '80s pop culture love letter. Give it a listen. Great song.

One reason '80s pop culture continues to resonate is John Hughes's incredible ability to tell the human story through so many unique characters and tell it in a way that resonates with people — particularly youth in decade after decade. I often tell the story of being at the grocery store with a buddy and his girl-friend on a 4th of July weekend a few years ago, getting our BBQ shopping done. I was wearing a Breakfast Club t-shirt with the iconic shot of them in front of the lockers. The girl bagging our groceries looked at my shirt and said, "That's my favorite movie." From there our conversation went like this:

> **Me:** "Really? That's cool. It's one of my favorites too. Wait, how old are you?"
>
> **Girl:** "I'm fifteen."

Me: "Fifteen? I was fifteen when this movie came out and I'm 50 now. How can this be your favorite movie?"

Girl: "My friends and I all love *The Breakfast Club* and all of those movies from back then."

Me: "Can I ask why? I mean there are movies about high school that are much more recent. Probably some that came out this year."

Girl: "We love the characters. They are more real and have similar problems to what we have and feel today. They have conversations that we have with each other and the same issues with cliques, parents, acceptance, bullying. Things like that."

Me: "Wow. This is so cool. And the high school movies today?"

Girl: "No way. The guys drive hundred-thousand-dollar cars and the girls look like they are 30. Not realistic, at least where we go to school."

Me: [Laughing] "Yeah the '80s was definitely a different time."

Girl: "You were so lucky to grow up then. We all wish we did too."

Me: "Well, you've made my day. Thank you. Happy 4th!"

Girl: "Happy 4th to you. Hey, does Barry Manilow know that you raid his wardrobe?"

Okay, she really didn't say that last part but I'm sure she knew that quote. Just like Shakespeare is the bridge to the pop culture of the 16th and 17th centuries, John Hughes is both the 1.21 gigawatts and the flux capacitor to the pop culture of the '80s.

Another reason '80s pop culture continues to resonate is because of the pop culture genres that were either created or drastically expanded upon during the decade. In music, there was hip hop, which went from a few songs in the late '70s to multiple sub-genres in the '80s, producing eclectic voices and sounds ranging from the hardcore — like Public Enemy, The Geto Boys, Boogie Down Productions, and N.W.A. — to the house party sounds of Tone Loc and Young MC, to the socially conscious flows of A Tribe Called Quest and De La Soul, and the somewhere-in-between-it-all sounds of Run DMC, LL Cool J, and The Beastie Boys. And how about "heavy metal?" Sure, there was a bit of a metal scene before the '80s, with bands like KISS, Black Sabbath, and even Judas Priest's first album, but '80s metal saw the same sub-genre growth as hip hop. From arena rock/metal with Van Halen, AC/DC, Dokken, and Def Leppard to hair-metal with bands like Poison, Motley Crue, Ratt, and Warrant to thrash-metal led by Anthrax, Metallica, Megadeth, and Slayer, to Top-40 metal from Bon Jovi, Night Ranger, and Loverboy. Okay, maybe those last three aren't exactly metal but they were considered "harder" rock back in the day.

Me with Don Dokken, the founder and lead singer of '80s rock band Dokken.

When it comes to the expansion and explosions of genres and sub-genres, the same goes for the movie industry, although the '80s really took existing movie genres (which previously had fits and starts) and expanded them considerably — essentially making it the decade of record for genres like rom-coms, coming-of-age movies, slasher films, and over-the-top action-hero blockbusters.

The Quintessential Do-Over

The '80s are also known for the explosion of the movie sequel. I can't list all of them here since my publisher told me: "Please, less than 70,000 words, Chris." I think I failed her here, so a little list wouldn't hurt too bad. On the contrary, it might "Hurt(s) So Good" as John Cougar Mellencamp sang back in 1982. Movie franchises were built on multiple sequels in the '80s. Movies like *Raiders of the Lost Ark*, *Lethal Weapon*, *Beverly Hills Cop*, *Rocky*, *The Karate Kid*, *Police Academy*, *Halloween*, *A Nightmare on Elm Street*, *Friday the 13*[th] (all 193 sequels), *Star Wars*, *Back to the Future*, *Ghostbusters*, *Vacation*, *Missing in Action,* and so many more, both good and terrible. Remember the sequels to *Poltergeist*, *Gremlins*, and *Eddie and the Cruisers*? Yeah, me neither.

So why all this talk about sequels in a chapter for a movie that thankfully didn't have one? Well, this *chapter* is actually a sequel (yes, I've published some thoughts on *The Breakfast Club* before), but I'm hopeful this one will be more like *Rocky II* than *Poltergeist II.*

When I sat down to write my first book on lessons from '80s pop culture, my mind went right to classic and iconic movies of the decade — movies like *The Goonies*, *Back to the Future*, *Stand By Me*, *Ferris Bueller's Day Off*, and, of course, *The Breakfast Club*. I really had no idea what I was doing, and my initial book was really just a result of seeing surprising interest in a LinkedIn article I wrote, titled "What the Breakfast Club Taught Us About Problem Solving" and a desire to create something of my own and not "lead a life of quiet desperation" as Henry David Thoreau said way, way back in the day. You've seen that Thoreau quote in multiple chapters throughout this book. Yes, it means that much to me.

I had no idea what that first book would launch in terms of my career as a keynote speaker and author on the topic of lessons for life and the workplace from '80s pop culture. And it shows. Look, I'm so proud of that first book for multiple reasons, starting with the fact that without it, I would likely still be toiling away at a marketing job in a cubicle or office with little control over my workday and my future. Now I get paid to talk about '80s pop culture. "Surreal" doesn't even begin to define it. But that first book is not a great book. I can say that now. I think the content is fun, the idea and lessons were certainly unique and new, and it had a good dose of nostalgia — but it's more like a novelty item than an actual book. It's all of 70 pages and that includes the blank pages at the end so it's more like 60 pages of actual content, if that. And that's using a smaller trim size than a typical book. It also had 10 chapters — just like this book and my 2ⁿᵈ one, which are both almost four times the length of Book #1. Instead of being on the shelves at your local mall bookstore, Walden Books, it would have likely been sitting next to the newest *Truly Tasteless Joke*s book at Spencer's Gifts, which I would have actually preferred.

I know I'm beginning to sound a little like a pessimistic Cameron Frye from *Ferris Bueller's Day Off* or the always-devastated Lane Meyer from *Better Off Dead*. But looking back, that first book does resemble the beginning of one of the best music videos ever made and what should be the anthem for rebellious youth for centuries to come — "We're Not Gonna Take It" by Twisted Sister. At the beginning of the video, the dad walks into the kid's room when he is playing the electric guitar and says: "Alright mister, what do you think you're doing? You call this a room? This is a pigsty. I want you to straighten up this area now!"

Replace the word "room" with "book" and I'm sure that if I had an editor, she would have said the exact same thing. But a wise person once told me that getting better is part of the creative process, and if you enjoy creating, you hope that the *first* thing you did isn't the *best* thing you'll ever do. Just like anything in life, the goal is to continue to get better and improve as you go. The big difference, of course, is when you create stuff, it's out there for everyone to see and consume. It also means that they get to see you grow and, hopefully, they will take that totally awesome journey with you. All that is to say that if you read my take on *The Breakfast Club* in my first book, I can assure you that this discussion is far more robust.

Now some of the lessons in that first book were literally a paragraph or two and the shortest chapter was the one on, you guessed it, *The Breakfast Club*. How I decided to give one of the most iconic and possibly the most influential movie for Generation X — my generation — the least amount of love, well, I have no idea. Thank Gozer the Gozerian (that's a *Ghostbusters* reference for those not completely immersed in the '80s paranormal movie monster manual) that we were given the gift of sequels. For some, the sequel is to add to the story and for others it's a shot at redemption. The quintessential do-over. That's what this sequel is. Take two.

In offering up this do-over, I'm also deviating from my standard template (i.e., the introduction of two lessons, the trip back in time to my life when the movie came out, an overview of pop culture that month and year, and a deep dive into the lessons). This time, I'm going to give *The Breakfast Club* the attention it deserves, so rather than dive into what I was doing in February of 1985 (I was in detention for wearing a "Who Farted" shirt in Spanish class, if you must know) and talk about the movies, TV, and music during that timeframe, we are going to just focus on a brain, an athlete, a basket case, a princess, a criminal, a principal, and a janitor.

I do have to mention just one thing about the music at the time. As iconic and influential as the movie was, the main track on the soundtrack could arguably be the defining song of the 1980s. "Don't You Forget About Me" by Simple Minds and it's "hey, hey, hey hey, ooohhhh, whoa" opening is a Generation X anthem and just a damn-good song whose sound is both totally '80s and totally timeless. What is really interesting though is that the movie came out on February 18, 1985, but the song itself didn't break into the Top 40 until the week of March 23, when it came in at #36. It did climb all the way to #1 but not until the week of May 18, when it supplanted Madonna's "Crazy for You" in the top spot. Just like the movies stayed in the theaters for months in the '80s, the music did the same on the charts. "Don't You Forget About Me" didn't drop out of the Top 40 until the week of June 29, 1985. Four months in the Top 40 and very well deserved. How *Stranger Things* didn't find a way to include it in the series is beyond me. It's about the only thing they missed in an absolutely fantastic show.

■■■■■■■■■■■■■■■■■■■■■■■■■■■■■■■■

⚏ **FUN FACT:** Whether you are too young to have known the '80s firsthand and are new to John Hughes movies or if you are of a certain age — like me — and bow at the altar of everything John Hughes, it's clear that music was core to who he was as a filmmaker and human. Besides "Don't You Forget About Me," there are three songs from Hughes movies that immediately transport me back to my days of parachute pants, feathered hair, Drakkar Noir, and checkerboard Vans. I also immediately see so many Hughes characters — Ferris, Cameron, Sloane, Jake Ryan, Farmer Ted,

Samantha, Neil Page, Del Griffith, Chet, Wyatt, Gary, Lisa, Duckie, Andie, Uncle Buck, The Griswold crew, and, of course, the brain, the athlete, the basket case, the princess, and the criminal — when I hear those same three songs. For those who are just getting into John Hughes's wonderful films and for those who want to feel nostalgic, may I suggest:

- General Public — "Tenderness"
- Dream Academy — "The Edge of Forever"
- Thompson Twins — "If You Were Here"

These songs will transport you to the steps of Shermer High School or the aftermath of a wedding ceremony where Jake Ryan awaits next to his candy-red Porsche and even a train station on Thanksgiving Eve. And that, my friends, is the longest Fun Fact in my book series and I can't think of a better one to hold the record.

■■■■■■■■■■■■■■■■■■■■■■■■■■■■■■■■

Life Lessons from *The Breakfast Club*

On February 15, 1985, *The Breakfast Club* hit theaters. It was a movie that the studio was not interested in making. John Hughes ultimately scared up a $1,000,000 budget for the film and shot it concurrently with *Ferris Bueller's Day Off.*[49] *The Breakfast Club* tells the story of five students at Shermer High School — Brian (the brain played by Anthony Michael Hall), Andrew (the athlete played by Emilio Estevez), Allison (the basket case played by Ally Sheedy), Claire (the princess played by Molly Ringwald), and John Bender (the criminal played by Judd Nelson) — all from

---

49 https://screenrant.com/breakfast-club-details-behind-scenes-making-trivia/.

very different walks of life and all in detention together in the school library on Saturday morning, March 24, 1984.

The detention monitor is Principal Vernon, who immediately makes himself known at exactly 7:06 a.m. and informs this "demented and sad but social" party of five that they will each write an essay of no less than 1,000 words describing to him who they think they are. He tells them they will not talk, move from their seats, or sleep. Of course, they ignore all three rules, most importantly the first one because talking is exactly how they truly get to know each other and ultimately understand and appreciate each other's differences.

One thing that is really cool and unique about the movie is that it is shot in one location — Shermer High School — and 90% of the movie is shot in one room, the library. It's for this reason that I think it would make a fantastic Broadway show. Anyone who knows me also knows that I loathe remakes and I've probably mentioned that in this book a few times, but I do think a theatre production would be really awesome.

Another deviation from the other chapters in this book is the number of lessons I'm about to offer up. Each of the previous chapters had two in-depth lessons, but *The Breakfast Club* characters and their dialogue present so many opportunities for lessons that I decided to find at least one lesson from each character. It wasn't difficult. So the lessons will be shorter but you'll also get to hear from all the unique voices in the movie, each teaching us something about life.

So, what can a group of awkward teenagers in detention, plus their principal and a janitor named Carl, teach us about life? Let's start with "The Brain."

Brian "The Brain" Johnson
The Essay

Just like the ocean, the really cool stuff in human beings is found beneath the surface.

Nerd. Dork. Geek. These were all a different category of four-letter words that people, usually kids, used to describe someone who kicked ass in the classroom but may have struggled in social and athletic settings. Of course, all that fun at their expense came with a price in adulthood. For the "cool kids," spending four years berating the nerds, dorks, and geeks in their "Glory Days" (as The Boss sang back in 1985) was likely the high point in their life, while the nerds, dorks, and geeks had a lifetime of success, accomplishment, and, in many cases, wealth ahead of them. The cool kids? Well, if you've been to a 20-year high-school reunion, I think you know the answer.

Now that is not to say that all cool kids acted uncool. On the contrary, I'm sure there are a lot of cool kids out there who act cool in their interactions with everyone, regardless of their high-school social status. And there are, of course, cool kids (i.e., popular kids) who go on to do great things. Many of my lessons, including this one, have an underlying theme around not general-izing, so I certainly don't want to do that myself. However, except for portions of *Revenge of the Nerds* and one episode of *The Big Bang Theory*, you don't see too many examples of groups of nerds pushing around and making fun of the cool kids. But it is specifi-cally because of *Revenge of the Nerds* in 1984 that a character like Brian Johnson could be a protagonist and someone we cheer for in 1985.

If we use the standard definition of a "nerd," then Brian was it in every sense of the word. He was a "neo maxi zoom dweebie," as Bender would say. He was in the math, Latin, and physics clubs, and his mom packed his lunch and made sure that all five food groups were represented. When Principal Vernon said, "You will not move from these seats," Brian moved back to his original one. He has a fictitious girlfriend who lives in Canada, and he has a fake ID so he can vote. And the reason he is in detention is because he was failing shop class because he couldn't get his elephant lamp to light up when you pull the trunk, which would have brought down his perfect GPA, so he brought a gun to school that went off in his locker. Not a hand gun. A flare gun.

Being a "nerd" is also why it's likely that at the beginning of the movie, the rest of the characters were probably thinking about leaning on him to write their essays required by Principal Vernon. After all, the nerds do everyone else's homework — especially for the cool kids, right? Remember that each breakfast clubber was supposed to write a personal 1,000-word essay describing who they thought they were to Principal Vernon, which made sense because they all came into detention as individuals from different cliques with nothing in common (or so they thought). By the end of the movie, they were a club in the truest sense of the word. They knew each other better than their own families or the groups of friends they each had prior to that morning. They knew each other's secrets and now respected each person's life journey and individuality. Most importantly, they realized that they had more in common than they could have ever imagined. They were a team. They were friends. They were The Breakfast Club. Brian wrote one essay to represent all five of the breakfast clubbers, but it was something that he chose to do and something that they all entrusted him with because they truly knew him at that point. The essay read as follows:

They were a team. They were friends. They were The Breakfast Club.

Dear Mr. Vernon,

*We accept the fact that we had to sacrifice a whole Saturday
in detention for whatever it was we did wrong. But we
think you're crazy to make us write an essay telling you who
we think we are. You see us as you want to see us — in the
simplest terms, in the most convenient definitions. But what
we found out is that each of us is a brain and an athlete and
a basket case, a princess and a criminal. Does that answer
your question?*

Sincerely Yours,

The Breakfast Club

Powerful. And they attacked their essay "As One!" as General
Maximus (played by Russell Crowe) said in his inspirational
pre-battle speech in the 2000 Oscar-winning film, *Gladiator*. The
most important line in the essay is "You see us as you want to see
us — in the simplest terms, in the most convenient definitions
..." So many people go through life seeing people only through
the lens of perception and labels. It's stupid and it's lazy. It's also
where we find ourselves at this moment in time. In human terms,
it's shallow. In marine terms, it's like living in the shallows but:

Just like the ocean, the really cool stuff in human beings is found beneath the surface.

And, also just like the ocean, the coolest stuff is *super* deep and
way below the surface. I only know this because my sister is
a marine biologist and a totally awesome diver, so she shares
all her really awesome pictures and videos with me. I, on the
other hand, have issues with scuba diving. I do love the ocean

and being in it, but my scuba-diving career was super short.
Just two dives. After getting certified in college and getting two
credits for it, which was pretty awesome, I took my skills to the
open ocean. Big mistake. On my second dive, I was floating
around the bottom — about 50 feet below the surface — when
I got the feeling something was looking at me. You know that
feeling if you have a dog or cat that is staring at you while you
sleep until you open your eyes. Kind of freaks you out, right?
Now imagine being on the bottom of the ocean and having that
feeling. I turned around to find a 400-pound Goliath Grouper
staring right at me! Scared the holy shit out of me, causing
my regulator (which is what you use to breathe) to fall out of
my mouth. Thankfully, I was aware enough to grab it and put
it back in my mouth but here was this massive creature still
staring at me. I was wondering if it was going to try and eat
me if I made a sudden move but not wanting to wait to find
out, I went to the surface a little faster than I should have. The
Goliath didn't follow me, but when I got to the boat, the dive
captain asked me what happened and if I was okay. I told him
the story and he laughed and said, "Dude, they aren't dangerous
at all. Super docile and plant eaters. Not predators. He was just
curious." I said, "That's all well and good and kind of the point.
A non-predator, very overweight, plant-eating fish snuck up on
me like a ninja and stealth isn't even in his skillset, yet here we
are. If that thing can sneak up on me with no predatory instinct
whatsoever, well, I'm not really interested in being down there
anymore." And with that, my scuba career ended two dives in.
But I did see some really cool stuff beneath the surface.

All the characters in *The Breakfast Club* are so well developed
by Hughes and brought to life in an incredibly believable way by
the entire cast. The characters all have a lot of depth and layers,
but Brian, in my opinion, is the deepest of the characters. He's in
a very delicate position in his life. Of all the groups in high school,
the brainy kids tend to have it the hardest but if they could just
jump in a time machine and see where their life is heading 10,

20, 30 years down the road, they would have a very different impression of themselves and those around them. The pressure from being a bit of a social outcast combined with the pressure from the family and themselves to perform at the very highest levels academically has got to be overwhelming. I'm guessing here because, as my dad once told me when I came home for the holidays around the age of 30 after being in Florida for eight years and establishing a career of my own, "I never really thought you were the smartest guy. I mean if I was to compare you to a dog breed, I'd say golden retriever. You walk into a room smiling, happy, and wagging your tail and everyone is happy to see you, but you know there isn't a whole lot going on in that dog's head. Goofy and happy but not very bright." To this day, he says he was complimenting me on my unexpected success at the time, but I'm still not convinced.

Brian was smart enough to be a border collie. But being smart isn't the same thing as being cool, and he felt so much pressure to be accepted that he holds Bender's stash of weed in his pants when asked to do so and makes up a girlfriend who lives in Canada — "you wouldn't know her," he says — so they won't think he's a virgin. Now these may seem like small things in the overall spectrum of things that will happen in our lifetime, but to Brian they are monumental moments. For the first time in his life, he is getting to spend quality time with the cool kids and, yes, in Brian's mind, Bender — with his rebellious streak — is a cool kid as well. We see this when Principal Vernon comes in after Bender creates a commotion falling through the HVAC ducts while "exploring" the school and Vernon says, "What was that noise? I heard a ruckus" — to which Brian says, "Could you describe the ruckus, sir?" Yes, I do have a shirt with that saying on it. It's Brian coming out of his shell, but it is also shows us three things about Brian that the other breakfast clubbers and the rest of the students at school don't know about him:

1. He does have a rebellious streak in him, and he isn't afraid to challenge authority.

2. He's quick-witted with a sharp sense of humor.

3. He will protect his friends even at his own expense. Remember when Bender told Principal Vernon that his dope was actually hidden in "Johnson's pants," he knew Vernon wouldn't actually think that to be true even though it was — so this really is the first time we see him step up and take a real risk.

The reason this moment is so important is because (a) we and the breakfast clubbers learn about what is below Brian's surface and (b) it feels like the first time we see him express himself not for the acceptance of the others but because it is really who he is underneath it all.

This is what happens when we take the time to explore others and go beyond what we perceive someone to be based on a label or how we view them from afar. When you go beneath the surface, the human underneath might surprise you and when given the opportunity, like Brian, they just might surprise themselves. Just like what is below the surface of the ocean, we are all full of beautiful colors, variety, wonderment, and a bit of the unknown. Explore a little. It will do you and others some good.

Andrew "The Athlete" Clark
"We're all pretty bizarre. Some of us are just better at hiding it, that's all."

 Be unique. Be bizarre. But most importantly, just be you.

What is it that makes you bizarre? Do you still hide it as an adult or have you just decided to let that freak flag fly?

On the surface, Andrew "The Athlete" Clark would likely be chosen for the school yearbook as "Most normal," "Most stable," or "Most likely to succeed." At a later point in the movie, the breakfast clubbers are sitting in a circle having a very honest and sometimes contentious conversation about who they really are. They expose themselves and are exposed by the others with everyone's flaws on display for the group to see. It is perhaps the most authentic and most important scene in the film. It's John Hughes doing what he did best — exploring the teenage soul and spirit.

At one point, Allison (The Basket Case) finally talks and gets Claire (The Princess) to admit something personal that she didn't want to share by lying about herself. Claire fires back, saying how weird Allison is and how she doesn't open her mouth all day and when she finally does, she throws out a bunch of lies. Andrew tells Claire that she is just pissed because Allison got her to admit something she didn't want to admit to, and the scene goes from there:

> **Claire:** "Fine, but it's still bizarre."
>
> **Andrew:** "What's bizarre? We're all pretty bizarre. Some of us are just better at hiding it, that's all."

The lesson?

Be unique. Be bizarre. But most importantly, just be you.

As teenagers, we often felt the pressure to be someone we're not just to "fit in" with friends, family, or other social groups that demand it. We were young and impressionable so it's understandable. So much of what we did was a façade, a way to find acceptance, and we didn't even have social media to assist us in creating our fake and "acceptable" lives. But we still do the same thing as adults. So many people take a life journey based on what other people want or expect rather than what their soul is telling them to do. And often times, it's because what they really want to do or who they really want to be would be considered unorthodox, different, non-traditional, or that dreaded word, bizarre.

I'm 52, I've never been married, and I have no kids — and apparently there are a lot of people who think that's bizarre. So many in fact that it was the most consistent topic of conversation whenever I met people at personal events, work events, or black-tie events because I usually attended solo. Typically, when I would be introduced to a new group of people, which were usually couples, the first few questions were the "normal" ones like: what do you do, are you married, do you have kids? We call them normal, but they do seem kind of intrusive if you really think about it. In any case, I would always answer the last two questions the same — no and no — and it would always get the same response. The head cocked to the side like a dog when they are confused and have no idea what you are saying, followed by a "Never married? No kids? How come?" There was absolutely no comprehension of the fact that someone just might be different, dare I say bizarre, or might possibly have a non-traditional journey. Regardless of the look I was given, I was always polite. Until one night, when I had a few bourbons and decided I was tired of nodding, smiling, and then making up some excuse for why I wasn't like all the other reindeer. I was introduced to a couple and the conversation went like this:

Man: "Nice to meet you."

Woman: "Nice to meet you. So what do you do?"

Me: "I'm in marketing."

Woman: "Are you married?"

Me: "No."

Woman: "Divorced?"

Me: "No."

Woman: "Have you been married?"

Me: "No."

Woman: "Do you have any kids?"

Me: "No."

Woman: "So never married and no kids?"

Me: "Yes."

Woman: "WHY?"

Me: "Let me ask *you* a question."

Woman: "Okay."

Me: "Married?"

Woman: "Yes, of course. You just met my husband."

Me: "Kids?"

Woman: "Yes, a boy and a girl."

Me: "WHY?"

Woman: "Ummm … I don't understand the question."

Me: "Exactly. Neither do I."

I still don't know what she mumbled under her breath as she walked away but I would imagine it might have been something like what *Qbert* used to say in the '80s arcade video game of the same name. Whenever you got the character in trouble, a dialogue bubble would come up that said "@!!!?@!" which translated means, well, nothing good.

Now that may not seem like something super bizarre, like say being a grown man and singing Kelly Clarkson at the top of your lungs in your car with the windows rolled down every time a song of hers comes on a Pandora station. I know someone who does that. He's an author and speaker as well. You might know him a little bit by now. But honestly, never being married and having no kids at the age of 52 does put me in a tiny little group of people, so maybe it is a little bizarre after all. I've also been in a New Order style "Bizarre Love Triangle" as they sang back in 1986. Not really, but maybe. You'll never know.

Any way. Whether the way we live our lives is a little bizarre or a lot bizarre, as we grow, we realize that our happiness is in accepting and being who we really are and that our strength lies in the fact that each of us is uniquely different from every other person … and that is awesome.

Ultimately, what Andrew was saying is: Be you. Embrace who you are. We get one shot at this crazy awesome life, and it's gone in the blink of an eye. Be unique. Be different. Be bizarre. Most importantly, just be you.

Allison "The Basket Case" Reynolds
"When you grow up, your heart dies."

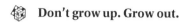 **Don't grow up. Grow out.**

In the early '80s, Toys R' Us launched an ad campaign with a jingle that has lasted longer than the toy-store chain itself. The last store officially closed on June 29, 2018, but the "I don't wanna grow up, I'm a Toys R' Us kid" jingle is likely to be part of pop culture for generations to come.

■■■■■■■■■■■■■■■■■■■■■■■■■■■■■■■

FUN FACT: One of the most famous crime writers in history, James Patterson, wrote the "I don't wanna grow up" Toys R' Us jingle along with Linda Kaplan Thayler when they were both co-workers at the advertising agency J. Walter Thompson (now Wunderman Thompson).[50]

■■■■■■■■■■■■■■■■■■■■■■■■■■■■■■■

During the same amazing scene where the Breakfast Club kids are sitting in a circle having that very honest and contentious conversation, the focus turns to their parents and growing up. That part of the scene goes like this:

Andrew: "My god. Are we going to be like our parents?"

Claire: "Not me. Ever."

Allison: "It's unavoidable. It just happens."

Claire: "What happens?"

Allison: "When you grow up, your heart dies."

---

50 Kathleen Elkins, "How James Patterson, the Richest Writer in the World, Helped Create the Iconic Toys R' Us Jingle," CNBC, March 19, 2018, www.CNBC. com/2018/03/19/james-patterson-helped-create-the-toys-r-us-jingle.html

Bender: "Who cares?"

Allison: "I care."

"When you grow up, your heart dies." It's an incredibly real and raw moment. One that still hits me right in the gut because it's true for so many people and you can really feel the authenticity from Ally Sheedy. As we move from the carefree world of youth to the very real world of adulthood, we tend to lose so much of what makes us truly individuals and, in some ways, even human. It's partly our fault and partly the way the world has defined what it is to be an adult. We are told to stop daydreaming, but creativity and imagination fuel our communities and organizations. We are told it's time to be mature, but a little bit of immaturity is what helps us get into situations that spawn stories for a lifetime. (Sidenote – I almost said "lifetime stories" but I realized that could be misconstrued for Lifetime Movies. Wrong kind of movies for this guy.) "Grow up," we are all told. "Settle down." But when has settling in any aspect of your life really helped you grow? We are told "you're too old" for this or that, and then we start to believe it. Think about how many things you haven't done that would have brought you joy simply because you were told by someone, "oh, you're too old for that." You may not know the name Irene O'Shea, but she is the oldest skydiver on record at the very young age of 102. That whole "too old for this or that" is absolute nonsense. We are told to grow up. "You're an adult now, act like it." No one tells us that taking that imperative too seriously can make your "heart die." No one except Ally Sheedy as Allison in *The Breakfast Club*. The lesson she teaches us?

 Don't grow up. Grow out.

We're told to grow up and so we do. Most of us oblige and do all the things we are told to do when you grow up. We stop daydreaming. We stop playing. We stop focusing on our friends. We stop being creative and daring and authentic. Go ahead and tell me that if you stop doing all those things in favor of "growing up" that your heart won't die. Allison was right. When you grow up, your heart dies. So instead of growing up, try growing out. Growing out requires doing all the things that you are told not to do as an adult. Just like anything else that goes (or grows) up, there is an eventual ceiling and in this case the ceiling is adulthood. Growing *out* doesn't have a cap or a limit. The expansion of your personality and your experiences and your interests is limitless. Every time you "grow out," you are learning or creating a new experience or new memory.

Growing out is spending time with people from different backgrounds or different cultures.

Growing out is taking a class to learn a new skill or to educate yourself on something new.

Growing out is saying yes to the bungie jump when you're 60 or the skydive when you are 102.

Growing out is taking that passion or talent that you've bottled up for way too long because it was "immature" or "childish" or "just a dream" and sharing it with whomever you choose.

Growing out is doing whatever it is that you dreamed of doing as a kid on those long bike rides with friends when you had no destination, no end game, and no limitations in your mind on what was possible in that exact moment.

And if you're busy growing *up* right now and you don't feel like you have the luxury of growing *out*, just know that you can grow out later. If the Grinch's heart could get bigger as he amassed new experiences and perspectives, yours can too.

Clarie "The Princess" Standish
"I hate it. I hate going along with everything my friends say."

 "Group think" isn't thinking at all. Don't blindly follow anyone. Ever.

As I've mentioned a few times in this book, I've never had kids but so much of *The Breakfast Club* is really targeted to teenagers that it would only make sense to have a few lessons that are for kids and adults alike. Now even though I don't have kids, I can speak from a place of understanding because, well, I used to be a kid. I was a high school freshman when the movie was released and my first viewing of it was when I was 15 years old and facing many of the same issues as the Breakfast Clubbers. My dad actually saw the movie first with a few of his friends, called me and said, "This is a really important movie for you to see. I think it is going to be one of the movies that defines your youth." Remember that my dad was in the entertainment business so he definitely understood the impact of movies beyond just that they were "good," "fun," or "entertaining."

It turned out he was right, but at 15 years old, I'd much rather have been forced to sit through a triple feature of *Yentl, A Chorus Line,* and *Terms of Endearment* than admit that either of my parents were right about anything.

So many of the lessons I'm sharing about *The Breakfast Club* come from the scene where they are sitting in a circle in the back of the library. This one is no exception. The beginning of this conversation starts with Brian (The Brain):

> **Brian:** "I was just wondering what is going to happen to us on Monday? I mean, I consider all of you my friends. I'm not wrong, am I? C'mon, what happens on Monday?"

Claire: "Are we still friends you mean? Friends now after this?"

Brian: "Yeah."

Claire: "You want the truth?"

Brian: "Yeah, I want the truth."

Claire: "I don't think so."

It's a super harsh answer but also the likely truth. The conversation continues from there, with all five characters getting involved and directing much of their ire at Claire for being both honest and obnoxious. She pushes back and puts mainly Bender and Andrew on the spot, asking them if they would invite the others to hang out with their group of friends. Andrew doesn't say anything, and Bender gets into a shouting match with Claire over her privileged and spoiled life.

They go back and forth, and it gets very heated. At one point, when Brian realizes that none of the others would include him in their group of friends (or as Simple Minds sings in the film's featured song, "call his name as he walks on by"), he asks Allison, "Would you do that to me?" She replies, "I don't have any friends." Brian smiles and says, "But if you did?" Allison smiles back and says, "No. I don't think the kind of friends I'd have would mind." I feel like Allison was and is representative of so many kids in high school who were just really ignored or considered weird by the "popular" crowd. And many of those kids went on to do big, dynamic, or creative things as adults — which is why her character is the most important one in the movie for real-life teenagers going through something similar.

At this point, Claire is put on the spot once again when Brian asks her why she is so full of herself in the sense that she won't acknowledge him, Allison, or Bender on Monday at school.

Claire responds: "I'm not saying it to be conceited. I hate it. I hate having to go along with everything my friends say."

In that moment, we get our key lesson from her:

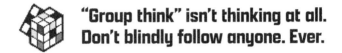 **"Group think" isn't thinking at all. Don't blindly follow anyone. Ever.**

Of all the dialogue in this conversation, this may be the most important line delivered. So much of the movie revolves around issues of acceptance or rejection (inclusion or exclusion) and this line perfectly sums up the issue that so many of us had in our youth. It didn't matter what group you belonged to, honestly. The "popular" kids typically take the rap for being cliquey, uninviting, and downright obnoxious to others and it is a well-earned stereotype but the vast majority of groups in high school could also be very uninviting. We all tend to be insular with our groups — groups like "the sportos, motorheads, geeks, sluts, bloods, wastoids, dweebies, dickheads" as Grace the assistant said when telling Principal Rooney about all the groups who thought Ferris was a "righteous dude" in *Ferris Bueller's Day Off.* High school is what the word clique was created for, but unfortunately too many people end up bringing that dynamic and way of thinking well into adulthood. The difference, of course, is that — by design — we should be more impressionable in our youth and that need for acceptance (regardless of the group whose acceptance we're seeking) is a real thing. It drives kids to do stupid things, like the things you've heard me tell stories about "yours truly" in this book. It also drives them to do and say hurtful things to their peers and, unless you are a Cyborg, that is something that the kid who becomes an adult will regret for the rest of their life.

If I had kids, I would share this lesson with them as early as possible and I would remind them of it every chance I got. That lesson is:

**Group think isn't thinking at all. Don't blindly follow
anyone. Ever.**

This isn't just about how you handle things in your youth.
Inevitably at one point or another, kids are going to bow to peer
pressure. The hope is that it is something small and silly that
can be a starting point for an important life discussion about
independent thinking and the importance of leading or at least
questioning rather than just blindly following. Make friends and
create relationships simply because you like that person and they
like you. Nothing more. Those types of friendships and relationships typically evolve into deeper friendships or a partnership
in either the personal or business sense. Those are your people.
Don't make friends or create relationships to be accepted into
a particular group. That's what Claire did, and she didn't even
realize she was doing it until the rest of the Breakfast Clubbers
lit her up and exposed her. That's what real friends do. Yes, they
support you, but they also call you out. That's what happens
when you don't have "group think." And not having group think
is how you grow. Thankfully for Claire, she unexpectedly found
her people on that Saturday of March 24, 1984, in detention at
Shermer High School and she was better for it. My guess is that
she didn't "walk on by" but said hello to Brian and Allison in
the hallway that next week and thereafter. We know she said
hello to Bender, as she kissed him in the parking lot to the likely
chagrin of her parents waiting in the car. And I suspect that she
didn't blindly follow anyone ever again.

> *Quick sidenote here: The Breakfast Club touches a number of times
> on bullying, and we see the kids bully each other on multiple occa-
> sions although they do come together at the end and embrace each
> other's differences. Bullying is a topic that I think '80s movies covered
> really well so here are three films that really focus on the issue that
> you could share with your teenagers: My Bodyguard, Lucas, and
> Three O' Clock High.*

John "The Criminal" Bender
"Screws fall out all the time. The world's an imperfect place."

The proverbial screws are going to fall out. The *why* is important but it's how you put them back *in* that really matters.

Have you ever felt like your screws were just falling out? That your life or your career or your body was falling apart? Yeah, me too. In fact, the reason that I am doing what I do today as a speaker and author is directly related to my career screws falling out all over the place. And for a lot of us, our careers are a major part of our life; so, I suppose you could say that my life screws were falling out as well. I was 47 years old and in a job that just wasn't working out for me and as I really looked around, I realized that the career path I had chosen for the better part of 22 years wasn't working out for me either. Yes, I'd had the chance to work for some great companies and I'd climbed that very unstable corporate ladder — so, from the outside, I'd imagine people had a very different perspective. But I wasn't fulfilled at all, and I hadn't been for a very long time. I was happy in my personal life but downright miserable in my career and I'm sure my co-workers could see it. I was, like a lot of people, caught up in the cycle of career advancement and a singular focus on a bigger title, more compensation, and that extra week of vacation (which so few of us took anyway) — the coveted extra "days off" that came after five years on the job or with a new position at a new company with a better "workplace culture."

I felt like Siouxise (of Siouxise and The Banshees) was singing to me in their 1985 song "Cities of Dust" when she sang, "Your city lies in dust, my friend." City being my career and my life in a sense. So, there I was lying on my couch and having a self-pity party of one while watching *The Breakfast Club* for the 121st time. With all the amazing dialogue and interaction throughout the movie, it was easy to miss some of the lines and their potential impact in the first 120 viewings. What's really cool about '80s movies for me besides, well, everything, is that as I grow, have new experiences, and add to my life journey, there are lines of dialogue that I didn't hear before. I mean *really* hear. They resonate in a way now that they never did before, and they mean something new to me now.

When Bender said, "Screws fall out all the time. The world's an imperfect place," he was answering Principal Vernon's question of "Who took the screws out of the door?" after he found the library door slammed shut. It, of course, bought him another week in detention but in all the times that I'd watched the movie, that line never really jumped out at me until that day. I sat straight up and rewound back to that line and listened again. My proverbial screws had most definitely fallen out and were all over the floor. What was I going to do to put them back in? I knew that it required finding something new to do with my life, but what exactly? The only way those screws were going back in is if I left the career path I'd been in for over 20 years and started fresh. Ironically enough, I had just recently rewatched *The Outsiders* and one of the characters named Johnny Cade (played by Ralph Macchio) said, "You'll still have a lot of time to make yourself be what you want." This crazy-ass universe of ours was trying to tell me something. At this point I had three choices:

1. Put the screws back in just as they were and continue living my life of "quiet desperation," as Thoreau said.

2. Get a new set of screws — meaning get a new job, essentially putting a fresh coat of paint on my current career that would eventually weather and peel … putting me right back in that area of "quiet desperation."

3. Get a new set of screws, a whole new door and doorframe, and use it as an entranceway to an entirely new path.

Circa 1974: Dimestore fashion monster, stylin' and profilin'
on my Big Wheel, choosing my path.

I chose #3 and transformed my life and my career starting with an article on LinkedIn entitled "What *The Breakfast Club* Can Teach Us About Problem Solving." From there, I built a keynote speaking series and a book series around the workplace and life lessons we can learn from '80s pop culture. Five years later, my 3rd book is in your hands and I'm bringing lessons from '80s pop culture to organizations around the country, including DHL, VISA, University of Florida, UPenn Medicine, and more.

Look, here's the truth:

 The proverbial screws are going to fall out. The *why* is important but it's how you put them back *in* that really matters.

The *why* is the past and it's always important to understand why something happened so you can avoid it moving forward or solve for it in the present. Maybe the screws fell out by no fault of your own. Maybe they had some assistance from you and choices that you made. Maybe you let them stay in there so long in the same place with no maintenance that they just rusted and fell out. Maybe the universe just decided to let you know that it was time for you to have a little test or challenge and they fell out in a way that felt completely random (but wasn't really random at all). Or maybe it was a combination of factors. But the why or the past is not where you want to live. It's not where you want to dwell. Understand it and then move forward.

The *how* is the future. How you put those screws back in is what really matters. That will dictate the rest of your life or at least the next stage in it. Robert Frost said, "Two roads diverged in a wood, and I — / I took the one less traveled by, / And that has made all the difference." Most people will choose the path *most* traveled — the comfortable one. The popular one. The safe one. The one that just puts the screws back in exactly as they were. The non-disruptive or non-John-Bender path. Bender defied the rules in an instructive way. I mean, he was pretty disruptive and at one point when Andrew was given permission to get up to go to the bathroom, Bender said, "If he gets up, we'll all get up. It'll be anarchy." Now, if you do choose that whole new set of screws, new door, and new doorframe, you may find yourself doing the Carlton dance from *The Fresh Prince of Bel Air* to the Pointer Sisters 1982 smash hit, "I'm So Excited." Trust me, this comes from a place of experience and no, I won't put it up on YouTube but I may just do it for the right price. The right price being a sizable donation to an animal rescue. I'll dance for dogs.

A life well-lived is going to have some screws fall out. It's inevitable. I can't imagine anyone's entire life is just a straight line from point A to point B. If so, well what a mundane, boring, and unentertaining life that would be. A well-lived life is going to have ups, downs, peaks, and valleys. That's what makes it worth living. As David Lee Roth sang in his 1986 cover of, "That's Life":

"That's life.
That's what all the people say.
You're riding high on Monday,
Shot down in May.
But I ain't never gonna change my tune,
When I'm back on top in the month of June."

That is definitely life. Remember to focus on "how you put those screws back in." That's your future and as Timbuk 3 told us in 1986, "The future's so bright I gotta wear shades." Get a new set a screws, a whole new door and doorframe, and grab those shades. Your future is bright, indeed.

Principal Vernon
"You ought to spend a little more time trying to make something of yourself and a little less time trying to impress people."

Time spent on you is time well spent. (Kids' lesson! But great for grown-ups too.)

So, similar to the lesson from Claire, this is one that is geared more toward kids than adults (although I do know people in their 50s who are still concerned with what others think about them and their life choices even down to the shoes they buy). Yes, it's "Sad but True" as Metallica sang in 1993. I know it's a bit of blasphemy to have a '90s song in this book about the '80s, but its Metallica ... so hopefully you'll let it slide.

I'm going to keep the discussion of this lesson fairly short, but I do want to acknowledge and appreciate Principal Vernon for a moment. Like Mr. Hand in *Fast Times at Ridgemont High*, I didn't appreciate his character when I was a kid. In actuality, Mr. Hand was pretty cool — considering he recognized Spicoli's limitations and met him halfway by going to his house to give him a verbal exam in American History so he could ultimately go to his senior prom and graduate. But *The Breakfast Club*'s Principal Vernon was everything I loathed in an educator. He was super strict, inflexible, authoritative, and one of those adults who, as a kid, you were convinced was never a kid themselves. Just popped right out at age 40. But looking back as an adult, I can appreciate that he really was exactly what some kids — kids like John Bender — absolutely needed. He also had a quick wit and showed it in his exchanges with Bender. The big issue he had, that you realize as you get older, is that he really hated his job. And if you've ever hated your job, then you know the kind of negative impact it can have on you and your life in general. Having said that, Principal Vernon's approach at the beginning — when he told the kids that they should not talk to each other and that they were to write 1,000 words about themselves — was rooted in a very old-school mentality. That isolating mentality kept people from getting to know people who were different from them and kept us in the bubbles that have become such a huge problem in modern society. Separating us, instead of inspiring us to collaborate, did more harm than good.

Throughout *The Breakfast Club*, we see that Principal Vernon has difficulty building relationships — with kids and adults alike — as evidenced in his approach to Carl, the janitor, who is of a similar age. However, he does dole out some good advice to the Breakfast Clubbers during those thoroughly entertaining conversations with Bender. When Principal Vernon sees that the door to the library is shut because Bender took the screws out, as you heard earlier in this chapter, he is not happy. He knows that Bender was the cause of the problem but he can't prove it. So they get into a back-and-forth argument through which Bender earns an additional two months of detention by saying things like "eat my shorts," "you really think I give a shit" (when Vernon tells him he just earned another Saturday in detention), and answering Vernon's question of "You through?" with a "Not even close, bud." It's an intense scene and it really does show how much Bender needs and likely craves a male figure who shows any sign of caring about his well-being, which Vernon signals in his own way when he says to Bender during their exchange, "Instead of going to prison, you'll just come here."

As Principal Vernon is walking out of the library — having won the battle of wits and struggle for power with Bender — he says this: "You ought to spend a little more time trying to make something of yourself and a little less time trying to impress people."

The lesson?

Time spent on you is time well spent.

In so many ways, we can all benefit from the wisdom in spending "more time trying to make something of yourself and a little less time trying to impress people." Decades after the '80s, now in a world of selfies and social media, we're spending even more time trying to impress people, and we sometimes do it to our detriment. That's one of the reasons why I think *The Breakfast Club* should be required viewing for every high school student. The earlier in life you can learn to spend time on *you*, the better. Too many people go through life spending their time trying to impress others instead of spending that time impressing (and nurturing and accepting) themselves. Time spent on you is time well spent. It's really that simple. And although, to some, this idea may seem a bit selfish, it is not at all. We often hear that you can't help others until you've helped yourself and all the way back in 1985, Whitney Houston sang that "learning to love yourself is the greatest love of all." She was right.

When your life revolves around impressing others, you don't really have a life at all. It's all fake. Every single minute of it. And those people who you are trying to impress? They won't be there when you need them because they don't care about you. And that isn't all on them. They don't even know who you really are because you've never shown them — so how could they possibly care about you as a human being? You should be proud of who you are and take pride in your accomplishments rather than base your worth on what others think of you. It's hard when you're a kid to see this and recognize it, which is why it is incumbent upon all of us to impart this wisdom on the kids in our little circle of family and friends. Time spent on you is time well spent.

And for any parents who are looking for a good line to use when you've had to ground your kids for something they did (that you probably did too when you were their age), Principal Vernon gave you a great one when he said: "Don't mess with the bull ... You'll get the horns."

Carl the Janitor
"When I was a kid, I wanted to be John Lennon."

The best lessons come from the most unexpected places and people.

Let's do a little exercise here. I want you to think about the people in your life who are around you the most and who have the most influence on who you are and what you do. Parents, spouses, partners, siblings, best friends. Now I want you to think about a few people who were in your life for a very short time. A bit player in your life journey. It might have been a dating relationship, a manager or co-worker at a job that didn't last very long, someone who owned a business that you frequented for a moment in your life, a person you contract for work from time to time, or just someone who came into your life through another acquaintance, and you ran into periodically.

This second group — the memorable bit players — is where Carl the Janitor resides in the movie. In one of his appearances, he is cleaning in the library when Bender asks him how one becomes a janitor. The conversation goes as follows:

Bender: "How does one become a janitor?"

Carl: "You wanna be a janitor?"

Bender: "No, I just wanna know how one becomes a janitor because Andrew here is interested in pursuing the custodial arts."

Carl: "Oh really? You guys think I'm just some untouchable peasant? Serf? Peon? Well, maybe so. But following a broom around after shitheads like you for the last 8 years, I've learned a couple of things. I look through your letters.

I look through your lockers. I listen to your conversations. You don't know that, but I do. I am the eyes and ears of this institution, my friends."

He is a bit player. He comes into the film's scenes from time to time and just for a few moments, but his impact lasts much longer than his interactions. Have you had someone like this in your life? For me, it actually was a custodian at my middle school. Our paths crossed one day when I was the last one to leave baseball practice and the school was essentially empty. He looked old to me at the time, but the reality is that he couldn't have been more than 40 years old and seeing that I am now 52, I take offense when anyone says, "40 is so old." I was coming out of the locker room carrying my bat and glove over my shoulder when he said to me, "Are you the last one, son?" "Yes," I said. "Man, I miss playing baseball," he said. "Whenever I get a break, I sit up on the hill and watch you all play." "Did you play baseball?" I asked. "Sure did," he said, "Played in college. Was pretty good too. Hurt my elbow and, well, that was that."

It was this simple exchange that started a conversation and ultimately a cross-generational friendship for the remaining three months of my middle-school career. Our conversation continued and I asked him if he finished college after getting hurt, to which he said, "Nope. I was always much better at hitting and throwing a baseball than I was with the books." We talked about our hometown Orioles who were actually pretty good back then and had just won a World Series several years prior with a 2nd-year shortstop named Cal Ripken leading the way. Ripken went on to play in 2,632 consecutive games — breaking the previous record of 2,130 held by the immortal Lou Gehrig. My new friend shared with me that he grew up in what would be considered an upper-middleclass neighborhood and that he had a wife and two boys who he hoped wouldn't choose to chase a profession that could be derailed by a simple injury, but really just wanted them to be happy in whatever they decided to pursue and do — even if it meant taking that chance. "So, Chris, what do you want to be when you grow up?" he asked. Without hesitation I said, "A baseball player. I mean, I wanted to be an ambulance driver when I was in first grade but now, yeah, a baseball player." He smiled and nodded. It was my turn to ask a question. With respect, I started: "Can I ask you question?" "Sure, shoot," he said as he leaned into his mop and bucket. "Do you regret not finishing college after you got hurt?" I don't think this was the question he was expecting. There was a bit of a pause before he looked me straight in the eyes and said, "Not one bit. Did you ask that because I'm a custodian at a middle school?" "No, not at all," I said. Now, I'm sure the answer that follows isn't the word-for-word (as I was 14 and it would be impressive to get every single world correct here), but it was the broader message that stuck with me and that's why it's important to me. "Good, because I am going to share a little wisdom with you. Sometimes what we perceive to be the worst thing that happened to us is actually the doorway to the best thing that ever will. I met my wife, the love of my life, because I hurt my elbow and lost the ability to play baseball at the highest level. She was an intern at the rehab center they sent me to for my elbow injury. Never would have known she existed if not for the worst thing that happened to me. Life isn't just about awards or titles. To use a baseball term, it's about finding your sweet spot. For some, that's the biggest house and the most money. For others, it's stability and managing the risk in their life. For me, it's family. It's spending the most time possible with my wife and kids. That's my sweet spot and doing this job gives me that time."

At 14 years old, I learned that life is about finding your sweet spot. Not someone else's vision of your sweet spot. *Your* sweet spot. The one you want and the one that you make for yourself. The one that makes you happy regardless of whether it would make someone else happy. And I learned that from a modern-day Socrates posing as a middle school custodian. It took me until 47 years of age to apply his advice to my own life, when I finally went out and chased my '80s pop-culture dream ... but here I am in my sweet spot and as happy as I've ever been.

The Breakfast Club and the life I have lived have taught me that:

 ## The best lessons come from the most unexpected places and people.

I wasn't expecting to hear a powerful story or be taught a meaningful lesson by my middle-school custodian. But as it turns out, you never know when or where it might happen and who just might provide you with the advice that will change your life forever.

You should know that I wrote this whole chapter while wearing Barry Manilow's wardrobe. Bender would be proud.

I hope you enjoyed reading this journey back to the '80s as much as I enjoyed writing it. And I hope you learned a little something along the way, besides that fact that I am deathly terrified of spiders. But if you take nothing else from the book, please take this one final lesson from those most excellent dudes — Bill and Ted — when they said:

"Be excellent to each other."

THE END

"Here's where the story ends.
Ooh, here's where the story ends."

— THE SUNDAYS

Hope you loved it.

Acknowledgments

As I've mentioned before, writing a book is such an isolating process and it can be difficult for someone who considers themselves a bit of an extrovert. But what's interesting about the process is that although it is a solitary exercise, it cannot be done without an incredible team of people who each provide support in a multitude of ways. My publisher, Kate Colbert, told me to think of this section of the book — the Acknowledgments — as "my Academy Award Speech." Based on the amount of people I would like to thank, I'm pretty sure the red light would come on, the music would come up, and a cane would appear from the side curtain ... yanking me right off the stage. So, here we go:

First, I want to thank everyone who made the investment in me and have purchased one or more of my books like you've just done here. It is incredibly humbling when someone spends their hard-earned dollars (and their limited time) on your creation.

To my family — I am so lucky to have the support of this incredible group of people who have believed in me from the very beginning. Thank you to my **mom** (miss you every day) **and**

dad for raising me right (I think) and always supporting my endeavors. Whether it was a move to Florida right after college with $200 in my pocket or quitting the corporate world to pursue this dream, you've always believed in me. Everyone should be so damn lucky.

To my sister, Ashleigh, who inspires me daily and whose courage to pursue her dream encouraged me to pursue mine. I'm a very lucky and a super proud big bro — I love you more than you will ever know. Now move to Florida and hang out with me!

To my stepdad and stepmom (miss you, Carol) for their unwavering support throughout the years. I also want to thank my stepdad for his service to our country and, most importantly, for caring for Mom when she couldn't care for herself. Thanks to my stepbrother, **Todd** (Big T), for being a great brother. The "step" in stepbrother has always been non-existent for us and now you get to tell your dates that you are mentioned in an acknowledgement in a book for a second time. Love you all.

To all my friends — of whom there are way too many too mention — who put up with my years of '80s movie quotes and, well, just put up with me in general. Your continued support and dedication to my dream is what pushes me every day to make this happen. I would love to list everyone here but that might take a book in itself, so just know that I see you and I appreciate everything. I've been so fortunate to have such amazing circles of friends from elementary school all the way through 50+ years of living on this planet. It's really amazing when someone I haven't seen since 6th grade pops up on Facebook to tell me that they purchased my book or that they are proud of me or that they are recommending me to their organization for a keynote-speaking opportunity. Thank you from the very bottom of my heart.

Thanks to my Fantasy Football league. I can now say I am a Fantasy Football champion, circa 2020! And my team, ironically enough, has been "Cobra Kai" since 2008. Strike first. Strike hard. No mercy.

To my good friend, graphic designer and one of my strongest supporters, **Jim Zielinksi** of Zielinkski Creative. When I decided to write my first book, I had no idea how I was going to design and produce it. Jim stepped in and learned how to do the whole self-publishing thing on Amazon and gave so much of his time to me and my dream.

Thank you to my friend, manager and speaking agent **Kristin Haggar** of the Haggar Agency. You were one of the first people to jump on board with my new journey into keynote speaking a handful of years ago and have been there every step of the way. What an interesting few years we navigated together!

To **Christian Boswell**, President of BFW Advertising, for his friendship and mentorship through the years and the team at BFW for your support in helping to make my brand look totally awesome!

To the Silver Tree Publishing team, including my publisher and editor, **Kate Colbert**, who took my books to an entirely new level when we first started working together in 2019, and to **George Stevens** for his totally awesome cover design and layout as well as just being a cool guy to work with.

To **Penny Tate** for trying to do something really cool for me. I appreciate you.

To my publicity team at Smith Publicity, including **Marissa Eigenbrood**, **Erin MacDonald-Birnbaum,** and **Katie Schnack**. Thank you for all your hard work with finding new audiences for me and my content through media opportunities across every conceivable channel.

Thank you to the early readers who provided me with some incredible endorsements: **Kyle Autrey** and **Justin DiSandro**

(*Back in Time Podcast*), **Briane Fleming** (University of Florida instructor and *Making the Brand* podcast host), **Robert "Bo" Brabo** (Former Presidential Communications Officer for Presidents Bush & Obama and author of *From the Battlefield to the White House to the Boardroom ... Leading Organizations to Values-Based Results*), **Zak and Dustin** (*Two Dollar Late Fee Podcast*), **Tamara Dever** (author of the *Ultimate Mix Tape* series, TotallyCool80s.com), **Steve Spears** (creator and host of the *Stuck in the '80s* podcast), **Kevin Barnett** (Producer, Director, and Writer of T*he Heartbreak Kid, Hall Pass, The Do-Over, The Wrong Missy, The Righteous Gemstones* ... and so many other Rotten Tomatoes-producing productions), **Patricia Stark** (author of *Calmfidence: How to Trust Yourself, Tame Your Inner Critic, and Shine in Any Spotlight*), and **Evan L. Kropp, PhD** (Director, Online Graduate Programs, University of Florida, College of Journalism and Communications).

To **Shaun Urban** of The Inception Company for entrusting me with the organization's marketing strategy during an unprecedented time.

To **WonderPaws Rescue** in Fort Lauderdale for saving my Bodhi boy and giving me a chance to give him his best life.

I'd like to thank **Stephen King** for inspiring me with all his writing and in particular his book *On Writing,* which is an absolute must for any author, aspiring or otherwise.

Thanks, as always, to **Adam Sandler** for making me laugh through the years and for providing all of us with movies that provide humor with a heart. He also seems to have an affinity for the '80s as well and his movie *The Wedding Singer* was on constantly in the background to set the '80s nostalgia mood as I wrote this book — as it was when writing my previous book.

Thanks to my man — **Patrick Swayze** — for helping to make my teenage years totally awesome with movies like *Red Dawn,*

The Outsiders, Road House, Youngblood, UnCommon Valor,
and — of course — *Point Break,* which gave my rescue Bodhi his
name. Wolverines!

It's always good to thank all the people who didn't return my
phone calls or emails as I built out my speaking and author
career. You inspired me more than you will ever know and made
me grind even harder to be successful. Thank you ... and I'm still
available for a chat.

A big thank you to all of you who had me as a guest on your
podcasts and gave me the platform to promote my books
and content.

A huge and totally awesome thank you to everyone who has
recommended or hired me as a keynote speaker for an event,
especially for in-person events in 2021 and 2022, during such
a weird time. Thank you to **Crislyn Lumia** and **Laura Dooley**
of SGAC; **Adalyn Tello** of RCC Associates; **Kim Pasquale**, **Jeff
Morgan**, and **Jim Cardamone** of CMAA; **Angela Carlos** and **Amy
Stout** of Commerce Lexington; **Kathy Collins** of GCMAA; **Carole
Enisman** and the team at Premier Wealth Planning; **Joseph
Siegel** and **Patricia Buchanan Jeanneau** of DHL; **Logan White**,
Leah Antovel, and **Evan Kropp** of the University of Florida
College of Journalism and Communications; and **Cindy Morgan**,
Young Un Cho, **Jennifer Rader**, and **Gretchen Kolb** of Penn
Medicine. I'm sure I missed someone, so please accept my apolo-
gies and email me for a signed book. ☺

An awesome (totally awesome!) thank you to everyone involved
— both in front of and behind the camera — in making '80s
movies, '80s music, '80s television, and '80s pop culture in
general. It goes without saying that you inspired me and were
the building blocks for my formative years. I'm so glad to see so
many of you back in the spotlight again! And an even bigger thank
you to those who keep '80s pop culture alive and kicking through

shows like ***Stranger Things, Cobra Kai, The Americans, Halt and Catch Fire, The Goldbergs***, and so many more!

Lastly and as always, I want to thank my best friend **Dexter Ashford** for whom this book (and this entire series) is dedicated. I thought we would end up old and gray together somewhere on a front porch in our rocking chairs, laughing about stories from our youth, but it was not meant to be. Dex passed way too soon. Fortunately for all of us, his smile will be imprinted on the world for eternity. Thank you, my friend, for so many incredible memories and thank you for continuing to be there for me. I know I can always turn to you when I need support, encouragement, or a smile. If you, the reader, ever need to smile, just look at *his* smile in the picture in this book. It will make your day.

About the Author

Chris Clews is a keynote speaker and author of the book series "The Ultimate Series on Essential Work and Life Lessons from '80s Pop Culture," which is currently made up of three books including *Raised on the '80s* and two editions of *What '80s Pop Culture Teaches Us About Today's Workplace*. His love for '80s pop culture stems from a number of things, including his formative years — ages 10 to 19 — having taken place in the '80s, such that everything he did for the first time (good, bad, or indifferent) happened in the '80s. He's also very proud of the fact that at the ripe old age of 12, he paid $2.00 for a movie ticket to see *E.T.* and then used that ticket to sneak into *Fast Times at Ridgemont High*, which also contributed to his love of '80s pop culture.

As a keynote speaker, Clews has spoken to a diverse set of organizations and companies, including VISA, University of Florida,

UPenn Medicine, DHL, Women in Insurance and Financial Services (WIFS), DisruptHR, FuturePharma, HR Healthcare, Club Management Association of America (CMAA), State Government Affairs Council (SGAC), Nostalgiacon, and more. He's a frequent guest on podcasts with topics ranging from workplace culture to '80s pop culture and he has been referenced or interviewed in numerous publications, such as Entrepreneur.com and *Esquire UK* magazine.

A graduate of Elon University in North Carolina, Chris has 20+ years of marketing leadership experience with companies ranging from Planet Hollywood to DHL. He's built brands, led brands through transition, and spearheaded sports sponsorships with NCAA Basketball, the PGA, MLB, International Soccer, and the UFC.

Chris is passionate about animal rescue, with a particular fondness for rescue organizations that focus on bully breeds, such as Stand Up for Pits and others. He donates a portion of the proceeds from his book sales and speaking engagements to WonderPaws Rescue, which is the rescue that saved his dog, Bodhi. Chris lives in Deerfield Beach, Florida, just skateboarding-distance from the beach. He lives by the quote from the poet laureate Ferris Bueller: "Life moves pretty fast. If you don't stop to look around once in a while, you could miss it."

Keep in Touch, Go Beyond the Book, and Bring Chris Clews to Your Organization's Stage

"Everything I needed to know I most definitely learned from '80s pop culture."

— CHRIS CLEWS

Yes, believe it or not, '80s pop culture — and particularly the great movies that defined the decade — can teach us a lot about our workplace cultures, our business operations, our careers, and our lives.

Chris Clews, author of *The Ultimate Series on Essential Work & Life Lessons from '80s Pop Culture* (now with three books!), combines 20+ years of marketing experience — in a variety of industries with global brands and ad agencies — with his unmatched passion for all things '80s to bring a fun, informative, relatable, interactive, and unique presentation to your group.

When you engage Chris to speak at your event, your audience is guaranteed to learn, laugh, and discover valuable lessons to use in their lives and the workplace.

Chris can even customize the lessons to your organizational needs or themes and include movies and a few musicians that fit your conference, workplace, or classroom from several categories, like:

- *Workplace culture*
- *Leadership*
- *Inclusion*
- *Teamwork*
- *Marketing, sales, and communications*
- *Life*
- *And more.*

Some of the most popular work and life lessons from '80s pop culture that Chris can integrate into presentations for your audiences:

- Find out how **Billy Ray Valentine** from *Trading Places* can teach us about the difference between confidence and arrogance.

- Hear what the kids from *The Breakfast Club* can teach us about problem-solving and being your authentic self.

- Learn how a bouncer named **Dalton** from *Road House* can teach us about how Simplicity Rules *and* how trusting the process requires trusting the person.

- See what **Prince Akeem** from *Coming to America,* the musician **Prince,** and **Ellen Ripley** from *Aliens* can teach us about leadership.

- Discover how **Axel Foley** from *Beverly Hills Cop* demonstrates that your best resource is you.

> Find out how ***The Outsiders*** taught us that it's never too late to "create you."

> See how **Inigo Montoya** from ***The Princess Bride*** shows us the importance of message consistency.

> Learn what ***E.T.*** teaches us about social responsibility.

> Hear what **Jeff Spicoli** from ***Fast Times at Ridgemont High*** taught us about making your business the greatest and coolest place to work, as well as the power in saying "I don't know."

> See how **Mr. Miyagi** in ***The Karate Kid*** teaches us about handling stress and putting our health and wellness first.

> And hundreds of more lessons from '80s pop culture!

Learn more about Chris, how to hire him as a keynote speaker for your conference, and his book series *The Ultimate Series on Essential Work & Life Lessons from 80s Pop Culture* at:

ChrisClews.com

✉ **Send an email:**

Chris@ChrisClews.com

↪ **Find, follow, and share on social media:**

🐦   Twitter.com/80sPopCulture

❶   Facebook.com/ChrisClews80s and Facebook.com/ Chris.Clews.10

in   www.linkedin.com/in/ChrisClews

🖸   Instagram.com/ChrisClews80s

▶   YouTube: "Chris Clews - Author and Speaker"

If you really enjoyed the book and want to read more, please keep in touch with Chris — and don't forget to read the other books in the series! Tell your friends and colleagues about the books, leave a review online, or email Chris directly about keynote speaking engagements or just to tell him you want more rad stories from *The Ultimate Series on Essential Work & Life Lessons* from '80s Pop Culture!

Made in the USA
Las Vegas, NV
27 August 2024